ROCK CULTURE IN LIVERPOOL

Rock Culture in Liverpool

Popular Music in the Making

SARA COHEN

CLARENDON PRESS · OXFORD
1991

Oxford University Press, Walton Street, Oxford OX2 6DP
Oxford New York Toronto
Delhi Bombay Calcutta Madras Karachi
Petaling Jaya Singapore Hong Kong Tokyo
Nairobi Dar es Salaam Cape Town
Melbourne Auckland
and associated companies in
Berlin Ibadan

Oxford is a trade mark of Oxford University Press

Published in the United States
by Oxford University Press, New York

British Library Cataloguing in Publication Data
Cohen, Sara
Rock culture in Liverpool.
1. Merseyside (Metropolitan County) Liverpool. Pop music,
history
I. Title
782.421630942753

ISBN 0–19–816178–6

Library of Congress Cataloging in Publication Data
Cohen, Sara.
Rock culture in Liverpool/Sara Cohen.
Includes bibliographical references and index.
1. Rock music—England—Liverpool—1981–1990—History and
criticism. 2. Liverpool (England)—Popular culture.
I. Title.
ML3534.C63 1991
781.66'09427'53—dc20   90–42402

ISBN 0–19–816178–6

Set by Pentacor PLC, High Wycombe, Bucks
Printed in Great Britain by
Biddles Ltd, Guildford & King's Lynn

For my father

Preface

In writing this book I have depended upon the support and generosity of many people.

I am grateful for the financial assistance of the Economic and Social Science Research Council, and for the encouragement and support of Peter Lloyd, Kenneth Kirkwood, Shirley Ardener, and, most of all, the late Edwin Ardener.

Particular thanks go to all those in Liverpool who so kindly helped me with my research, especially Barry Jenkins and the bands at Vulcan Studios but, most importantly, the members of the Jactars and Crikey It's The Cromptons! who put up with my presence, relentless questioning and note-taking with great patience, humour and hospitality. From them I learnt a great deal. Karen, Trav, Huw, Tog, Dave, and Tony also took the time to read the text and their comments on it were extremely generous and perceptive, enabling me to write a postscript. I was deeply touched by their understanding, thoughtful, and fair-minded approach and I will always appreciate it. I must also thank them for granting me permission to use their names and their lyrics and to publish the text in its original state. I wish them much luck for the future.

For further comments on the text I would like to thank: Adam Hussein, Nick Allen, John Baily, David Horn, Simon Frith, Wendy James, Ruth Finnegan, Dave Keen, and Paula Cannon. I am also grateful to participants of seminars at Oxford University's Institute of Social Anthropology and Centre for Cross-Cultural Research on Women, London University's School of Oriental and African Studies, the John Logie Baird Centre at the Universities of Glasgow and Strathclyde, and a conference of the International Association for the Study of Popular Music held at Oxford Polytechnic, for their responses to papers I presented.

In addition, I would like to thank my friends in Oxford and Liverpool who have helped me in so many different ways. I am particularly grateful for the support and kindness of Melissa Parker, Jeremy Coote, Nemat Shafik, Georgia Kaufmann, Rebecca Adams, Louise Traynor, Gary McGuinness, and Graham Jones; but special thanks must go to Colin Hall, who has lived through the preparation and writing of this book, sharing the associated traumas and offering much-needed sympathy and encouragement.

Finally, I would like to thank my family for their support and comments: Simon, Tammy, and my parents Abner and Gaynor, to whom I owe the greatest debt. They provided continual encouragement and advice and without them I would not have had the necessary motivation or perseverence. My father in particular has been a tremendous source of inspiration and played a central role, reading and discussing the text with endless patience. I therefore dedicate this book to him with much love and gratitude.

Contents

Introduction

Rock bands have been an important part of Liverpool's culture and identity since the 1950s. It is impossible to determine the exact number of bands on Merseyside, but a survey conducted for the *Liverpool Echo* early in 1980 discovered the existence of more than one thousand. When I first arrived in Liverpool in 1985 full of strategies on how to seek out bands and establish contacts in the music world, I found myself immersed in an overwhelmingly musical environment where many people seemed either to be in a band themselves or to know someone who was in a band, and where many of those not in bands spent much of their time talking of forming or joining one. I learnt about bands from taxi-drivers, hairdressers, waitresses and waiters; and in cafés and bars conversation on bands could be overheard.

Each time I changed residence, fellow residents put me in touch with more bands and each new neighbourhood slowly revealed to me its musical populace. Through my window I watched music equipment being loaded into vans, saw people emerge from houses carrying guitar cases, and heard the echoing sounds of bands rehearsing. In Liverpool itself, clothes and music shops displayed notice-boards crowded with advertisements placed by bands searching for new members or by individuals looking for bands. Some bands had daubed their name in all sorts of places in what seemed a frenzy of self-promotion whilst long stretches of walls were continually plastered, layer upon layer, with posters advertising performances and records.

With so many bands existing in an area of great economic decline, frequenting a fairly small city centre, with a music scene thwarted by lack of funds, the competition for resources and venues for live performance, media attention, and local as well as national fame was intensive. The music scene was rife with gossip, legend, and feud. It lacked a focus such as a major club or centre for live performance, and many bands had formed factions and cliques based around particular studios, clubs, and organizations. Within and between them there was rapid movement and fluctuation as bands came and went, split up and reformed, changed their name and membership, so that interrelations between them were often complex, and plotting the course of individuals through a series of bands was as laborious a task as charting family trees within the most intricate of kinship systems.

Such rapid change also occurred with the clubs, studios, and venues for live performance that continually opened and closed. The city was littered with boarded-up clubs, some supposedly burnt down for insurance claims, existing side by side with empty and decaying buildings and warehouses. Economic decline had not only reduced the number of venues for live music but also its audiences. Well-known bands were no longer attracted to Liverpool to perform and music facilities for young people were sorely lacking. All this despite the fact that Liverpool was still famous world-wide for its bands and their music and had consistently, over the previous twenty-five years, produced an average of two new charting bands a year. Few of those successful bands had been able to remain in Liverpool, if only because of the London-based monopolies in publishing and recording, and had thus left, taking their wealth with them. One local disc jockey often told the story of a promoter of local music who in the 1960s stood on the London-bound platform at Lime Street Station begging the departing bands not to take their equipment out as well. It was not just the bands that left the city. Liverpool's population declined from around 900,000 in 1951, to 483,000 in 1986. (The population of Merseyside at that time was 1,467,600.)

Liverpool was no newcomer to poverty and unemployment but since the 1970s the rate of unemployment had risen dramatically. By 1985 it was 27 per cent, double the national average. 53 per cent of those unemployed persons had been out of work for more than a year, compared with 39 per cent nationally (Parkinson, 1985: 13.) The highest rate of unemployment was amongst the young. A report by the City Planning Officer (October 1987: 'An Economic Development Strategy for Liverpool') stated that in 1986 only approximately 13 per cent of the economically active young people had jobs if placements on various temporary employment schemes were discounted. The national unemployment rate was also highest amongst young people but was no more that half that in Liverpool. Consequently, many school leavers in the city were no longer even thinking in terms of jobs. For most, life revolved around the fortnightly Supplementary or Unemployment Benefit cheque which might occasionally be supplemented by periods of semi-employment —usually at cash-in-hand jobs exploited as cheap labour—or broken by some government scheme entitled 'Youth Training', 'Community Programme', or 'Enterprise Allowance.'

That dramatic rise in unemployment and the increasing awareness of it had been accompanied by a mushrooming of bands. (It has been

said that, 'Unemployment brings out the guitar in everyone'—
Channel 4, *Europe A Go Go*: 5 January 1985. A journalist from
Liverpool wrote: 'large numbers of people seek to escape the
boredom of the dole by forming bands and playing music'—*Next
14*: 6 September 1986.) There existed a general feeling that being in a
band was a legitimate career to follow rather than a 'drop-out' phase
some adolescents might pass through before going on to a more
'serious' occupation. Thus in a city where the attitude of many young
people was that you might as well pick up a guitar as take exams,
since your chances of finding full-time occupation from either were
just the same, being in a band was an accepted way of life and could
provide a means of justifying one's existence. 'It's an alternative to
walking around town all day', said one band member, while another
asked, 'What else is there to do?'

A band could provide a means of escape where fantasies were
indulged but it could also play an important cultural and social role,
providing an outlet for creativity and a means by which friendships
were made and maintained. Basically, most people were in bands for
these social and cultural factors. They enjoyed it. They loved playing,
performing, and socializing, and since alongside that there always
existed the possibility of 'making it', that is earning a living from the
band in one way or another, then the quest for success became a
major motivation and preoccupation, a ray of hope in a grim reality,
and band members were drawn into all kinds of plans, strategies, and
activities designed to achieve that success. It might sound cliché'd but
it cannot be denied that being in a band was seen by many, whether
employed or unemployed, to be a 'way out' of their current situation,
'a way out of the jungle', as some phrased it. A local promoter of
bands described it (Radio 4, *Dancing In The Rubble*: 29 October
1982) as being, along with sport, the 'fastest way out':

In such a run down area people look around, see how depressed it is and
decide they have to get out . . . It's the only way for young kids. Everyone
you meet is in a rock band these days. There's more go in people here
(Liverpool band member quoted in Chappell, 1983: 6).

Thus for many bands the major problem was how to 'make it', not
only in a period of economic decline, unemployment, dwindling
audiences and performance venues, but also during a recession in the
national recording industry that made record companies cautious,
taking fewer risks and signing fewer bands. In reality, the chances of
getting a record deal were remote. During my year in Liverpool only
five or six bands signed record contracts and it was estimated by a
few people with relevant experience that less than one per cent of

bands would ever get one and fewer still would attain success thereafter: 'There's got to be approaching one thousand bands, I suppose, at any given time . . . and I can tell you that between . . . 1977 and 1980 about four or five actually made it . . . got chart placings, made money . . .' (Roger Eagle, Radio 4, *Dancing in the Rubble*: 29 October 1982). Most bands were thus precariously balanced between fame and obscurity, security and insecurity, commerce and creativity. Life was a series of successes and failures, periods of optimism followed by periods of depression. The longer a band struggled and the older its members got, the more harshly the failures were felt.

This book discusses that struggle in detail within the context of the bands' social and cultural lifestyle. In doing so it considers the interrelationships between art and society, attempting to explore the tension between creativity and commerce through description and analysis of the processes of musical production and performance by the bands, with particular reference to two specific bands. It demonstrates the way in which both bands perceived commerce and women to be a threat to their creativity and solidarity and indeed their very existence, and argues that in response those bands expressed notions of purity and impurity in the production, performance, and marketing of their music, emphasizing in that distinction certain ideals such as those of masculinity, democracy, egalitarianism, honesty, naturalness, and cleanliness.

Liverpool was chosen as the location for the study because of its history of involvement and achievement in rock music. I have used the name 'Liverpool' even when referring to Merseyside as a whole because the music scene on Merseyside was focused upon Liverpool and because Liverpool has become a familiar name since the success of the Mersey Beat bands in the 1960s. I lived in Liverpool for one year, from October 1985 to October 1986. Research was largely restricted to 'rock' bands, with the term 'rock' being used to encompass those bands that made music with reference to the national 'independent' or 'commercial' music 'scene' (with the exception of 'heavy metal' bands whose music-making and under-lying conceptions and ideology of music were so specific as to require study on their own.) This therefore excludes jazz, cabaret, folk, and country-and-western bands from the study (although many members of those were also members of rock bands) but includes a variety of music labelled in many different ways, such as 'alternative' or 'pop'—although 'rock' is generally distinguished from 'pop', which is seen as more commercial. It must be emphasized that on its own 'rock' was not a commonly used term because whilst bands might refer to their music as 'rock' or 'pop' they nearly always accompanied those terms with qualifying descriptions.

Research focused upon cultural production in a local context, covering bands without record contracts that therefore functioned on the margins of the industry. However, an important part of the study dealt with the way in which those bands were influenced and affected by cultural production of a commercial nature at a national, mass media level. Throughout the year, unstructured interviews were conducted with musicians and music personnel. Co-operation was rarely a problem and many were eager for the attention and were particularly flattered at being asked questions on the most detailed aspects of their music-making. Participant observation involved a smaller circle of bands, including the two used as case-studies. Gradually I became an accepted part of this group. I did not participate in the actual composition, rehearsal, or performance of the music—though occasionally invited to do so, largely because the music-making was taken so seriously and depended upon such a delicate balance of different factors (e.g. the personalities, concentration, and musical techniques of each band member) that I decided it would be better not to get involved in that particular activity of the band. However, I did attend rehearsals and 'gigs' (live public performances) and participated in many of the bands' social activities. Most of the information gathered was written down in note form either during or after it had been collected. Some conversations, particularly those on the most intricate aspects of music-making, were tape-recorded, as were many rehearsals and performances.

The social, cultural, and artistic impact that rock music has made throughout the world is outstanding. Its mass production has become exceedingly complex and costly and a great deal has been written about it in the popular press. Yet despite the enormity of the industry and the ubiquity of the music it produces, academic study of rock music has been slow to emerge in Britain and remains as yet underdeveloped in comparison with the literature on other forms of popular culture. As a result, the available literature is fragmented.

Of the few writers who have studied rock music, some (e.g. Benjamin, 1970; and Willis, 1978) have celebrated it as counter-culture, a folk or art form that directly expresses the needs and values of an active audience. They do so in opposition to mass culture critics such as Adorno and Horkheimer (1977) and Burchill and Parsons (1978) who argued that rock is a meaningless reflection of the evil machinations of the commercial record industry which debases its performers and audience. Others, such as Harker (1980), Coffman (1972), Burchall (1965), and Frith (1983), have located rock somewhere in between those two positions. Coffman and Harker discussed the conflict of roles experienced by rock stars caught between the demands of their audience and the record industry. Frith has analysed the way in which rock music expresses the contradictions and tensions of capitalist culture. 'The music doesn't challenge the system but reflects and illuminates it' (Frith, 1983: 272.) Nevertheless, youths can still use it to create their own meanings; thus although rock music is not a folk form, its ideology incorporates a notion of authenticity, i.e. claims to the music as 'folk' or 'art': 'Rock is a mass-produced music that carries a critique of its own means of production; it is a mass-consumed music that constructs its own "authentic" audience' (ibid.: 11.) Frith's work represents a major contribution to the study of rock music, and this book follows many of his concerns and ideas and examines some of them in detail.

Much of the literature on rock music has concentrated upon lyrics, youth culture, rock stardom, or the record industry, focusing upon the ideological and theoretical issues involved with rock as mass culture. There has also been a preoccupation with rock's origins and relatively short history—which is perhaps to be expected from any new discipline trying to establish itself by historicizing and documenting its own development. What is particularly lacking in the literature is ethnographic data and microsociological detail. Two other important features have been ommitted: the grass roots of the industry—the countless, as yet unknown bands struggling for success at a local level—and the actual process of music-making by rock bands. It is those bands and that process that form the subject of this book.

In pursuing such a subject I follow the example of Bennet, Finnegan, and White, three exceptions to the above literature. Bennet (1980) described the process of becoming a rock musician in America. Finnegan (whose book, *The Hidden Musicians*, 1989, only became available as this book was going into press—though I am grateful to the author for sending me draft copies of two chapters) studied the 'practice' of music-making by rock bands in Milton Keynes, describing the social processes by which they and other 'amateur' 'musical groups' in Milton Keynes learn, rehearse, perform, compose and organize their music. White (1983) studied two 'semi-professional' bands in another part of Britain, one a rock band, the other a jazz band, highlighting both the musical and non-musical conventions and constraints upon their music-making and focusing in particular upon the way in which their music-making was directly influenced by the legal factors that governed it. These writers provide valuable ethnography on the music-making and musical environment of rock bands. Many of their findings were confirmed by my own, which supports their use, following Becker (1982), of the terms 'art world' and 'musical world' to describe the ideological and practical circumstances within which rock bands operate.

Apart from Finnegan and White, British anthropologists have rarely dealt with popular culture or even with music, and it is only recently that more attention has been focused upon 'anthropology at home'—in this case modern industrial Britain. Those studies that have included analysis of music often considered it only as a reflection of the social structure within which it was made, or in its relation to the functioning of the society as a whole. This study attempts to redress that by focusing upon the processes of music-making and the complexity of social relationships involved, analysing the way in which the music not only reflects but affects the social environment, and highlighting the underlying conceptions of music which determine the musical terminology and categories used and the evaluation of music, musicians, musical knowledge and skills. The study thus reflects the influence of ethnomusicology (particularly that embodied in the seminal works of Blacking, 1973; Merriam, 1964; and Keil, 1966), a discipline closely related to social anthropology, which has addressed such issues in its cross-cultural approach to the study of music.

However, although ethnomusicologists have studied Western musics, they have rarely looked at rock music. Nor have musicologists, who (with the exception of Adorno) have tended to avoid the study of popular music in general, often considering it not worthy enough for study. In addition, they have rarely adopted a sociological or anthropological approach to their material, unlike literary critics such as Finkelstein (1976) and Durant (1984), who have analysed the way in which music's structures and forms embody certain ideas and meanings.

Because of the paucity of anthropological analyses of music and popular culture, the gap that has been identified in the academic literature on rock music, and the absence of musicological and ethnomusicological data on Western popular music, the discussion presented in this book is inevitably exploratory and much of the literature surveyed has been gleaned from non-academic periodicals, papers, and rock biographies. It must be emphasized that musicological transcription and analysis would be applicable to the study but is not within the scope of the book. It must also be noted that although the discussion will highlight a continuous ideology, organization, and structure amongst the bands and the music 'scene' in which they operated, those bands and that 'scene' nevertheless comprised a situation of such rapid change and fluctuation that to follow traditional anthropological practice of writing in 'the ethnographic present' would have been misleading. Consequently, the past tense has been employed throughout. Pseudonyms have been used very occasionally.

The book is divided into eight chapters. The first presents some background material on Liverpool and its rock music 'scene', whilst the second introduces the two bands featured as case-studies throughout the book and examines the social factors involved in the structure of the bands. Chapter 3 outlines what is involved in the organization and running of such bands, Chapter 4 describes and analyses their public performances, and Chapter 5 considers their endeavours to 'make it' and achieve success. Chapters 6 and 7 focus upon the making of the music itself and the band members' underlying aesthetics and conceptualization of music, whilst Chapter 8 considers the relation of women to those bands and their music-making and focuses upon tensions and contradictions within the bands.

I

Scene and Personae

It is difficult to describe and characterize a city, particularly one as complex and varied as Liverpool. For the media, Liverpool has been a newsworthy place, a provider of headlines, a colourful backdrop to inner-city decline, scene of numerous soap operas, documentaries, and socially relevant plays. It is famous for its football teams and supporters, its rock bands and other performance arts (poets, playwrights, comedians), and for passionate politics.

It is also a city of contradictions. The wealth of its past contrasts sharply with the poverty of both past and present. Today, sites of great beauty and grandeur such as the waterfront and spacious, landscaped parks, lie in between areas of squalor and ugliness. Streets littered with rubbish and rubble are flanked by huge, decaying buildings once grand and ornate; rotting reminders of a former age of splendour and decadence. Tales of past achievements and glories contrast with present problems (such as unemployment), disasters (such as Heysel and Hillsborough), and defeats (such as the abolition of Merseyside County Council.) Yet it is a city associated not only with depression but with a unique humour and wit. In addition— and this will be reflected throughout the book—it is a city divided by social differences and rivalries yet at the same time it projects a strong sense of loyalty and solidarity and a spirit of co-operation.

Liverpool's role as a seaport has also endowed it with an 'outward-looking' character, a sense of detachment from the rest of Britain and thus a sense of being somehow different. It is a characteristic shared by New Orleans, its new sister city in the United States, which has a similar economic, social, and cultural history and strong musical identity. Stemming from the traditions of the port has grown a reputation for vitality, exuberance, toughness. Lane (1986: 8) suggested that the 'flamboyant', 'assertive, blunt' individualism of Liverpool and its egalitarian and masculine character reflect the nature of sailors at sea:

In a city saturated with port activity it is not so surprising that the idealized seafarer should come to be regarded as the ultimate expression of what it meant to be a man . . . Here was the free born, free-spoken, foot-loose male who respected those who earned it and was unswervingly loyal to his equals . . . There is a raw egalitarianism at the core of the cultural currency of working class Liverpool and this has long been seen in shipboard relations (ibid.: 10).

The 'hard-living, hard-drinking' stereotype sometimes associated with Liverpudlians might also reflect the activities of, and facilities for, sailors on leave in the city centre. In 1986 there were still hundreds of different types of clubs within the city centre.

Aggression and trouble-making were also characteristics associated with Liverpool and sensationalized by outsiders as well as by many Liverpudlians themselves. A lecturer from Liverpool Polytechnic pointed out that Liverpudlians have been continually portrayed through the media as 'work-shy, difficult anarchists, violent hooligans, disrespectful' (Channel 4, *The Media Show*: 2 April 1989.) Lane (1987: 103) showed that this was not a recent phenomenon and quoted a British master who wrote of Liverpool and its seamen in the 1890s:

It has a good name, so far as ports go, though its seamen are reputed to be responsible for more than half the misdeeds and mysterious happenings on board ship. When something goes wrong, or some wrong is done and none comes forward to admit culpability, then, 'it was the Liverpool feller wot done it'.

There was, undoubtedly, a certain bluntness or combative spirit apparent on the surface of life on Merseyside and acknowledged by many. It manifested itself, for example, in the humour for which the city was so famous and which so many local comedians had popularized. One local described it as being based upon an 'I'll-put-you-down-before-you-put-me-down' attitude, one that might have arisen from a general feeling of oppression and of being 'hard-done-by' which generated a feeling of hostility towards the outside world—a 'two-fingers-to-the-world-attitude' as another person put it. Lane (1987: 161) wrote of it as 'the equivalent of spitting defiantly in the face of adversity and a refusing to accept the pessimism they often feel.' For Liverpool had suffered economic decline for some time. Most port activity had long since ceased and silent and deserted docklands stretched mile upon mile along the Mersey.

Consequently, a strong sense of identity and loyalty to the city had arisen. Local papers and characters focused upon, and thus engendered, a great pride in Liverpool and its achievements:

No matter what happens to Liverpool people will always defend the place. Michael Heseltine could drop a bomb on the place and they'll still say 'Liverpool's a cracker, wouldn't go nowhere else', you know what I mean? (Pete Wylie, Radio 4: *Dancing in the Rubble*: 29 October 1982.)'

That sense of identity was so parochial that even those living a few miles outside the city centre were spoken of derogatorily as 'woollybacks' i.e. country folk and therefore associated with sheep. References I made to those from the Liverpool area about bands in outlying areas such as Widnes or St Helens, typically met with scornful remarks such as, 'You'll need a passport to get there', or comments that such areas couldn't possibly produce any kind of band activity—'You'll only find an old man in the corner of a pub playing the spoons.'

That fierce sense of identity and individualism expressed itself in the rich cultural life of Liverpool, and was particularly suited to the glamorous and brittle world of rock music which thrives upon challenge and attention. 'And then came rock'n'roll and its social subversiveness', wrote Lane (1987: 147), 'which Liverpool with its long-standing American associations and its democratic temperament, drank down in quarts.' The rock music scene in Liverpool was rife with competition, rivalry, and factionalism, revolving around particular characters and egos. The strong sense of loyalty to the city was revealed in the general attitude to local stars such as the Beatles and Frankie Goes to Hollywood who were frequently criticized or treated as deserters if they left the city to live elsewhere. The media often reported what such stars were supposed to have said about the city, or quoted the amount of money they were supposed to have (or not have) donated to it. Thus, shortly after my arrival in Liverpool there was much emotional debate surrounding a comment a member of Echo and the Bunnymen was reputed to have made to a national music paper in which he referred to Liverpudlians as 'scum.' The *Liverpool Echo* devoted its front page to the matter. There existed, therefore, a desire to pull such stars down to the same level as everyone else and the view that 'if they can do it so can we.' That attitude undoubtedly encouraged the formation of many bands and could perhaps be likened to the 'independent-mindedness' that Lane attributed to Liverpool's sailors, and their 'scepticism towards authority and rank' (1987: 85).

ROCK MUSIC IN LIVERPOOL

Music has always been an important feature in the cultural life of Merseyside and a broad range of styles existed. The region had a strong tradition in styles such as music hall, cabaret, and Irish folk, and it had spawned many well-known performers. Country-and-western music was particularly popular. According to Joe Butler (who ran a country-and-western programme on local radio), Liverpool was the first city in Britain to realize, appreciate, and appropriate country-and-western. The department of programming at the local BBC radio station reported that of all its specialist music programmes, country-and-western was by far the most popular, so much so that they classified it as 'mainstream' and broadcast it during the day rather than in the evening along with other specialist music programmes.

The classical music scene on Merseyside was also healthy and the Royal Liverpool Philharmonic Orchestra was a growing asset for the region from a cultural, educational, economic, and tourist perspective. In the late 1980s it became the only orchestra of its kind in Britain to own its own building and appoint a music animateur through its newly established educational subcommittee. Meanwhile, in 1989 the Merseysippi and Blue Magnolia jazz bands celebrated their fortieth and twenty-fifth anniversaries respectively.

This wealth of music-making partly reflected an influx of foreign cultures and influences entering Liverpool through its port. The music and music-making of Welsh and Irish immigrants had always been prevalent, with everyone encouraged to join in regardless of age or talent. Thus many band members spoke of collective music-making at family gatherings. Russell (1987) pointed out that Liverpool was a pioneer of the free concerts for the poor in the latter half of the nineteenth century, and according to a 1934 *Social Survey of Merseyside* (p. 284), there was in Liverpool, 'no lack of societies and organizations giving musical performances. Some years ago, indeed, there was probably a superfluity of such institutions.'

The outward-looking character of Liverpool made it more susceptible to American cultural trends brought over by sailors in the 1950s and 1960s and by American servicemen based at Burtonwood. Some of them brought records and guitars which at that time could not be found anywhere else in Britain:

Liverpool has a direct shipping line to New York. For centuries sailors brought music from other countries back to Liverpool. Now the so-called 'Cunard Yands' obtained American records. As John McNally of the n Searchers recalls, 'Most people in Liverpool had some relation who went to sea and could bring record imports in' (Leigh, 1984: 30).

Such trends influenced the hundreds of skiffle bands performing in the city in the 1950s and gradually a large number of rock bands emerged which encouraged promoters to bring American rhythm and blues artists to Britain and, in particular, to Liverpool. Fletcher (1966) described how gangs of youths started turning to music and formed bands which became the gangs' 'totems.' Local disc jockey Bob Wooller referred to Liverpool as a 'city of gangs' and said:

After 'Rock Around the Clock' played here, a lot of gang members formed groups ... As jobs became scarce they devoted more and more time to following the beat scene. The noise may be deafening but it's better than having them in the streets with chains (quoted in Braun, 1964: 58).

Facilities for informal entertainment in Liverpool grew rapidly. Between 1958 and 1965, according to the Liverpool Corporation, the number of teenage 'beat' clubs doubled, and similar increases occurred with gambling and cabaret clubs (Masser, 1970: 468). Rival gangs mixed together in clubs such as The Cavern which lay in the heart of the city and became a focal point for bands and their audiences. Liverpool's clubs were so popular during the late 1950s and early 1960s that many bands found it difficult to get a chance to perform. At the Cavern, bands played one after another from early evening until the following morning, and it was there that the Beatles performed during their earlier years.

The Beatles and their rise to fame has been well documented elsewhere. They became a symbol for teenagers world-wide and were the first band to make their local identity and cultural background a part of their success. 'Perhaps the greatest wonder and delight of the Beatles was that they came from Liverpool', said Derek Taylor speaking on ITV (*It Was Twenty Years Ago Today*: 1 May 1987). Lane (1987: 146) wrote that, 'the elevation of the Beatles to the status of folk heroes had its effects in Liverpool. Liverpudlians, already confident in being taller than anyone else; were now grown even higher', and inevitably, the Beatles' success spawned hundreds of similar groups in the city. Through the Beatles Liverpool became a tourist attraction, though that tourist potential has only recently begun to be capitalized upon—partly perhaps because only now have the teenagers of the 1960s emerged as city councillors. Today Liverpool has a Beatles museum; a daily Beatles coach tour; an official statue of the Beatles erected in the Cavern Walks—a modern shopping complex built by the site of the original Cavern near shops selling Beatles memorabilia; and an annual Beatles convention which attracts many visitors from abroad.

Although there exists an extensive literature on the Beatles and the Liverpool music scene of the 1960s, little has been written about that of the 1970s and 1980s. After the 'Mersey Beat' era much of the focus of rock music-making in Liverpool shifted to London and the number of bands performing on Merseyside decreased substantially, with hardly any playing their own material. That situation was reflected all over Britain and it wasn't until the 'punk' phenomenon in the mid–late 1970s with its 'do-it-yourself' ideology that the numbers of local bands increased. In Liverpool a club called Eric's became the focus of the local music scene, attracting up-and-coming bands and journalists from all over Britain and encouraging those in the audience to form bands of their own which were able to perform there regularly and build up a strong following. The club, however, suffered financial problems. When it eventually closed after a police raid in March 1981, a large demonstration took place to oppose its closure just as in 1966 a similar demonstration occurred over the closure of the Cavern. Eric's is now legend on Merseyside and I was often reminded of all the successful local bands it had spawned (e.g. Big in Japan, Deaf School, Orchestral Manœuvres in the Dark, Dead or Alive, Echo and the Bunnymen.) Many who had been there spoke nostalgically about the place and its atmosphere and many who hadn't resented the constant reminders of what they had missed. Time and time again I was told that what local rock music needed was another Eric's.

Local journalists talked of the 'two waves' of Liverpool music. The first occurred in the 1960s and focused upon the Cavern, the second occurred in the 1970s and focused upon Eric's. Both influenced the music scene of the 1980s. The Beatles were still spoken of a great deal and several bands admitted to being influenced by them although others were embarrassed by them and their music and resented the legacy they had left. Many band members of the 1960s now had sons of their own who were also in bands. The music produced by those two waves of bands was thus reflected in some of the music produced when I was there and the cliquishness and compactness of the city centre might well have made those influences stronger. Outside and inside Merseyside many people still spoke of a 'Mersey Sound'—a term that arose in the 1960s along with 'Mersey Beat'—and several proclaimed their ability to distinguish Liverpool bands from non-Liverpool bands. Yet when I enquired as to the characteristics of that sound each gave a different answer pointing to a particular quality of voice, use of keyboards, rhythm, and other factors. In the city centre some bands were anxious not to end up sounding like all the other bands whilst some of those on the outskirts believed that their distance from the city centre gave them a better chance of creating a different, more original sound.

It is difficult to put into words particular sounds and styles of music and the same piece of music may be heard differently by different people. When I arrived in Liverpool I was struck by the number of bands producing what I took to be a rather melodic, lyrical style of 'pop' music and by the lack of bands producing music of a harsher, angrier style such as 'punk', and that impression did accord with the way in which many locals also described or typified the music produced. Some attributed it to the influence of the Beatles or to the absence of students from the music scene, who tended to favour more 'alternative' types of music. Some suggested that the lack of 'angry' music or music of a more overtly political nature reflected the escapist tendency of the bands that produced instead music of a 'dreamy' and 'wistful' style. Others pointed out that Merseysiders had understandably grown cynical about politics and therefore avoided writing about it. One said, 'People are fed up with political bands who don't offer a way out.' 'What are the chances of *singing* Thatcher into submission anyway', said another.

I made a point of talking to bands that produced music generally distinguished as 'alternative', 'harder', 'angrier', and found that the majority had originated from outside Merseyside or from bordering areas such as St Helens and the Wirral, an area of Merseyside that lay across the River Mersey from Liverpool and was commonly referred to as 'over the water'. It is hard to say whether those bands produced such music because of outside influences. Certainly, when asked, that is what many suggested. But regional variation in music might also have reflected geographical distribution of facilities for music or individuals, groups, and organizations who encouraged music-making.

Outlying areas did, however, tend to be ignored by the record industry, either because as part of the provinces they did not figure on the record companies' map of Britain, or because the better-known bands had usually been based in Liverpool. Often therefore, bands living in the outskirts lacked local role models to follow and emulate and were less orientated towards the record industry, and less confident than the Liverpool bands in their ability to 'make it.' That was noted by local music journalists who complained that bands in the city tended to be overly ambitious with high expectations—'After two weeks they think they should be on the cover of the *NME* [*New Musical Express*]' said one, whilst those from the outskirts were said to be more relaxed about their music-making, less competitive and ambitious. The music scenes in those areas were described as flourishing and enthusiastic due to a recent discovery of local musical identity.

Although many bands on the outskirts liked to distinguish

themselves from Liverpool bands, some of them saw, at the same time, the value of labelling themselves a 'Liverpool' band since the industry paid particular attention to Liverpool and the Liverpool label had always been associated with success. 'Besides,' said one, 'who has ever heard of Widnes?' Strong regional identity occurred even amongst bands within Liverpool itself so that a band might be known as being 'from Bootle', for example, and might feel a particular sense of rivalry or comradeship towards other bands from the same area.

THE BANDS

There was much variety amongst rock bands on Merseyside. They originated from many different localities, and social and educational backgrounds. There were, however, some common characteristics. On average, most seemed to last two to three years and comprise four or five members aged between 20 and 30 years of age, playing roughly the same arrangement of instruments. Nearly all were white and male. The number of women involved was negligible, and I never found or heard of one all-black or Asian band, although a few were racially mixed.

The absence of women from the local music scene will be considered later on. The absence of blacks is harder to explain. To begin with, music made by black musicians was traditionally of a style different from that made by white rock bands, much of it being made outside a band format amongst social gatherings in private homes. The majority of Liverpool's black population, unlike that of cities such as Manchester and Birmingham, were of African descent which could partly explain why West Indian styles of music such as reggae were less noticeable. During the 1960s and 1970s there had been several well-known black bands in the city such as the Chants and the Real Thing, influenced by popular American vocal soul groups, but when I was in Liverpool hardly any seemed to be performing, whether reggae, soul, or otherwise, although I did attend performances of some individual singers, musicians and teenage female vocal groups singing well-known soul numbers to backing tapes. The vocal, cabaret tradition was therefore still quite strong among the black population and was encouraged by the Charles Wootton Centre, the only one of several black community centres to hold music workshops. Besides those cabaret and vocal musical styles 'dub', 'toasting', and 'rapping' were performed to tapes in some clubs and private homes, but I was told that even those forms of music-making had died down in recent years.

One likely explanation for the lack of a visible black presence in the local music scene seems to be the racism that existed in Liverpool despite the images of unity and solidarity the city often projected (see Parkinson, 1985: 15; Lane, 1987: 12; Kettle, 1981: 60; the foreword to a study by Law, 1981; and the Gifford Report, 1989, which concluded 'that the situation with regard to racial discrimination in Liverpool is uniquely horrific', p. 82), and the inherent racism of the music industry itself (see, for example, Frith, 1983: 17). A feature of life in Liverpool was a noticeable racial segregation. Liverpool 8—which had a large black population—was situated barely a mile away from the city centre yet within the centre few blacks were seen either on the streets or in the shops and clubs though one or two clubs nearer Liverpool 8 were frequented by blacks. One local described how clubs in the 1960s and early 1970s operated a racial bar. Consequently, black musicians played in clubs where black audiences were not allowed. Many believed that a racial quota system still operated in a lot of clubs, and around the time my research was conducted two or three clubs were convicted for barring entry to blacks.

This situation arose despite the fact that black people had lived in Liverpool since the nineteenth century and despite the high incidence of racial intermarriage. It had obviously made many blacks wary of the city's club and music scene and had affected their music-making. Within Liverpool 8 there were few facilities or venues for music-making. Increasing economic deprivation had forced the closure of many clubs, and unemployment in the area was higher than anywhere else on Merseyside. Kettle (1981: 61), quoting from a report submitted to the racial disadvantage inquiry by the Merseyside Area Profile Group, wrote that unemployment was four times higher in inner Liverpool than in the city as a whole. Financing a band was thus difficult. Racism and lack of resources had affected not just black music but black culture in general—though some white people attributed the absence of blacks from the music scene to the lack of organization amongst the black community, their 'paranoia' about being 'ripped off' (i.e. cheated or swindled), and the fact that they smoked a lot of marijuana which made them 'lazy.' Irrespective of such stereotypes, the general impression was that of an oppressed and consequently disorganized population with a complex and shifting sense of identity, and cultural activity that was frustrated through racism and lack of resources.

According to Channon (1970: 193), the contribution of students in higher education to the cultural life of the city had always been small. Students from the art college, however, made an important contribution to the city's artistic and musical life in the 1960s and 1970s. Liverpudlians were said to have traditionally expressed hostility towards students—though there was a sizeable proportion of indigenous students—and many students, particularly those from the university and polytechnic, tended to keep to themselves and restrict their social activities to a few clubs and bars. I only saw or heard of one or two all-student bands and was told, when I visited the University Entertainments Office, that students were discouraged from participation in the local music scene by the strength of indigenous music-making and the large number of local bands. Student bands probably did exist but had a lower profile because the students couldn't afford to devote a lot of time and commitment to them. Nevertheless, students were important to the local music scene because they patronized record shops and various clubs, and because the university and polytechnic provided large venues that booked well-known bands from outside Merseyside.

Many band members, particularly when talking of their school-days, tended to make a distinction between themselves and the 'scallies.' 'Scally' was a term derived from the word 'scallywag' and used by Merseysiders to refer to a typical working-class, football-following lad, though with a certain style of dress and leisure activities. On the whole 'scallies' tended to be viewed as conservative and narrow-minded—hence the term was often used in a derogatory sense. Generally, scallies had not participated in local music as band or audience members though there were exceptions, such as a band named the Farm that, for various reasons, attracted a scally following and was labelled a 'scally band'. Members of the Farm were involved with the production of a local fanzine (a cheaply produced magazine usually locally based and distributed) called *The End* which was aimed at a 'scally' readership. One local journalist believed that through *The End* scallies had gained a sense of identity but I cannot remember anyone applying the term 'scally' to themselves except when referring to their youth.

Although they were not usually thought of as consumers of local music, like most other people scallies generally followed national trends in commercial music. Once local bands such as China Crisis and Echo and the Bunnymen became famous they might sometimes lose the loyalty of local fellow musicians but gain a scally following that latched on to them through national media channels. When I was in Liverpool, however, many scallies had turned to what was often referred to as 'dope culture.' They smoked marijuana and listened to music from the late 1970s produced by bands such as Dire Straits, Genesis, and Pink Floyd. Upon visiting a school in Huyton, I discovered that many of the pupils in fact listened to the same music as their parents. (An article on this phenomenon entitled 'The Dark Side of the Mersey' and written by J. McReady appeared in the January 1989 issue of *The Face*.)

Most bands on Merseyside were young. Youthful bands were continually forming and participating in the local music scene. Fewer people seemed to leave it and there were a lot of promoters, band members, managers, and others of 25–30 years and over. Many seemed to find it hard to sever contacts with the music scene and financial hardship meant that it attracted those who were trying to earn extra money or had no alternative employment to turn to. Above all, Liverpool had a great tradition in music and a strong identity built around it. For many their involvement with it had become a way of life, preferable to working in some nine-to-five job. 'It is difficult to get it out of your system', said one. Another explained that the longer one continued the harder it was to give up because of the experience, sacrifices, and commitments one accumulated. As they got older, many band members went on to playing and performing of a different kind such as 'cabaret' or 'session' work, or moved on to production, engineering, management, and music educaton.

It is not the intention of this book to suggest that the situation in Liverpool regarding rock bands was particularly unusual. There was a large number of bands in the city (major record company representatives said their companies received the highest number of tapes from both Liverpool and Glasgow, but it could be that bands in other areas did not approach those companies as much) yet there were large numbers of bands in other cities, towns, suburbs, and villages all over Britain. (Finnegan, for example, has estimated that in 1985, Milton Keynes, with a population of 122,000, had around one hundred practising rock bands—though Milton Keynes has, among other distinctions, a particularly youthful population.) What I would like to emphasize, however, are the ways in which those bands and the local music scene in which they participated, reflected not only characteristics of the music business in general, but those of Liverpool itself.

The factionalism and rivalry that existed between various political, social, community, and arts groups and amongst bands and the rock music scene has been emphasized. This reflected, in part, the 'individualism' attributed to Liverpudlians and might explain the failure to co-ordinate and structure the rock music scene despite several plans and proposals directed towards that end. In addition, a fierce sense of identity and pride in the city existed alongside strong ambitions aimed outside it: the desire for attention and a thriving upon it, the desire to be someone and achieve something when perhaps much had been denied and thwarted. Such identity and ambition inevitably focused upon the music, football, and humour that made the city famous and inspired, motivated, and raised the expectations of so many within it.

Yet the strong feelings of solidarity and egalitarianism within the city have also been emphasized, reflected amongst its crews of sailors, its large, close-knit families, its workers and the trade unions that represented them, its loyal football supporters, and its rock bands which generally displayed a democratic, co-operative structure and inspired strong feelings of loyalty and identity amongst members. The strength of such ties might have contributed to the rifts and barriers that existed, leading to family rivalries and strong ethnic, religious, political, and gender divisions. The combination of such contrasting qualities perhaps inspired Liverpool's creative talents.

The attribution of such characteristics is inevitably impressionistic. The intention of this chapter, however, was to 'set the mood' for those that follow and indicate ways in which the central themes of the book might be extended to apply to the bands' surrounding social, cultural, and economic environment.

2

Collective Creativity

Members of the Jactars and Crikey it's the Cromptons! originated from the Wirral but their social and cultural activities had become focused in Liverpool. The four members of the Jactars were from West Kirby, a pleasant-looking borough situated along the seafront, whilst members of Crikey it's the Cromptons! were from neighbouring areas. All of them were good friends and the two bands usually performed together.

The Jactars

In the Jactars were Trav (lead guitar and vocalist), Dave (bass guitar and rhythm guitar), Tog (bass guitar and keyboards), and Gary (drums). All were of the same age (22 when I first met them) and had attended the same secondary modern school which they left when they were 16. Three of them had even attended the same primary school. Trav described them as having a working/upper working-class upbringing. He himself lived with his parents who worked in the catering trade. He had a married older brother who worked in the Civil Service, and an unmarried younger sister with a baby. His family took an interest in his musical activities and his sister and her friends often attended his performances with the band. After leaving school with few qualifications Trav began a catering course at a local college but was expelled a year later. He had since been unemployed but studied History and English A levels part-time at Liverpool Polytechnic. In the summer of 1986 he began applying to various Community Programme Schemes but eventually started a temporary job working with the mentally handicapped.

Dave, unlike the others, had been in the top stream at school and went on to sixth form college to take two A levels. He then attended Newcastle Polytechnic where he studied Media Communications. Afterwards he returned to Merseyside and joined a Community

Programme Scheme in Liverpool working on a nature magazine. He lived with his mother in West Kirby until January 1986 when he rented a flat in Liverpool. His parents were divorced. His mother, who owned a café, was supportive of his band involvement and had once or twice attended his performances accompanied by his older brother who worked in London in marketing. His father, whom he never saw, was in the navy.

Tog was an only child. His father was a carpet salesman who played the organ in church on Sundays. His mother was a retired teacher. After leaving school with a few CSEs Tog trained to be a psychiatric nurse but gave it up, largely so he could concentrate on the band he was with at the time, and had since been unemployed. His parents had been upset about this but gradually came to accept it saying that they did not want to alienate their son and understood that in this age of high unemployment alternative occupations had to be sought.

Gary left school with a few O levels to work in a restaurant and a bakery. In 1983 he took a part-time course in drama, art, and music. When I met him at the beginning of 1986 he was working as a labourer on a Community Programme Scheme but he later quit to go back on the dole. He had recently left home to live in a flat nearby but moved back after a few months, having experienced problems with fellow flat-mates. His mother worked part-time in an old people's home. His father had been made redundant by the local Birds Eye factory. Both parents had initially been supportive of his involvement with bands and attended some of his performances but became critical after he left the bands to do something different. His older sister also lived at home and was unemployed. His older brother was head caterer for a local football team.

The biography of the Jactars is complicated and is intertwined with that of Crikey it's the Cromptons! Trav and Gary had known each other at school but only met Dave after they left when Dave and Trav attended the same college. The three of them lived near each other and began to socialize together. They shared a common interest in music and from around 1979 began to make music together under various names such as Cultural Disease (a name that reveals the influence of 'punk rock' which was popular at that time.) Trav described that period as 'playing about for a few years.' They had little equipment to start with but gradually accumulated more.

Dave went to live in Newcastle and Gary joined other school-friends in a band named the Riders of Discord. They rehearsed in a cottage in North Wales but never performed live. It was at that cottage that Gary met Tony (now in Crikey it's the Cromptons!) who had come to watch Gary's band rehearse. When Gary left the Riders of Discord he and Tony began to make music together with many other friends including Trav. (Trav described it as 'messing around', Tony as 'self-indulgence in the bedroom and the kitchen'.) They rehearsed at each other's houses, recorded a few tapes on cassette machines, and called themselves the Zyloids. It was an unstructured group with a floating membership.

In 1983 a band formed out of the Zyloids that was named the Crompton Vest Band by Tony, who used to call himself 'Crompton Vest'. There were seven in the band including Gary and Trav. They rehearsed at Trav's house and at the house Tony's parents bought for him. By sticking egg boxes on the walls in an attempt to alter the acoustics they converted Tony's tiny bedroom into what they called 'Giraffe studios.' All seven of them, and sometimes additional friends, would cram into the room to record songs such as 'Never Trust a Fish' and 'American Toilet' on a small cassette machine. The band performed in public once at a local youth club which, according to Trav, 'ended up with the kids playing our instruments and the band getting drunk.'

In 1984 the group split up. Gary joined a band named Sunrise Sa Blues with friends he met at college. They rehearsed in a rented basement and performed regularly. Trav joined Dave in Newcastle for six months and the two of them continued to make music together. When they returned to Merseyside in September 1984 they formed a band named the Jades with Tony and Gary (who had by now left Sunrise Sa Blues.) 'After a couple of months', said Trav, 'the Jades actually formed into a real band.' They were no longer able to rehearse at Trav's house owing to complaints from the neighbours, so they began to rent by the hour a room in Liverpool city centre in an old warehouse converted into rehearsal studios and called the Prison, a name that suited its dingy and decrepit state. They knew no other bands and never performed live.

After several months Dave met Tog for the first time although they had been in the same year at school. Dave, Trav, and Gary decided to bring Tog into the band in place of Tony (since according to Trav a 'clash of egos' had occurred), and Tony agreed to leave on condition that Trav and Gary helped him start his own band. Meanwhile the Jades were renamed the Jactars and began rehearsing at Vulcan Studios just outside the city centre. By the time I met them they had been together for just over a year, had recorded two 'demo tapes', and had performed live several times around Merseyside, usually with Tony's band Crikey it's the Cromptons! They had also begun to meet and socialize with some of the other bands that rehearsed at Vulcan Studios.

In appearance and manner members of the Jactars seemed introverted and modest. Dave was rather nervous and sensitive and was a bit of a loner. He was easy going but often revealed strong views on issues he had obviously thought deeply about. Gary was also quiet and was probably the most difficult of all the members of the Jactars and Crikey it's the Cromptons! to get to know. Once or twice the other members expressed surprise at the realization of how little they knew him. Tog was the most outgoing member of the band—although according to his friends he had until recently been very shy and lacking in confidence—and Trav was the most dominant personality. On the surface Trav appeared calm and quiet but he held very definite views, particularly on music, and could be stubborn and argumentative. He was popular with the others and respected by them and he and Dave were the main creative force behind the band.

Generally, members of the Jactars got on well with each other and saw each other frequently. Other bands' members described them as a very close-knit group. They shared the same age, education, background, and interests and had many friends in common. They were even all vegetarians. All were supportive and encouraging of each other, but tension did lurk beneath the surface and, due to a variety of factors, emerged later on to threaten the functioning and existence of the band.

Crikey it's the Cromptons!

The members of Crikey it's the Cromptons! were Tony (rhythm guitar and vocals), Huw (drums), Dave T. (lead guitar), Midi (bass guitar), and Karen (backing vocals).

Tony (aged 21) came from the wealthiest background. His father was a chemist and his stepmother a doctor. Neither approved of his band activities. They lived in one of the more affluent areas of the Wirral and had sent Tony to boarding-school at the age of 9. Tony hated the school. He was expelled from it and went to the local secondary modern school instead, which he left at 16 with few qualifications. He left home at the same time. He got on badly with his family, especially his stepmother. He had an older brother who was training to be a solicitor, and a younger sister who was still at school. Eventually he moved into a small house bought for him by his father which became a centre for drug-taking, music-making, and other social activities. His father sold the house and for two years Tony lived with his girlfriend Margie until she threw him out and he found a flat in Liverpool. After leaving school Tony joined a

Community Programme Scheme where he met Huw. He had since been unemployed.

Huw was 22 years old and came from a working-class background in Birkenhead. He lived with his retired parents but often thought of moving. He had an older brother who was an electrician and an older sister married to a sailor in Bermuda. Huw left school with six O levels. In 1980 he went to a local art college but was later expelled. He worked on a Community Programme Scheme for six months and then went on the dole. He applied unsuccessfully for jobs and training schemes until in the summer of 1986 he became eligible for another Community Programme Scheme working as a craft instructor with the mentally handicapped.

Huw's family were quite supportive of his involvement with a band (though his father had earlier been against his older brother joining a band). Huw's mother once sang with a vocal group and expressed an interest in attending Huw's performances with the band but her husband was against it. Huw's brother, however, did attend Crikey it's the Cromptons!' performances and helped the band in other ways. He had been playing guitar since he was 13 years old and recently played with a cabaret band. Now however, at the age of 29, he had just got married so Huw didn't think he would stay with the band though he would probably continue to make music alone on his portastudio (a small 4-track, portable recording machine).

Karen and Midi also worked with the mentally handicapped. Karen was a religious 23-year-old from an upper working-class background on the Wirral. She left school without A levels but was taking evening classes in A level psychology. Her father was a truck-driver and market gardener. Her mother worked in a home for the elderly. She had two sisters. The elder planned to take a course in psychotherapy, the younger one was a hairdresser. Midi was 27 years old and lived with his retired parents. His father had been a Methodist minister and his mother a teacher. Midi took A levels before going to Liverpool University where he gained a degree in politics. He then got the job at the centre for the mentally handicapped and described his occupation there as 'professional bum-wiper'. It was a low paid, demanding job and he was trying to find something better in the same field. With each job application he considered whether or how the job would allow him to remain with the band. He had an older brother who worked in London and played guitar in a folk band.

Dave T. was 27 years of age, divorced, and lived with his mother. He had a 6 year-old son who lived with his ex-wife. He worked in insurance but owned PA (public address) and recording equipment which he hired out to earn extra money. In the summer of 1986 he moved to London and took a new job, also in insurance. His younger sister Kathy lived in a flat in Liverpool and was unemployed—though she had occasionally practised fortune-telling. She often attended his performances with the band and had in fact managed Crikey it's the Cromptons! for a brief period before Dave became a member.

It was Tony who brought them all together. After leaving the Jades he decided to form his own band and asked Huw if he would play drums. Trav and Dave agreed to stand in on guitar and bass until Tony found replacements. Tog brought Midi along to audition for bass player and later suggested that Karen sing backing vocals. Midi, Tog, and Karen had known each other for years. They all met through their local wine bar and church youth club. From 1979 to 1982 Midi and Tog had been in a gospel band together named Pieces of Glass. They rehearsed in the church hall, mainly during the holidays since all the members except Tog were either doing A levels or were at university. Midi was the songwriter. Tog didn't play an instrument but mixed the band's sound. They made one record and performed regularly, occasionally at religious festivals, but the nature of the band and its lyrics gradually became less religious before they split up. After the split Tog, one of his co-members, and Karen formed another band which was named La Voix Celeste and existed for two years. Tog then joined the Jades and later Midi and Karen joined Crikey it's the Cromptons! Trav continued to play lead guitar with Crikey it's the Cromptons! for just over a year until Dave T., whom they met at Vulcan Studios, made it known that he was interested in joining.

Members of Crikey it's the Cromptons! were more diverse than the Jactars, not only in age, interests, and background, but in their personalities. Midi was affable, good-natured, and popular with the others who teased him constantly. Dave T. was easy-going but more reserved. Karen was more difficult to get to know because she wasn't around very much and was less forthcoming when she was, but she also seemed easygoing, tolerant, and good-natured—though strongly independent-minded as well. Huw was quieter and moodier than the others but thoughtful and perceptive. Tony was the main creative and driving force behind the band. He was highly imaginative, inventive, and enthusiastic but was also insecure, emotional, and petulant. Thus although likeable he could be frustrating and annoying and, unlike Huw, was not a reliable commentator. He fluctuated from moods of extreme enthusiasm to those of depression. He was eager for praise and approval and became frustrated when things went badly for the band. He was also keen to be different from everyone else and to be perceived as such. He once showed me a colourful portrait he had done at school which his teachers refused to display on the wall because he had incorporated writing in the design of the hair. His class-mates had all drawn in a more conventional style in black and white. 'That's when I knew I was different', he said.

Although members of Crikey it's the Cromptons! saw less of each other and had less in common than did members of the Jactars, they were good friends and rehearsals were usually relaxed and jovial— although tension often arose between Huw and Tony. Tony pointed out to me on several occasions that he got on better with Huw 'outside of the band.'

The early bands of Tony, Trav, Dave, and Co. were different from the Jactars and Crikey it's the Cromptons!. They comprised a group of friends with a common interest in music who had been influenced by 'punk rock' and its 'do-it-yourself' philosophy and began making music together in each other's houses in groups of fluctuating membership that went under a variety of different names. Their music-making was thus unstructured, experimental, improvisational, and was taken less seriously than that of later years. It was a preoccupation—or 'self-indulgence' as Tony described it—rather than an occupation, and their few public performances were usually relaxed, taking place in church halls or youth clubs.

Unlike many young people living on the Wirral whose bands dissolved when they went to college or got married, members of the Jactars and Crikey it's the Cromptons! progressed from band to band, gaining more experience with each and becoming gradually more committed and ambitious about their music-making, moving on to bands with fixed membership and name. This was accompanied by a shift in the focus of their music-making from their original locality on the Wirral to Liverpool city centre, where facilities and opportunities for bands and for a social life were much improved. They began to rehearse and socialize in the city centre and one by one several of them moved over there. Thus when they were in need of new band members, the two men recruited were from Liverpool and had nothing to do with their previous social network on the Wirral.

That shift of emphasis and increasing ambition necessitated greater organization of the bands and more investment of time, money, and emotion into them. The following chapter will show that in addition to arranging and financing rehearsals the band members were required to become involved, as other bands did, in the recording of demo tapes and the organization of gigs, publicity, and finances. The changing nature of the bands was well illustrated by a compilation tape they presented to me before I left Liverpool. It consisted of various recordings made by members of both bands over the previous eight or nine years. They ranged from early compositions performed on hairdryers, typewriters, milk-bottles, and hoovers, and mock interviews of each other pretending to be journalists and famous rock stars (constantly interrupted by fits of giggling), to excerpts from their latest recordings of a more serious nature, compiled in professional recording studios.

As the bands performed and became more organized, relationships between their members intensified which often, as this chapter will highlight, led to stronger solidarity and egalitarianism. Although some members might contribute more towards the composition of a band's music than others, the structure of the band's music-making was a collective experience which emphasized group rather than individual activity and excellence. 'The glory of music', wrote Hughes (1973: 151), 'is its ability to demand and receive co-operation from performers and to create a sense of common purpose and communal enjoyment.' The discussion will also indicate, however, some of the problems and friction that such collective creativity could give rise to, thus illustrating ways in which a band could not only unite, but also divide its members.

MUSICAL COLLABORATION

Members of the Jactars and Crikey it's the Cromptons! socialized together outside their music-making activities. Most of them shared the same interests, friends, and a similar sense of humour. They drew cartoons of each other with amusing captions, wrote graffiti on the toilet walls at Vulcan Studios to entertain each other, teased each other, shared jokes, catch-phrases, and speech styles (for example, all the Jactars used the word 'like' at the end of, or in the middle of, sentences) and gave each other nicknames. Their main topics of conversation were music and sex. Very occasionally Trav and Dave discussed politics but usually when they were drunk and on their own.

Music was discussed and listened to at parties, gigs, in pubs, in each other's flats, and wherever else they happened to be. Conversation and debate centred around particular bands and their records, local bands—especially those that rehearsed at Vulcan Studios, gigs they had attended, and of course their own bands. Plans and decisions concerning the Jactars and Crikey it's the Cromptons! were

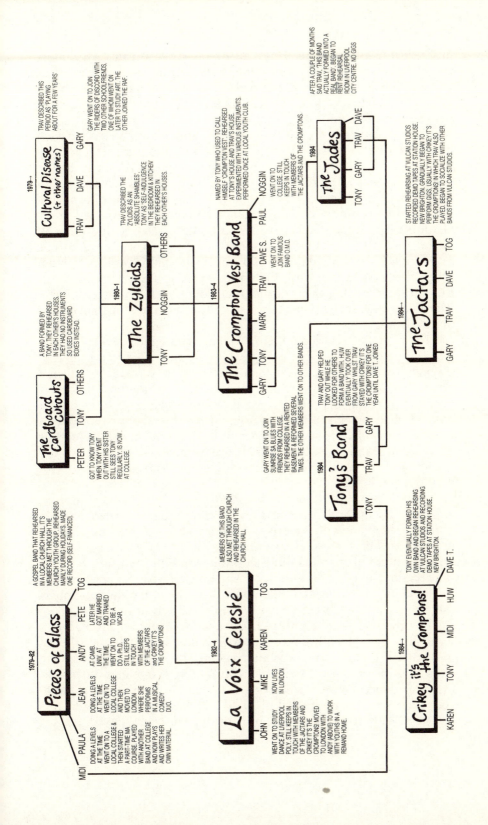

1979→

Cultural Disease (+ other names)

TRAV   DAVE   GARY

TRAV DESCRIBED THIS PERIOD AS 'PLAYING ABOUT FOR A FEW YEARS'

GARY WENT ON TO JOIN THE RIDERS OF DISCORD WITH TWO OTHER SCHOOL FRIENDS, ONE OF WHOM WENT ON LATER TO STUDY ART. THE OTHER JOINED THE R.A.F.

The Cardboard Cutouts

PETER   TONY   OTHERS

A BAND FORMED BY TONY. THEY REHEARSED IN EACH OTHER'S HOUSES. THEY HAD NO INSTRUMENTS SO USED CARDBOARD BOXES INSTEAD.

GOT TO KNOW TONY WHEN TONY WENT OUT WITH HIS SISTER. STILL SEES TONY REGULARLY, IS NOW AT COLLEGE.

1980-1

The Zyloids

TONY   NOGGIN   OTHERS

TRAV DESCRIBED THE ZYLOIDS AS AN 'ABSOLUTE SHAMBLES'. TONY AS 'SELF-INDULGENCE'. IN THE BEDROOM & KITCHEN THEY REHEARSED IN EACH OTHER'S HOUSES.

1983-4

The Crompton Vest Band

GARY   TONY   MARK   TRAV   DAVE S.   PAUL   NOGGIN

NAMED BY TONY WHO USED TO CALL HIMSELF 'CROMPTON VEST'. REHEARSED AT TONY'S HOUSE AND TRAV'S HOUSE. EXPERIMENTED WITH VARIOUS INSTRUMENTS. PERFORMED ONCE AT LOCAL YOUTH CLUB.

DAVE S. WENT ON TO JOIN FAMOUS BAND O M.D.

NOGGIN WENT ON TO COLLEGE. STILL KEEPS IN TOUCH WITH MEMBERS OF THE JACTARS AND THE CROMPTONS.

The Jades

TONY   GARY   TRAV   DAVE

1984

AFTER A COUPLE OF MONTHS SAID TRAV, THIS BAND ACTUALLY FORMED INTO A 'REAL BAND'. BEGAN TO RENT REHEARSAL ROOM IN LIVERPOOL CITY CENTRE. NO GIGS.

The Jactars

GARY   TRAV   DAVE   TOG

1984→

STARTED REHEARSING AT VULCAN STUDIOS. RECORDED DEMO TAPES AT STATION HOUSE. NEW BRIGHTON. GRADUALLY BEGAN TO PERFORM GIGS, USUALLY WITH CRIKEY IT'S THE CROMPTONS! IN WHICH TRAV ALSO PLAYED. BEGAN TO SOCIALIZE WITH OTHER BANDS FROM VULCAN STUDIOS.

1979-82

Pieces of Glass

MIDI   PAULA   JEAN   ANDY   PETE   TOG

A GOSPEL BAND THAT REHEARSED IN A LOCAL CHURCH HALL. IT'S MEMBERS MET THROUGH THE CHURCH YOUTH GROUP. REHEARSED MAINLY DURING HOLIDAYS. MADE ONE RECORD (SELF-FINANCED).

PETE LATER HE GOT MARRIED AND TRAINED TO BE A VICAR.

ANDY AT CAMB. UNIV. AT THE TIME WENT ON TO DO A Ph.D. STILL KEEPS IN TOUCH WITH MEMBERS OF THE JACTARS AND CRIKEY IT'S THE CROMPTONS!

JEAN DOING A LEVELS AT THE TIME WENT ON TO LOCAL COLLEGE AND THEN MOVED TO LONDON WHERE SHE PERFORMS IN A MUSICAL COMEDY DUO.

MIDI DOING A LEVELS AT THE TIME WENT ON TO A LOCAL COLLEGE & DID A PART-TIME MA COURSE. PLAYED WITH ANOTHER BAND AT COLLEGE AND NOW PLAYS AND WRITES HER OWN MATERIAL.

1980-4

La Voix Celesté

JOHN   MIKE   KAREN   TOG

MEMBERS OF THIS BAND ALSO MET THROUGH CHURCH AND REHEARSED IN THE CHURCH HALL.

JOHN WENT ON TO STUDY DANCE AT LIVERPOOL POLY. STILL KEEPS IN TOUCH WITH MEMBERS OF THE JACTARS AND CRIKEY IT'S THE CROMPTONS! MOVED TO LONDON WITH ANDY (ABOVE) TO WORK WITH YOUTHS IN A REMAND HOME.

MIKE NOW LIVES IN LONDON.

Tony's Band

TONY   TRAV   GARY

1984

GARY WENT ON TO JOIN SUNRISE SA BLUES WITH FRIENDS FROM COLLEGE. THEY REHEARSED IN A RENTED BASEMENT & REFORMED SEVERAL TIMES. THE OTHER MEMBERS WENT ON TO OTHER BANDS.

TRAV AND GARY HELPED TONY OUT WHILE HE LOOKED FOR OTHERS TO FORM A BAND WITH. HUW EVENTUALLY TOOK OVER FROM GARY WHILST TRAV STAYED WITH CRIKEY IT'S THE CROMPTONS! FOR ONE YEAR UNTIL DAVE T. JOINED.

Crikey it's the Cromptons!

KAREN   TONY   MIDI   HUW   DAVE T.

1984→

TONY EVENTUALLY FORMED HIS OWN BAND AND BEGAN REHEARSING AT VULCAN STUDIOS AND RECORDING DEMO TAPES AT STATION HOUSE. NEW BRIGHTON.

made during all social activities. At one party I noticed that almost every conversation was about either band. Although much of what was discussed, debated, and decided upon never actually came about, those conversations about music, the listening to music, the exchange of tapes, records, and so on that occurred, were additional forms of rehearsal important to the functioning and maintenance of each band. Talking to outsiders about the band or about music generally was also a means of making contacts that could be of use to them.

Drink played an important part in most social activities and members of both bands were respected or teased according to the quantity of alcohol they could consume and the way it affected them. Getting very drunk was often the main aim of an evening out and they would talk of 'pacing' themselves in their drinking in order to be at the right stage of drunkenness at particular points in the evening. Often they would 'crash out' at Tony and Tog's flat afterwards. In the spring they began brewing their own beer to save money. Marijuana and speed were taken by a few members but never any 'hard' drugs.

Lack of money restricted their social activities and prevented them from going out more often but Dave, Trav, and Tog often preferred staying in and watching television or listening to records. Tog spent a great deal of his time watching television, even daytime children's programmes and soap operas, which annoyed Tony who lived with him. He had no desire to get a job. In contrast Tony went out as much as possible. He seemed eager to live the rock'n'roll stereotype of sex, drugs, and an early death. He occasionally talked of death and suicide and he drank a great deal, sometimes getting drunk on his own during the day.

By January 1986 Huw had been on the dole for several months and was fed up and depressed about it although he tried to keep himself occupied with creative pastimes such as reading, photography, and craftwork. Trav, on the other hand, was content to potter around his parents' house on his own and spent much of his time reading, playing his guitar, or watching television. Gary was less forthcoming about his activities apart from the other band members but seemed to socialize a lot with friends who lived near him.

The others were all employed. Dave worked two or three days a week and apart from his activities with fellow band members he sat in his flat listening to records and reading, or went to the pub with colleagues from work. Midi worked full-time, sometimes during the evenings. Since joining Crikey it's the Cromptons! he had come to spend more time with his fellow band members and with the Jactars and less with friends he had previously. He even played for the

Vulcan Studios football team on Sundays. In addition, he had a steady stream of girlfriends to keep him occupied. Dave T. had less free time because of work and family commitments but was still able to join in many social activities with fellow band members.

In addition to making music with their band, some members of the Jactars and Crikey it's the Cromptons!, like many band members, made music in other contexts, either independently or with each other. Midi, for example, persuaded Tog and Gary to accompany him playing some of his own compositions; Tony and Tog started making music together calling themselves the Vegetable Smutt Kraft Band and later got together with members from another band at Vulcan to play music of a satirical, 'heavy metal' style; and Tony and Dave rehearsed together several times using a drum machine for accompaniment. Such musical enterprises were experimental, humorous, self-indulgent, and short-lived. They were a relaxing alternative to the more stable and structured music-making of their main band and were not taken as seriously.

The fact that members of the Jactars and Crikey it's the Cromptons! were all such good friends whose involvement with bands took up so much of their activities, conversation, and energy, meant that they, like many others in their position, had less time for friendships outside the bands. Members of both bands did, however, have several friends in common who also came from the Wirral and had been to the same school or church youth club. Six or seven of them were men who had been with them in previous bands but were in bands no longer (see diagram on page 29). They regularly attended performances and sometimes rehearsals of the Jactars and Crikey it's the Cromptons! and went to the same parties. John and Andy, for example, originally got to know Midi, Karen, and Tog through their church youth group and all of them had been in bands together. They had been Midi's closest friends before he joined Crikey it's the Cromptons! and he, Tog, and Karen still saw them fairly regularly and had acqainted them with the other members of the Jactars and Crikey it's the Cromptons!

Similarly, Pete, Steve, Phil, and Noggin had at one time been in bands with Tony, Trav, Gary, and Dave and sometimes attended their performances with their current bands, largely because of their friendship with Tony in particular. Noggin was considered a 'real character' and his past exploits had become something of a legend amongst members and friends of the Jactars and Crikey it's the Cromptons! At a gig in the summer of 1986 he joined Tony, Trav, Dave, and Gary on stage for an impromptu performance of the song 'Never Trust a Fish' which he had composed with them several years earlier.

Besides Noggin and the others, Tony occasionally saw old friends with whom he used to take drugs, but he, Tog, and Dave also spent time with fellow residents of houses they had recently moved into. Dave shared a flat with Nick and both worked on the same Community Programme Scheme. Nick was also from the Wirral and had also once been in a band. Tog and Tony lived in another area in a house which two men named Steve—one an artist, the other a writer—also inhabited. The Steves already knew Nick through a common interest in art and the three of them began to attend gigs and parties with members of the Jactars and Crikey it's the Cromptons! Meanwhile Gary and Trav continued to live on the Wirral and occasionally saw a few of their old schoolfriends. Huw had a separate group of friends from Birkenhead, many of whom the others did not know though they attended one or two gigs during the year as did Huw's girlfriend's sister Fiona, and her boyfriend Wilf with whom Huw had become particularly friendly. Midi had once been out with Fiona and Tony and Huw had both worked with her on the same Community Programme Scheme.

Of all the members of the Jactars and Crikey it's the Cromptons! only Tog and Gary never had girlfriends, which, according to their friends, worried them considerably. Trav spent a lot of time with Karen (from Crikey it's the Cromptons!) and Dave had a steady girlfriend who lived in Newcastle, having just completed a university degree there. Dave T.'s girlfriend lived in London and worked in a bookshop. He saw her most weekends and eventually moved in with her. Huw went out for some time with Alison, who worked in an office, before their relationship broke up in the summer of 1986. Midi and Tony had a series of brief relationships with different women although for Midi this ended in the summer of 1986 when he met and settled down with a divorcee and her child. Tony still saw his ex-girlfriend Margie occasionally but they usually ended up arguing. Margie shared a flat with Trav's sister Sammie and her baby and both were friendly with Nula, an ex-girlfriend of Trav's.

Those girlfriends sometimes turned up at parties, gigs, and occasionally rehearsals. Otherwise they were rarely seen, which was commonplace amongst local bands. Many band members, as will be discussed later on, said that girlfriends conflicted with, or distracted them from, their band activities, which was why some of them, particularly younger members, insisted that they didn't want girlfriends at all. Others said that because of their activities with the band they didn't have time for a girlfriend, or said that if they did decide to go out with someone they would be sure to warn her beforehand of their band membership and all that it involved.

Friends and girlfriends were important as audience members, but because most of their friends lived on the Wirral, the Jactars and Crikey it's the Cromptons! could not expect them to turn up to many of their performances in Liverpool. The performances usually finished too late for the last train and taxis were expensive. There was a night tunnel bus but it was infrequent and unsafe and there was still the problem of transport at the other side. Furthermore, friends could not, as many other band members also pointed out, be expected to turn up to every gig and would get fed up if constantly asked to buy tickets. The number of friends who did turn up therefore depended upon the timing and location of the event and upon its importance for the band members and the amount of effort they made to recruit friends to it. If they were particularly anxious to get a larger audience they recruited acquaintances from a wider network. Two of Nula's girlfriends from college might be contacted for example, or Midi and Karen might recruit colleagues from work. Gigs rarely took place during the day but both bands once performed in a Liverpool café on a Saturday afternoon and were delighted when many friends and relatives (in addition to a group of mentally handicapped people looked after by Midi and Karen) were able to attend.

Through their music-making, members of the Jactars and Crikey it's the Cromptons! came into contact with other bands, particularly those that also rehearsed at Vulcan Studios. In this way further friendships were formed. Associations between bands were common. Band members met at performances; in studios, clubs, and pubs; through the transfer of members from one band to another; and in other contexts. Friendships were easily made since they all shared common experiences, preoccupations, and goals. Inevitably, cliques of bands had formed. Many band members, including members of the Jactars and Crikey it's the Cromptons!, often referred to 'the Clique' of Liverpool bands which they had no wish to be associated with. That clique was supposed to dominate 'contacts' and venues in the city centre like an 'old boys' network in the City.('They all think they are better than everyone else—if you're not in that clique, well you're out'—band member quoted in a local fanzine.) It was, in reality, several cliques, and those who abhorred it were associated with cliques themselves.

Some bands made a conscious decision not to associate with other bands for several reasons: because they had enough of bands with their own; because they wanted to make it clear that they had got where they were, or could get where they wanted to go, on their own without help from anyone else; because they felt their isolation would preserve their 'unique' sound or style; or simply because they did not want others to associate them with any clique. Members of Some Party, for example, assured me of their desire to achieve success on their own efforts outside of a clique and to have nothing to do with the Clique of Liverpool bands. Yet months later, after a series of disappointments, one member admitted that with hindsight this had probably not been a wise policy as there were several advantages to associating with other bands.

When the Jactars, for example, began rehearsing at Vulcan they knew none of the other bands apart from Crikey it's the Cromptons! and were regarded as introverted and elusive. Gradually, however, largely through Tog working in the office at Vulcan, they came to make friends and socialize with other band members. They established relationships with bands such as Ryan, the Da Vincis, the Decemberists, and One Last Fight, and with them built up a network of exchange and support. They joked and gossiped together; debated the merits of other bands; passed on contacts, advice, technical and musical skills, information about gigs, venues, and record companies; stood in for each other when a replacement player was needed, or helped each other during recording sessions. Between them instruments and equipment were shared, loaned, sold, and thereby continually circulated from band to band.

In addition, those bands often performed together on the same night, sharing the cost of publicity, transport, and PA hire, or attended each other's performances, even though their music was not always to each other's liking. (Some found it difficult to listen objectively to music made by friends anyway.) The Da Vincis, for example, attended performances of the Jactars and Crikey it's the Cromptons! and were upset when their members failed to reciprocate. The Jactars were invited to support Vanilla Beserk and later felt guilty for not staying to hear their performance. An exchange relationship such as this was obviously particularly strong between the Jactars and Crikey it's the Cromptons! They procured gigs for each other—though they often argued as to which band owed the other more favours and which should play first when they were performing together; Trav played with Crikey it's the Cromptons! while they were looking for a lead guitarist; and Huw drummed for the Jactars when they needed a drummer. Such collaboration encouraged bands to improve their music and the performance of it in order to keep up with the other bands and satisfy their critical appraisal. Relations with bands outside Vulcan were more difficult to maintain but Dave met several band members through his work on a Community Programme Scheme. Occasionally he and the others met members of different bands at gigs, such as a band from St Helens who invited the Jactars to perform in St Helens and challenged them to a drinking contest.

If one of the bands in such a group or clique achieved some degree of success the nature of its relationship with the other bands could change. The band's success meant that it became involved in new relationships, activities, and considerations that estranged it from its established network of support and obligations with fellow bands. Inevitably, rumour and gossip centred upon it. Half Man Half Biscuit was one of the main topics of conversation at Vulcan. One or two members of the band had been friendly with members of the Jactars, Crikey it's the Cromptons!, and others at Vulcan, but after the success of their first record Half Man Half Biscuit were obliged to perform frequently all over Britain as well as abroad, and therefore had less time or need to rehearse which meant they spent less time at Vulcan. Other band members were anxious to continue to treat them in as normal a manner as possible whilst in turn, members of Half Man Half Biscuit were concerned to attend the performances of those bands whenever they could.

In such a situation relationships were subject to particular scrutiny and could become strained if it was felt that someone was associating with the successful band *because* of its success. He or she might simply want to be associated with success or might perhaps hope to reap some benefit from the association. They were often called a 'ligger'. Tony, for example, was criticized by members of the Jactars and Crikey it's the Cromptons! for mentioning his association with Half Man Half Biscuit to people in an effort to arouse interest in his own band, and for loitering backstage after one of Half Man Half Biscuit's gigs when he hadn't been invited to do so and had never been particularly friendly with them.

Despite the friendliness and co-operation amongst many local bands, competition between bands was inevitable. So many of them were eager to attract attention and success that they became bitter if they failed to do so and envious and critical of bands that succeeded. In addition, styles of rock music and their associated images and attitudes are imbued with such social and cultural significance that they become badges of identity and allegiance. Thus in their criticisms the bands criticized not just each other's music but much else besides, so their competitive outlook could perhaps be likened to forms of gang rivalry which was sometimes friendly and sometimes not.

SOCIAL ATTRACTIONS OF BAND MEMBERSHIP

A band was formed or joined for a variety of reasons. It might have been seen, for example, as something different and separate from school, work, unemployment, and the family, but it was also generally considered an acceptable hobby, occupation, or career that relatives as well as peers approved of or participated in themselves. The opportunity to join a band might even have been more tempting to those with relatives or peers who encouraged them to join; or to those who were familiar with local rock stars who acted as role models, or lived in an area where such stars had come from or where certain youth clubs, community centres, or teachers encouraged music-making.

Some of the younger band members, for example, had fathers who had been in bands in the 1960s and had passed on their musical skills and enthusiasm. Others, like Midi and Huw, had older brothers who had been in bands. In fact, the number of band members with older brothers was striking (all of the Jactars and Crikey it's the Cromptons! for example—except Dave T. and Tog who was an only child—had older brothers). Obviously not all those brothers had been in bands, but it was suggested that because many of them had grown up 'in the family mould' (as Tony said of his brother)—taking up similar occupations to their parents and settling down early—they might act as negative role models for their younger brothers. The latter knew they wanted something different for themselves and turned to bands as a form of rebellion or escape.

The above discussion of the social relationships a band may involve or be involved in demonstrates the social benefits of being a member of a band. A band offered an active social life, enabling its members to establish, maintain, enrich, and deepen friendships by putting them in touch with new people and by consolidating already existing relationships. The band became a sphere of exchange of favours and of the borrowing of things such as money, equipment, cigarettes, records, and clothes. In this way it provided its members with both a context and a focus for their relationships and thereby a measure of security in their relationships and activities. One man described being in a band as 'a bit like being in a family'. Similarly, Finnegan (1986: 34) described it as a 'home', but it could also be likened to membership of a gang, club, or sports team (as the words 'band' and 'group' imply), all of which can arouse strong feelings of unity and solidarity, loyalty and identity, a sense of belonging.

Such sentiments were encapsulated by the band's name, which was carefully chosen not only to attract attention but to symbolize the band's character, aspirations, and ideology. Consequently, band names often fell into certain genres and fashions, perhaps indicating the bands' politics, image, or style of music. The few local punk bands, for example, had names like Decomposed, Dementia, Public Disgrace. Bands described as 'wacky' tended to make 'alternative' music under names such as Bob, Bob, Bob and Bob, Bogshed, the Revolutionary Army of the Infant Jesus, as well as Crikey it's the Cromptons! Several local bands had names that conjured up images of the East such as Come In Tokyo, Change to the East, the Entire Population of China, Big in Japan, and China Crisis. The names might indicate the bands' participation in a general trend or fashion towards the mysticism and exoticism of the East, or the 'dreamy', 'wistful', and 'escapist' character of their music (a description mentioned earlier of the music made by many local bands).

The Jactars took their name from a song by a band they particularly admired whilst Crikey it's the Cromptons! was named by Tony, after his pseudonym 'Crompton Vest.' The name represented Tony's quirky sense of humour although to outsiders it indicated another 'wacky' band in the same vein as Half Man Half Biscuit, playing a similar style of music. It did, however, attract attention. Some music journalists mentioned it for example, and in the Christmas edition of a popular national music paper one of the questions in the music quiz stated 'Crikey it's the . . .' and asked readers to fill in the rest.

It was under the name of their band that the band's members conducted their music-making activities. The name cemented their relationships, symbolizing the band to its members and to the outside world.

The name was a key focus in any promotional literature or visual symbols produced by the band . . . When a group was first formed it did not have an identity, but once it had a name the group took on a new quality. The very fact that the band had its own title gave its players a mark of unity and shared purpose for both themselves and outsiders (Finnegan, 1986: 21–2).

Under that name the band was seen, spoken of, and defended by its members as a thing in itself that was somehow more than just the sum of its members, existing above and beyond them, not just representing them but also defining them. Trav, for example, believed that Huw would never leave Crikey it's the Cromptons! because, 'He's a Crompton through and through.' Huw and Tony worried that Pete, their new bass player, did not really fit in with the band and its image. They got on well with him and he was a good musician, but could he be 'a Crompton'? Similarly, when the Da

Vincis acquired a new drummer the bass player described how the band had started to develop an identity and how excited and enthusiastic they all felt: 'We now feel like we're Da Vincis. Things could happen.' Thus in the naming of their band the band's members also gave the impression that they were inventing themselves, inventing a personality or something that would represent their personality, or project another personality on their behalf. Some joined bands that were already established, perhaps not in order to create an identity but for the security of the ready-made identity they could assume in doing so.

It was because the name of their band embodied to such an extent their individual and collective identity that band members got annoyed if they heard of another band with the same or a similar name. Members of Some Party, for example, were upset that three or four bands on Merseyside also included the word 'party' in their name and insisted that they had been the first to use it. They frequently discussed changing their name but were reluctant to do so. They rationalized that if they did change it people would not realize it was the same band, which might be harmful to their future career, but it was obvious that there was more at stake and that to change their name would be to relinquish much that was of importance to them.

Being in a band was thus a way of life. The sense of camaraderie and enjoyment involved was exhibited in the way in which musicians tended to fondly discuss and reminisce about past exploits with their band or with previous bands. Tales were told about wild goings-on travelling to and from gigs and what 'a laff' they had, or about how close the band had come to getting 'a deal' and what they should have done but did not. It was also revealed in the way in which band members charted the history of their band, describing in detail the movement of members from one band to another as if relating the genealogy of their own family. Finnegan (1986: 33) described such accounts as the 'mythology' of bands, which 'gave people an awareness of belonging to a wider band world, meaningful in its own right, a shared background to their own activities.'

Such accounts indicate further the sense of purpose that membership of a band entailed and the self-image it engendered. Dave from the Jactars described it as 'a challenge'. Another band member, whilst acknowledging the importance of the actual process of music-making within a band, particularly stressed the significance of all the paraphernalia that went with it. He described the feeling of owning a piece of equipment, 'something that is yours, that you can use to make your own sounds or emulate other sounds.' This indicates a feeling of identity, power, and control, but also a sense of creativity and of unlimited possibilities.

The confidence that membership of a band gave rise to is clearly revealed by the following quotes:

The only thing that keeps me going is being in a band.
If I wasn't in a band I'd be a failure.
If I wasn't in a band I'd be a really boring person.

Several said rather shamefacedly that if they weren't in a band they would probably be out drinking every night. The confidence of band members generally increased as they became more musically competent and skilled, as the songs they worked upon were developed and structured, and as audiences responded favourably to their performances.

That confidence was often reinforced by existing popular conceptions of band membership that attracted many. They varied along with the role models and notions of 'making it' adopted and all that they entailed. Many, however, involved the well-known image of the rock star performing on stage, guitar against groin, before an adulatory audience, a symbol of power and attraction that encouraged a lot of people, many of whom saw membership of a band as a means of enhancing their image and sexual appeal. Most band members, however, stressed the fact that they were in a band simply because it offered the opportunity of being successful at something they enjoyed doing, i.e. making music.

It was not only the structure and ideology of the band that played a social role for its members but the music itself and the performance of it. In Chapter 4 it will be demonstrated that although neither the Jactars nor Crikey it's the Cromptons! had followers as such and could only expect a few of their friends to attend their gigs, they were still able, given the right circumstances, to symbolically create a sense of community by becoming a focus of a group of friends and by refining and defining that group through their music and the performance of it. Live performance thus unites participants in common activity. They collectively concentrate upon, contribute to, and experience the production of a spectacle, and the relationship and dialogue between audience and performers can be such that even if they do not know each other a rapport is established, highlighting the social role of the gig. This binding and uniting of participants can be achieved through dance, music, or through the gig's symbolic forms.

A performance can thus establish and maintain social relationships, reflecting social divisions amongst participants but also transcending them:

> It adds to the stature of the work of art if its social function is not only fulfilled but also *seen* to be fulfilled. In the festive atmosphere engendered by its social setting the work of art becomes a public manifestation of humanity for humanity. There is a sharing of occasion and a feeling of intensity and communication which comes only to people exposed to the same experience at a social event and which is denied to the solitary person in front of the loudspeaker. (Mitchells, 1967: 373).

The sense of community and identity is heightened if the performers and their audience share the same or similar socio-cultural experiences and are thus disposed to interpret the performance collectively. It symbolizes, activates, redefines, and reaffirms values, meanings, concepts, identities, or myths that they might share. Herman (1971: 30) wrote of the Who's rapport with their audience: 'The excitement they generate is in direct proportion to the degree of closeness between them and their audience . . . a group of mods playing for an audience of mods.'

   The unity of audience and performers was sometimes particularly strong at performances of the Jactars and Crikey it's the Cromptons! where each band formed part of the audience for the other and leant its support orally or by assisting with equipment and sound production. Old friends who had previously been in bands with members of the Jactars or Crikey it's the Cromptons! also provided support. The few friends who were able and willing to attend performances regularly, did so mainly out of loyalty to the band and for the social contact and interaction occasioned by the event. Yet at the same time most of them took a genuine interest in the development of the band and its music and enjoyed the experience of seeing their friends perform familiar songs, songs that assumed a particular relevance since they knew the context and personalities that produced them. Pete, for example, once told me which of Crikey it's the Cromptons!' songs was his favourite and described how he used to visit Tony's house on the Wirral and listen to him playing his acoustic guitar. He had thus seen that particular song develop from an embryonic form.

   The division between audience and performers could not only be weakened by the interaction between them during the performance but by that which took place before and after it. At some of the Jactars and Crikey it's the Cromptons!' gigs, for example, band members chatted to friends who had come to see them play. If any music journalists were present they were usually cornered by Tony, who was anxious to confirm that a review of the performance would be written and printed. Trav, Dave, and Gary of the Jactars often dreaded mingling with audience members just after they had played because they found the sudden transition from the tension of playing to socializing and conversation difficult to cope with, particularly since they were expected to discuss their performance. But conversing with audience members directly after a performance was one way in which band members could make new friends and another means by which they could judge the success of their performance. If the response to it was favourable and came from those whose opinions they respected, or from people they had never met before, it was a great boost to the band's confidence.

The social benefits of collective creativity can be illustrated further by describing the formation of a collective of bands. Early in 1986 Fringe, a registered charity involved in community arts on Merseyside, began organizing the production of a compilation album of bands from the borough of Sefton on the understanding that those bands appearing on the album would together form a collective. Notices were distributed to various studios and shops to encourage bands from Sefton that had never before appeared on record to send demo tapes to Fringe, and from those applicants fourteen bands were chosen.

During the first few meetings with the bands, representatives from Fringe pointed out what the bands could achieve by forming a collective and recording an album. They would be in a stronger position, for example, to attract publicity and apply for funding from various trusts and arts groups (like Fringe itself) because they were collectively working for the 'common good' rather than each band for its own commercial ends. 'It's not a competitive thing between the bands,' they emphasized, 'the more you can work together as a democratic body the more we can help you.' The sharing of advice, expertise, and other resources would be to the benefit of all and, as a collective, the bands could work to improve rehearsal and performance facilities within the Sefton area and eventually set up a base there. They could then initiate other projects such as the recording of a second album or the establishment of a publishing company. The Fringe employees stressed, however, that although it would be better if profit from album sales went to the collective, the bands could still (if they were members of the Performing Right Society) claim their own royalties from the album if they wished, and each band would continue to be free to pursue its own ambitions: 'It's still your own material . . . it's still your band . . . it doesn't take away your self-identity. In a way it will add to everyone's identity.'

During those first few meetings many of the band members seemed cautious, shifty, even suspicious. That was also revealed by the questions they asked concerning, for example, distribution of royalties and profits.

During the last two weeks of April each band recorded its track for the album. The meetings continued. A committee was set up comprising a representative from each band, a bank account was opened, the collective was named 'The Sefton Area Musicians and Bands Association' (SAMBA), and a chairperson, treasurer, and secretary were elected. I found myself in the position of secretary, partly because I was already an 'observer' and note-taker, but also perhaps because I was the only female present since the one woman in the collective rarely attended meetings. Gradually the aims of the collective were established, a constitution was drawn up, and various trusts and organizations were approached for funds. Details concerning the album were discussed, a title and sleeve design were chosen, and a promotional event was organized to coincide with its release in October—a concert involving all fourteen bands on board the *Royal Iris*, a vessel that had been hired by bands since the 1960s to cruise up and down the Mersey during performances.

The atmosphere amongst the bands improved with each meeting as their members got to know each other and became more relaxed, good-humoured, and more involved with the album and its launch. Members of the committee drank together in the bar after their meetings and the two Fringe representatives joined forces with the chairperson in a separate music venture. Meetings continued to be well attended after the album's release though some had feared that many members would then lose interest because they had got what they wanted from the collective. More gigs by the collective were planned and some individual bands with gigs chose other bands from the collective to support them. No one seemed that concerned about the fate of the album or the publicity that individual bands might be getting, thus the emphasis had shifted from the ambition, individualism, and competitiveness of the bands to their joint creative and social co-operation.

SOCIAL STRAIN OF BAND MEMBERSHIP

A band could comprise a group of people who got together to make music and became friends—as happened with Crikey it's the Cromptons!, or it could arise from established friendships—as with the Jactars. However it was formed, the making of the band's music was affected by the nature of the social relationships involved, outside factors such as romantic entanglements, domestic or financial matters, and by the social context in which the music was made.

The music and the making of it could in turn enrich or even transform the social context and relationships and concepts within it, expressing, among other things, male solidarity. But it could also cause strain by imposing obligations and pressures upon the friendships involved. Music not only unites but also divides people, and may confirm existing divisions between them. Composition and rehearsal of music by a band depended upon commitment, concentration, and contribution from each member and intense communication between them. The social and emotional quality of experience engendered by such creativity added an extra dimension to the relationships involved which, on the one hand, increased the potential for harmony within the band, but on the other, imposed additional strain that increased the potential for conflict—which was why Tony said about Huw that he got on better with him 'outside of the band.'

Members of the Jactars and Crikey it's the Cromptons! were aware that the functioning of their band and the quality of its creativity depended upon the continuation of good relations and communication within the band, and that awareness itself imposed additional strain upon them. The manager of Up the Khyber, realizing that members of her band had little in common and barely knew each other, organized regular 'band outings' to improve the quality of their relationships and hopefully, therefore, that of their creativity. Some musicians, because of that pressure to get on well with fellow band members, preferred to work alone and only bring in other musicians when they needed to perform or record.

In addition (and this will be discussed in the following chapter), a band demanded commitments from its members such as regular and punctual attendance at rehearsals and financial organization and outlay. The social relationships involved thus took on additional economic significance. Relatives and friends helped with the band's organization and provided financial or moral support at live performances. Girlfriends in a position to do so often lent money for recordings or equipment. Meanwhile within and between bands the system of loans, debts, sharing and accumulation of property that existed tied their members closer together, with a manager often controlling the purse-strings, perhaps taking on a matronly and protective or paternal and financially supportive role.

The meeting of such obligations inevitably meant that sacrifices had to be made. Failure to do so created additional tension. (This could perhaps be alleviated if the band had a manager to meet obligations on its behalf, but managers could also add to the tension, depending upon the nature of their relationship with the band's members.) Many musicians, for example, gave up jobs or training and education courses to concentrate upon their band even when their band had as yet no involvement with record companies. All four members of Blue Nose B gave up 'dead-end' jobs for 'the chance of making it as musicians.' It was thus hardly surprising that most regarded their band as more than just a hobby. As a member of One Last Fight put it: 'The amount of work that goes into it doesn't make it a hobby. The amount of time we spend in a week is what others do in a month.' Another band member suggested that being in a band and on the dole should be seen as being like a student on a grant: the state funds you to do what you want to do and you work hard at it and aim towards a future career with it. That dedication, perseverance, and careerist attitude towards membership of a band could be traced back to the Beatles. In the 1960s most band members had day jobs:

Most of us didn't take playing in bands too seriously, we listened to our parents who said, 'Put that guitar down and do a job with your hands'. We took it half-heartedly, but The Beatles wanted to make a career out of it right from the beginning. Their attitude was, 'We're not messing about up here. We take ourselves dead seriously'. That rubbed off on a lot of bands, including us (musician from Manchester quoted in Leigh, 1984: 72).

The desire to 'make it' with the band could unite the members whilst at the same time straining their relationships. It drew them together by providing a common predicament and goal and many described the support system within their band whereby when one member became despondent or disillusioned the others would encourage them to continue and that member would later reciprocate. On the other hand, ambition increased tension and led to greater frustration when things went wrong or when some were thought to be contributing less than others. Midi, explaining why Pieces of Glass split up, said that while it had not begun as a serious enterprise, people outside the band, and hence those within it, began to take it seriously, which led to conflict within the band where previously there had been none. Similarly, a member of Ryan said that arguments within the band intensified when they realized the band had a chance of achieving something and 'getting somewhere.' Thus relationships between band members changed along with their feelings, attitudes, and conceptions about the band and their membership of it.

Inevitably, such ambitions pressurized the creative process. They were usually accompanied by a drive towards greater musical proficiency and a more professional outlook on the part of the band which meant that relationships were strained if members' musical skills and outlook did not match up. The 'sacking' of band members was commonplace. (Use of the terms 'sacking' and 'firing' was also noted by Finnegan, 1986: 15, amongst band members in Milton Keynes.) Members of Ryan had sacked a total of twenty-seven people throughout the band's two-year history, mainly because they lacked commitment. Members of another band, however (remarking, 'You definitely need a union in your band'), were horrified to hear that, and I never heard any of the Jactars talk of 'sacking' members and only once heard it amongst Crikey it's the Cromptons! when Tony talked of 'sacking' Karen. However, as will be discussed later on, the musical ambitions of members of the Jactars and Crikey it's the Cromptons! did sometimes, as with other bands, conflict with the bonds of friendship between them, a source of friction that led several to comment that one should not get friends involved in the same band because friendships 'got in the way' of band membership.

For many people in Liverpool, rock music and the band format provided one of the few opportunities to make music or indulge in any kind of artistic creativity. Their commitment to a band was one aspect of their lives they had control over and it gave them a means of self-expression and confidence, a sense of achievement and self-respect. Finnegan (1986: 33) suggested that, 'A player's work with his band was one continuing thread amidst the other activities in his life.' For those with access to that kind of music-making the rewards were thus immeasurable.

It is apparent, however, that such access was generally available to men and denied to women. The solidarity, egalitarianism, and creativity was thus overwhelmingly masculine. It was a male gang, a male family. The implication is that women were unwanted and even unnecessary. Membership of a band has been described as a way of life, a source of identity and self-image. The description of the social activities and friendships involved with the Jactars and Crikey it's the Cromptons! showed that that way of life could be so encompassing as to necessitate, to some extent, friendship with those who shared or had shared and experienced it. Thus it was obviously a way of life, an image, and identity formed and constructed apart from women, even in opposition to women because women were seen to threaten it and thus endanger the collective creativity involved.

It has also been shown that commerce was seen to conflict with and threaten collective creativity. The quality of the creative process

was dependent upon that of the collective, i.e. upon good relationships within the band, yet commercial ambitions and financial
matters could not only unite but divide the band, even leading to
'sackings.' Commercial success could again be divisive, as indicated
by some of the reactions to Half Man Half Biscuit. Thus although
there existed much co-operation and community spirit amongst
bands, commercial ambitions led to competition and conflict
between them in their striving for attention and success. In other
words, the bonds of friendship and co-operation within and between
bands and the democratic nature that many of them exhibited
contrasted with the nature of the business they were in and were
inevitably affected and strained by it. Bands didn't just provide their
members with a diversion and context for their social activities and
relationships but also with a series of goals and standards to aim for
and thus with a sense of purpose and justification. For many,
including the Jactars and Crikey it's the Cromptons!, their band
represented their future career and was treated accordingly.

3

Organization
and Management of Bands

The following discussion concerns the organization and management
of bands, indicating some of the activities, problems, and issues
involved and highlighting several features of the local music 'scene'
within which the bands operated.

REHEARSALS

Local rock bands rehearsed in all sorts of places including private
homes, pubs, youth clubs, community centres, and church halls.
Many, like the Jactars and Crikey it's the Cromptons!, used the few
privately owned rehearsal studios which offered adequate space and
the opportunity to rehearse without disturbing neighbours. It was in
the city's two main rehearsal studios that much of my research was
conducted: the Ministry was situated in a rather deserted area of the
city, whilst Vulcan Studios was situated further out in the docklands,
surrounded by scrapyards, empty warehouses, and factories. Each
was an old warehouse several storeys high with rooms converted in a
slapdash manner for rehearsing in. Both, particularly Vulcan, were
grim and dilapidated in appearance, very cold, and badly in need of
repair. Yet within each existed a hubbub of activity and creativity.
Walking towards Vulcan down silent, deserted dockland streets
flanked by hollow, ironclad buildings, an echo of music would
emerge, increasing gradually in volume. Inside, bands rehearsed,
socialized, exchanged tapes, records, equipment, and ideas, information, and advice. Much of that activity centred around one
particular group of bands that rehearsed there regularly. Their
members and friends gathered in the office to chat even when they
hadn't booked a rehearsal.

   To hire a room at the Ministry cost £2·50 per hour. Storage space
for equipment cost extra. At Vulcan prices were much lower. Each
owner operated a system of credit because many of their customers
found it hard to keep up regular payments. Every so often they called

in their debts, but both suffered from bands that disappeared without paying. Billy, owner of the Ministry, employed two or three men to look after the office and organize bookings. Those men also managed bands that rehearsed in the building and generally got on well with many of the other bands and attended their performances. Barry, who owned Vulcan, employed several band members to work part-time in his office. A few of them stayed alone in the building overnight to ward off burglars.

A competitive spirit had arisen between Vulcan and the Ministry whereby bands rehearsing in one stereotyped, slandered, or dismissed those at the other. I was made to feel a traitor by those at the latter when I shifted the focus of my research to the former. Vulcan had its own football team which practised every Sunday. Its opponents sometimes included teams recruited from the local music scene and Barry once tried to arrange a match against the Ministry. I was persuaded to present the challenge and act as go-between. Initially the idea met with enthusiasm from those at the Ministry and I was instructed to spy on the Vulcan team and report back on its membership and proficiency. Eventually, however, the enterprise collapsed, partly because those at the Ministry proved incapable of organizing a team.

The Jactars and Crikey it's the Cromptons! tried to rehearse at Vulcan at least twice a week. For the Jactars rehearsals were difficult to arrange as only Trav had a telephone, but Crikey it's the Cromptons! had to comply with Dave T. and Midi's working hours, and when Dave T. moved to London he was only able to rehearse at weekends. Rehearsals usually lasted three or four hours but rarely began or ended on time. More often than not one or two people arrived late. Often, members of the Jactars attended rehearsals of Crikey it's the Cromptons! and vice versa. Other friends were always welcome to drop in, but rehearsals were generally (as with most bands) rather private, involving hard work and concentration. Good communication between the bands' members was important, and creativity, which was quite a personal endeavour, depended upon it, so many bands banned all friends from rehearsals. 'It's a closed shop', commented one musician. A few, however, positively encouraged friends to turn up so their rehearsals became the focus of social gatherings.

Rehearsals of the Jactars and Crikey it's the Cromptons! were largely directed by those members who contributed most towards musical and lyrical composition and who probably, therefore, had the greatest confidence and emotional investment in the band and its music (generally this meant Trav and Dave from the Jactars and

Tony from Crikey it's the Cromptons!). After a rehearsal some might leave immediately, but usually they all lingered on in the studio or office, sometimes adjourning to a pub (particularly Yates' Wine Lodge opposite the station for trains to the Wirral). Rehearsals cost each band £1.00 per hour in addition to £2 weekly rent for a locker in which to store equipment. Each member also paid for transport to Vulcan Studios, which was more expensive for those living on the Wirral and took longer (it took Huw over an hour). Midi and Dave T. owned cars. Those who could not afford such costs were often lent money by the others and usually both bands owed a considerable sum to Barry.

In February 1986 Dave T. replaced Trav in Crikey it's the Cromptons!. The others were initially unsure whether Dave would suit the band but eventually decided to let him join, partly because of the financial benefits his membership offered. Dave had a room at Vulcan which he rented at £30 per week to use for recording purposes and both bands were now able to use it to rehearse in whenever they liked and could leave their equipment permanently set up in it. Each paid Dave T. £10 per week, which was less than they paid before. When Dave moved to London, however, he could not afford to keep the room so the Jactars and Crikey it's the Cromptons! began renting rooms by the hour again, in addition to storage space. By that time the rent had risen slightly.

INSTRUMENTS AND EQUIPMENT

Generally, bands spent a considerable amount of money on instruments and other equipment (collectively referred to as 'gear'.) The amount tended to vary according to the type of music played, which determined the gear used and the image the band wished to present. Bands wanting to produce a loud, powerful sound, for example, needed more amplification and therefore more money. The gear used by the Jactars and Crikey it's the Cromptons! was mostly second-hand and not of particularly good quality or condition. They sometimes bemoaned this sorry state of affairs, complaining about the poor quality of sound and the fact that their instruments kept going out of tune because they were so 'knackered':

You can just see what's gonna happen. If you go along and you don't get any success and your money back all the equipment's just gonna wear out and then you won't be able to carry on because you won't have any equipment (Trav).

They were also, however, quite proud of their instruments' simplicity and poor condition because it accorded with their general attitude to music-making. They often quoted Roger Hill (local disc jockey) who said 'all good bands come from something cheap.'

Other bands used more technologically advanced equipment such as a DX7 keyboard, which cost upwards of £1,400, had thirty-two pre-programmed installed voices, and took cartridges programmed with more sounds. Some saw the acquisition and accumulation of such gear as a means of achieving status or success and wanted the best and most sophisticated. I often wondered how some of them could afford the equipment they had and several recording and rehearsal studio owners, band managers, promoters, and journalists also expressed bewilderment over this. Most band members showed great determination in acquiring their gear and one must conclude that while many managed somehow to 'muddle through' their financial burdens, others employed considerable ingenuity in raising money and acquiring what they wanted. Some received instruments as presents from relatives but many saved up for months, took on local jobs, or spent time in London working as labourers or hotel workers. Pete (who later joined Crikey it's the Cromptons!) spent two weeks in hospital as a volunteer for drug experiments to raise money for his band. It was also common for those in employment, or with personal funds, to pay for equipment and other expenses on behalf of fellow members, i.e. for the good of the band as a whole.

Many musicians took up cabaret work to raise money for their band because local cabaret bands generally earned more than the rock bands and performed more often. Some earned a living from it. Many had what one described as a 'Jekyll and Hyde' existence. In public they performed cabaret, playing cover versions (songs composed by others); in private they played their own material. Members of rock bands like the Jactars and Crikey it's the Cromptons!, however, tended to regard cabaret as uninspiring, unadventurous, and demeaning and said they would never do it. Those who took it up generally did so just for the money, some describing it as prostituting themselves for money.

Many band members considered going on the government's Enterprise Allowance Scheme as an individual musician or a band, but as all the band's members had to be unemployed and the financial rewards amounted to little in the long term, few actually did the latter. One particular duo did take advantage of the government's Youth Business Initiative Scheme, which gave them the same weekly wage they would receive on Enterprise Allowance and an additional grant of £2,000 to set themselves up in business which they spent on equipment and backing tapes. The duo had to be under the supervision of two tutors who could report back on their progress. They were not, however, successful, and split up after one year.

The gear owned by members of the Jactars and Crikey it's the Cromptons! had been bought with money raised either from relatives or paid work. Tog's grandmother, for example, left him £150, which he used to buy a bass guitar. To buy his keyboards he worked part-time for a while. Neither his keyboards nor Gary and Huw's drums had proper cases. Bin liners were used instead. Dave T. had acquired a lot of equipment for his PA and recording work (most of which was jointly owned with members of his previous band), which both bands used. The upkeep of all this gear was expensive. A set of bass strings alone cost £13–14, and the skin for a snare drum, which had to be replaced every few months, cost £8. The only equipment communally owned by either the Jactars or Crikey it's the Cromptons! was one of the Jactars' amplifiers which belonged to Tog's earlier band until he bought out the others' shares in it after the band's demise. Tog once pointed out that since it was the only piece of equipment communally owned it was the only thing likely to cause a problem if the band split up—though he and Dave also shared the cost of strings for Dave's bass which they both used.

The majority of bands used second-hand gear or shared gear with other bands. A lot of it was bought on hire-purchase which was generally paid off over a number of years, and there was usually some 'knock off' (stolen goods) in circulation. The three best-known shops selling rock music equipment were Hessy's, Rushworths, and Curly Music situated in the city centre. Each had a long history of involvement in local music and together they had cornered the local market. They and other music shops acted as grapevine centres for musicians.

Some bands managed to raise money for other acquisitions such as a small PA system or a van. Three of the five members of the Viz Johnson Band were unemployed but the band took out a bank loan of £600 to buy a van. Blue Nose B also bought a van with compensation money awarded to one member after a car crash. A few bands even had 'roadies' to carry and set up their gear, either because they had so much of it their members found it hard to manage alone, or simply for the prestige. One such band employed as roadies two of their friends, paying them a small percentage of any earnings from performances. Several bands also spent money on stage outfits. More costly was the production of demo tapes.

DEMONSTRATION TAPES

A demo tape featuring recordings of a few (usually three) of the band's songs, could be sent to individuals and organizations in order to represent the band's musical style and talent, or was recorded for the band's own satisfaction. Every six months or so the Jactars and Crikey it's the Cromptons!, like other bands around them, produced one of those tapes. Each cost more and took longer to record than the previous one. The Jactars, for example, spent £45 and four hours recording their first, the second cost £60 and took longer, whilst the third cost £80 and took two days. Prices varied according to the band's financial resources and the studio used. The Da Vincis spent £150 on a three-day recording session at one studio whilst Ryan spent £320 for the same length of time at another, arguing that it was necessary to pay for a more sophisticated studio in order to do justice to the band's material.

For most musicians this was obviously a considerable expense and whilst recording they were under pressure to work as quickly as possible so as not to waste time and money. Hence recording was often a tense occasion. A number of bands, however, bought portastudios in order to make their own recordings. A small machine might cost around £400–500 and bands could compose and practice recording on it in a more relaxed environment with time to spare. Demo tapes could be produced on it but the sound was generally not up to the standards of a professional recording studio.

Geoff Davies, owner of a local record shop and label, insisted that bands should not pay huge sums of money to record in sophisticated studios: 'If you can't record on an 8-track you can't record on anything.' But most bands were concerned to produce something of 'good quality' in the best studio they could afford, not only to do their music justice but to satisfy the record companies for whom most demos were produced. It was generally assumed that larger companies preferred demo tapes of a fairly high standard of production and that was verified by an A&R representative (an employee of the 'Artist and Repertoire' department of a record company) speaking on Radio 4 (*Tuesday Call*: 8 April 1986), who only occasionally signed bands from 'rough' demos.

Among and within bands debates often arose concerning the quality and content of demo tapes. Members of both the Jactars and Crikey it's the Cromptons! discussed at length where to record theirs. Tony argued that he wanted a really good production and was willing to pay more for a better studio. Dave T. and Huw argued that such a high standard of production was unnecessary at their stage.

Trav from the Jactars argued along similar lines with Tog, who said in response that it was a well-known psychological fact that people responded more favourably to a tape of better quality and they should anyway be aiming for the best sound possible. Trav said that as far as he was concerned the quality was good enough and that what mattered was the music, whereupon Tog replied, 'I thought you had better standards than that.'

Amongst the Jactars and Crikey it's the Cromptons! payment for demos came from savings, and those in employment or with some outside source to borrow from usually lent the others their share. Sometimes those remained long-standing debts. Thus when the Jactars argued over the recording of their demo, Tog, obviously outnumbered, shrugged resignedly and said he hoped this time the others would pay him the money they still owed him for the previous demo. If a band was trying to get a record contract copies of the tape were sent to various record companies and radio stations, although many bands invested in a trip to London to deliver the tapes themselves. Some managed to get record companies (usually the larger ones) that liked the band and its music, to finance the recording of more material.

RECORD LABELS, STUDIOS, AND SHOPS

There were between fifteen to twenty commercial recording studios on Merseyside at any one time. Most were small (usually 8-track) and catered mainly for the production of tapes rather than records. They cost about £4,000–5,000 to set up (depending upon the premises), and had a short lifespan. They arose in the late 1970s with punk rock and the move to cheap recording. The larger studios owned more expensive, sophisticated equipment (one, for example, cost £52,000 to build). One or two had been financed by local bands with the advance payment on their record contracts. Such studios were hired out to other bands or used mainly by those who built them. The survival of a studio usually depended upon constant investment but could also be affected by the success of a band associated with it and the expertise of its recording engineers (who play both a technical and creative role operating the recording equipment and balancing the sound.) Few could afford such investment, even if they diversified into other money-earning activities such as the production of backing tracks or music for radio or TV advertisements; thus even the larger studios were struggling, confirming the conclusion of a 1984 feasibility study conducted on the music industry for Sheffield City Council (by C. P. Hadley in association with H. Barrow for McInlay marketing) that recording studios did not, on the whole, make money.

A few of the larger studios had their own record label, which attributes rights of ownership over a record and displays the identity of its owner. There were some small record labels on Merseyside but very few that dealt with several artists and outlived more than one record release. One of the latter was Skysaw run by Pete Leay on the Wirral, but Pete decided to terminate his involvement with local bands after a feud arose between him and Probe which moved on to the lawcourts before it was eventually resolved.

Many of the records produced independently on Merseyside were distributed by Probe record shop, which was part of the Cartel, a nationwide company of independent record distributors. Probe began in 1971, set up by Geoff Davies, an important character in the local music scene and a champion of 'alternative' music. It became a centre for news and gossip on local music. Past employees include two or three well-known rock stars. In 1981 the Probe Plus record label was started, run from an office above the shop. Both shop and office were usually crowded with musicians, some simply passing the time of day. The role played by other record shops besides Probe in the local music scene was not so great although most employed musicians and attracted them as customers, and the managers of one or two also managed bands.

Geoff advised and helped many bands finance, record, and distribute their own records, signing no contracts with them and receiving little or no profit. Most spoke warmly of him, describing his enthusiasm and encouragement of local music. Many praised the fact that he took on bands for no other reason than that he personally liked their music. Nevertheless, a few complained that they received less help than they might have since most of Geoff's efforts were put into the distribution and promotion of bands on his own label. Rumour had it that Geoff's casual approach to the business had resulted in one or two missed opportunities when bands associated with him moved on to fame and fortune elsewhere. During 1986, however, he did have success with Half Man Half Biscuit.

FINANCIAL ORGANISATION

With recordings, equipment, and facilities to pay for, bands had to organize their finances carefully. Amongst the Jactars and Crikey it's the Cromptons! financial matters were dealt with informally and discussed at rehearsals and various social gatherings. Other bands had a manager to deal with finances or were more organized. The five members of one particular band, for example, met on the first Saturday of each month to discuss issues concerning the band. (They didn't discuss such matters at rehearsals in case they got upset with each other, which would affect their playing.) One of the band's members was elected as treasurer and kept all financial transactions logged in a book. Every month each member contributed £10 to a general fund and their joint earnings as a band were added to it. When the treasurer once borrowed money from the fund to go on a drinking spree a new treasurer was elected and a system of interest on loans was introduced.

Other bands also organized regular meetings outside rehearsals and pubs and many had a bank account in the band's name and/or a band kitty. The four members of Blue Nose B each contributed £10 of their fortnightly unemployment benefit to their kitty. Most bands invested earnings from public performances back into the band to pay for rehearsals or recordings but some, including the Jactars and Crikey it's the Cromptons!, split the amount between them for individual use. Friction concerning finances often arose (though that had not yet occurred with the Jactars and Crikey it's the Cromptons!), particularly when a band signed a contract involving new financial and legal arrangements. If the band split up before the contract expired then further complications ensued, but that often happened even if the band had no contract. (Arguments often arose, for example, when bands held joint ownership of equipment.)

Sometimes relatives helped with the organization and management of a band. One man, for instance, managed his son's band and invested money in it, treating it like a family business from which he eventually hoped to profit. Often, relatives provided or assisted with transport and publicity. Huw's brother sometimes transported equipment for Crikey it's the Cromptons!, and he helped them record their first demo tape on his portastudio. He even offered to help finance the production of a record. If a band became successful its members could reciprocate. A well-known Liverpool band named China Crisis, for example, employed the brothers of the two founding members on a permanent basis as road manager and van driver.

Relatives also helped by providing emotional support and attending performances. The managers of a band that had just signed a contract with a large record company, were amazed and exasperated when at their first major recording session the band arrived with about a dozen relatives in tow who squashed themselves into the studio and shouted words of encouragement throughout the recording. Quite often, relatives were members of the same band. One of two cousins in Blue Nose B said that having a cousin in the band made him feel safer: 'I won't get kicked out because if I was my mum wouldn't speak to his mum.' The managers of another local band were unable to get rid of the guitarist because he was the brother of the band's founder and songwriter and again their mother would cause problems if he was dropped.

The type of music played by the band and the attitude of its members to the band, its future, and to the record industry, could affect the band's earning potential in a local or national context. Despite that, most local bands striving for a contract of some kind shared the same financial situation and faced the same economic hurdles. To overcome them required a great deal of commitment and sacrifice. A few had patrons (non-relatives) who helped financially, but for most, lack of money was a continual set-back and preoccupation. On more than one occasion I was told: 'Bands who've had their gear handed to them on a plate must have a very different attitude to bands like us who've had to work for it', and many were keen to point out: 'This band is not subsidized by any parents.' With money the bands could afford better equipment, promotion, and recording facilities and thereby, they believed, increase their chances of success. However, the general ideology of being in a band incorporated a notion of hardship, the suggestion that to struggle and perform for little reward over a substantial period of time was part of a process all bands should pass through. Many felt that bands that achieved success without having performed live or 'established contact with an audience', had not 'paid their dues.' Lack of finances often motivated bands and increased their sense of purpose.

PROMOTION AND PUBLICITY

The two main local radio stations were Radio Merseyside (BBC) and Radio City (independent.) Both ran only one or two programmes broadcasting music by local rock bands but the disc jockeys who presented them (Roger Hill for example) were well known and approachable and lent encouragement and support to the music scene in various ways. Airplay on their programmes could benefit a band. The Jactars, for instance, received phone calls from one or two small record companies who had heard their demo tape on local radio, and Roger Hill recommended Crikey it's the Cromptons! to promoters ringing from London to enquire about bands.

For a record to become a hit it had to be played on national radio but competition for such airplay was enormous and unless the recording was of a very high standard and had a record company to promote it, it would never be played. Many bands, however, including the Jactars and Crikey it's the Cromptons!, delivered tapes to disc jockeys John Peel and Janice Long at Radio One in London. Both were generally regarded as patron saints of 'local' and 'alternative' musics and since they originally came from Liverpool it was thought they might be more sympathetic to bands from there. A number of local bands, Half Man Half Biscuit for example, achieved success because John Peel liked and played their music. He received 100–150 demo tapes per week in addition to records, press cuttings, and photographs. He listened to the records foremost since he could play them on air straight away whereas he could not (because of copyright laws) do so with tapes. If, however, he heard a tape he particularly liked, his producer booked the band for a session, that is a recording played live on air.

In previous years several music magazines and fanzines had been produced on Merseyside, some by members of bands. During my stay in Liverpool, however, they were very few in number, largely because of the difficulty in selling advertising space within the city, which meant that the main outlet for bands in the local press were the few newspapers, the most important being the *Liverpool Echo* which ran a weekly column on local music featuring press releases and snippets of news and information on bands and forthcoming performances. Press coverage was thus desirable but hard to attain. One consequence of Liverpool's notoriety regarding rock music, however, was that it still attracted the attention of the national media. There were consequently about half a dozen music journalists who originated from and operated within Merseyside and wrote, at one time or another, for national music papers. Bands were constantly trying to persuade those journalists to review their gigs. The reviews could bring the band's name to the attention of a nationwide readership and were also read by record company personnel and disc jockeys.

By January 1986 the Jactars and Crikey it's the Cromptons! had only had brief mentions in a fanzine produced for a short period of time at Vulcan Studios and titled 'Vulcanburger' after the hamburgers sold there. The following month a brief review of the Jactars' latest demo tape appeared in a Manchester fanzine. Although it wasn't unflattering, it was not to their liking and they were depressed to discover that another Liverpool band reviewed well on the same page was friendly with the reviewer. They sadly concluded that whom a band knew counted far more than the quality of its music.

In July Crikey it's the Cromptons! got a gig at a local club and discovered that they were supporting a band from London that had recently attracted attention in the national independent music scene. Consequently, several journalists turned up to review that band and their reviews, published in three national music papers, also mentioned Crikey it's the Cromptons!—but were highly critical. Tony and Huw were initially shocked but soon accepted the reviews with good humour and were anyway flattered to get three in one week. Later, Huw even expressed delight at receiving such bad press and was pleased that the reviewers had been so moved by them, even if they had not been moved to give a particularly favourable response. It was better to get a very bad response, he rationalized, than a mediocre one; at least people would remember them, and hundreds of people would have read the reviews and would now know of the band's name and existence. The reviews seemed to give him added incentive to make it with the band so that he and the others could 'show them' (the reviewers) the error of their words. Tony was encouraged by Huw's optimism and decided that the reviewers were just too short-sighted to realize how brilliant Crikey it's the Cromptons! were. He suggested they gather together the worst bits from each review and print them on their posters.

A few months later both the Jactars and Crikey it's the Cromptons! were reviewed in a national music paper by a local journalist whom Tony had consistently invited to the bands' performances. Both bands were quite pleased with the review and thought it accurately summed them up. The Da Vincis were delighted by that journalist's review of one of their gigs printed in another edition of the same paper. They thought it 'spot on' and thanked her profusely for it the next time they saw her. Trav and Dave also thought it a good review. It was favourable 'without going over the top' and without making the Da Vincis seem 'pretentious.' I asked that journalist how she, in all honesty, would describe her review: was it favourable or non-committal? She seemed slightly offended but then said it was a combination of both and was 'about as good as you could do for a band at their stage . . . They aren't big enough to rave about.'

One or two other local journalists were often criticized for writing consistently bad reviews of local bands and for dismissing them in a sarcastic, offhand manner to make their reviews more interesting. However, when one of those journalists heard a recording by the Jactars he contacted them at Vulcan to tell them that he really liked it and thought they were the most exciting local band he had heard in ages. The Jactars were delighted but tried to remain cautious and nonchalant. They sent him another tape and invited him to a gig. The performance was not one of their best. Nevertheless the journalist said he enjoyed it and would attend another. He never did. When I spoke to him later he said he genuinely liked the band but had been unable to persuade his editor to print a review of, or interview with, them because they were so unknown. He particularly liked the band's 'offhand manner . . . as if they didn't give two hoots about me.' It made a change, he said, from all the other bands who were 'crawlers' and tried to 'suck up' to him.

Promotion of the band took many other forms. Some bands, for example, printed biography sheets which included reviews and photographs of them taken professionally or by a friend or relative (Crikey it's the Cromptons! had theirs taken by a friend but like the Jactars had no other promotional material). Those were sent to record companies, radio stations, and press personnel, along with tapes or records. Some bands also distributed business cards showing their name and a contact address. Others displayed their name on badges, pasted or wrote it on walls, or simply walked around town and sat in cafés so as to be seen together as a band. One such band had their name stencilled upon their leather jackets.

MANAGEMENT

To help them promote and organize themselves many bands sought some sort of management. Neither the Jactars nor Crikey it's the Cromptons! had a manager. The latter had one for a short while (Dave T.'s sister Kathy) but she was unreliable and uncommitted. The Jactars and their friends felt that they particularly needed a manager because they were disorganized, shy, and hesitant in their self-promotion. They thought carefully about whom they could approach to manage them and considered asking one of two men they knew through their management of other Vulcan bands. The merits of each were debated but no decision reached. Crikey it's the Cromptons! also considered management and once debated whether it was better for a manager to be a friend of the band, who would be more personally involved and loyal, or a complete outsider, who might be more objective, neutral, and pushy. Dave T. once met two men from London who expressed an interest in managing a Liverpool band. He invited them to a gig but they never turned up and the matter was dropped.

Perhaps half the local bands had some form of management. A manager was seen by most of those involved in the music business to be an asset because he or she would take over much of the organization and administration of the band and, by negotiating with people on its behalf, could protect the band's members from double-dealing and disillusionment. Most bands assumed that with a manager they would appear more professional, and that was confirmed by promoters and A&R personnel, some of whom refused to deal with a band unless it had a manager to represent it. Consequently, many bands got someone, sometimes a band member, to stand in as manager temporarily while approaching or negotiating with companies.

Some managers got involved with the creative side of the band and pushed the band to achieve better results, whilst others left that to the band's members. Generally the manager's role was to negotiate for the band a record deal and take charge of its career and in return he or she received a percentage of the band's earnings. Often the manager had to sort out any personal difficulties that might arise within the band. Ideally he or she was less emotionally involved in the music-making and thus more objective. Often a friend of the band took on the role of manager and became almost an additional band member, splitting costs and profits with the others. Usually no contract was signed and both parties could part company whenever they wished. Many other bands took on as manager someone with experience in some aspect of the music business, or had a more formal arrangement such as a partnership agreement with their manager. Occasionally, managers of clubs took on a management role and the band might play regularly at their club. Some bands approached and signed contracts with management companies but there were only one or two such companies in Liverpool.

If a band signed a contract with a record company, the company might consider the manager an important mediator between it and the band. Sometimes the manager was allowed complete control, able to arrange everything or appoint others to do it. That often worked to the detriment of less experienced managers who found themselves out of their depth with the contractual and business matters that had to be negotiated. Often the record company might then suggest that the band get rid of the manager, and usually the band's members could see that it was in their best interest to take on someone with more experience. Some companies were said to have a policy of cutting out the manager completely in order to gain control over a band.

Good management was regarded as gold dust and those involved in Liverpool's music scene held all kinds of opinions and theories on what qualities made for a good or bad manager. It was generally agreed that he or she should be confident and pushy and that was stressed by John Peel (Radio 4, *Tuesday Call*: 8 April 1986), who said, 'At some stage you have to have someone around you or working for you who is damned hard.' He described managers he encountered who were 'psychopaths' but added, 'perhaps that is what you need.' He thought it a mistake for bands to take as manager a friend or 'the guy who can't do anything' because bands 'have to be a bit more serious than that.' On the other hand, it was important for a manager to be able to get along with people and be prepared to ask for advice. Some managers irritated record companies by being overly aggressive. One musician seeking a record contract discovered too late that companies had been interested in offering him a deal but were put off by his manager. Ideally, a manager was someone with good contacts in the music business and, more importantly, good relations with those contacts. When a surprisingly large number of A&R personnel visited Liverpool to see one particular band it was rumoured that the band's manager supplied cocaine to various record companies and had got them to Liverpool by 'calling in his favours.'

The better known local managers were subject to considerable scrutiny and criticism by others in the music scene regarding their management techniques and dealings. One or two, for example, ran a record label and were criticized for ignoring the interests of other bands on the label in favour of the band they managed, or for attempting to sell one band on the strength of another's success. One such manager eventually ceased to run his label because it conflicted with his role as manager, a conflict also pointed out by Frith (1983: 108).

Managers were also criticized if they were personally involved with one of the band's members. Members of one band said they had been offered contracts by record companies on condition that they got rid of their manager but were unable to do so since she was the girlfriend of their founder member. Members of another band wrote a letter to the band's lawyer claiming that their manager's relationship with the lead singer made her unsuitable for the role. (The lawyer's reply, after consulting with the manager, stated that the manager's morals made her feel unable to go out with *all* the band's members.) Those managers who were personally involved with a band member, on the other hand, believed that though it did cause friction between the band's members, it also meant they were prepared to work harder for the band than someone else might.

Some bands approached the issue of management very cautiously, wary of the 'sharks' in management, i.e. those who pretended to know about the business but did not and were just out to make as much money from the band as they could. One man described them as the 'I-know-a-lot-of-faces-and-can-get-you-a-lot-of-gigs' type. Yet in turn, managers spoke of bad experiences with bands. Some spent a considerable sum of their own money on a band only to find themselves sacked by the band or have the band split up.

MUSIC EDUCATION AND COMMUNITY ARTS

Many bands sought advice and assistance from other sources besides managers. Few of the younger ones could do so through their schools since facilities for the teaching or performance of rock music in local schools were minimal, reflecting the situation nationwide where rock music was generally not considered a subject serious enough for pupils to indulge in. Despite that, bands formed at many schools, sometimes influenced and encouraged by one particular teacher, and, since the dramatic rise in youth unemployment and recent changes in school syllabuses, the role of rock music in youth education was gradually being considered more seriously.

That change in attitude was more apparent outside schools—in community arts groups, for example, which had previously avoided rock music because it was not considered worthy enough or because its commercial nature was problematic. Some of those groups organized rock music workshops and a few youth and boys' clubs also encouraged the formation of bands or provided facilities for them to rehearse in. When Merseyside County Council was abolished in 1986, Merseyside Arts took over the distribution of funds to local arts and community groups. That organization held music workshops and established a local songwriters' union but otherwise had little involvement with rock music. It did, however, fund bodies like Fringe and the Crawford Arts Centre which also ran workshops. In addition, as shown in the previous chapter, Fringe helped establish three collectives of bands on Merseyside.

Other local community groups included the Blackie, which had limited facilities for two bands based there and organized several musical events a year; Sons and Daughters of Liverpool, a small organization with facilities used by five or six bands which promoted a few musical as well as dramatic events, sometimes in collaboration with groups from other parts of the country; Gigs for Kidz, another small organization funded by the county council to organize gigs for local musicians and offer them information and advice. In addition, the Merseyside Trade Union Community and Unemployed Resource Centre (MTUCURC) employed two music 'fieldworkers' to promote popular music and built, during 1986, a 'community' recording studio with funds from the council and various rock stars, setting up a Music Working Group to supervise it. It also released, in collaboration with the Charles Wootton Centre, an anti-apartheid record.

It was possible for some community arts groups to seek funding from national organizations such as the Prince's and Jubilee Trusts which had a generous attitude towards rock music. Individual musicians and bands could apply independently for such funds but stood a better chance if they were linked to an organization. The records produced by the collectives of bands, for example, were partly financed by those two trusts. The North Liverpool Music Resource Centre was funded by the county council and the European Social Fund to build a small recording studio and train a group of unemployed youths in various aspects of music-making, paying them a basic weekly wage. Trainees on The Liverpool Youth Music Project, a training scheme funded by the Manpower Services Commission (MSC), learned a variety of skills, including sound engineering and music theory and notation. The Liverpool Youth Music Centre, a community education project, was financed through various sources. It professed some facilities for rock bands but was largely concerned with classical music, jazz, and brass bands.

Lack of communication and co-operation and frequent feuding and bickering existed within and between several of those community and arts centres. Accusations centred in particular upon corrupt squandering of community funds and during 1986 both Gigs for Kidz and the North Liverpool Music Resource Centre closed down after internal disputes over that issue. Opposition between Fringe and Merseyside Arts also intensified, and MTUCURC aroused hostility and criticism over its new recording studio which was said to be monopolized by a small group of bands affiliated both politically and otherwise to the centre.

Feuding often focused upon particular events those organizations were involved with. Three-day concerts such as 'Rock for Jobs', 'Rock for Rights', and 'the Peoples' Festival' were badly attended. They were sponsored by the county council, as was the 'Liver Aid' concert and 'the Drums Marathon', an anti-heroin event involving many musicians. Several of those involved in its organization spoke of embezzlement of funds by co-organizers and pointed out that the council donated thousands of pounds to the event, less than half of which was eventually raised. Bickering and backbiting also focused upon 'Larks in The Park', an annual event organized by an independent group of people, involving 70–80 local bands, which began in 1979 and grew in stature over subsequent years to become a media attraction. It was staged in Sefton Park over August bank holiday weekend but in 1986 the organizers decided not to hold it because of the amount of time and energy it required and because of its disruption in previous years by heavy rain. Nevertheless, the event was still the subject of much conversation and gossip throughout the year. Most complaints were directed at the organizers' criteria for choosing the bands that would appear.

PUBLISHING AND LEGAL PROTECTION

Some bands sought legal advice from solicitors (there were no solicitors on Merseyside who specialized in music—though two or three regularly undertook music-related work) or investigated for themselves the legal complexities of the music business, where income from recordings is modest in comparison to that earned from publishing. The decline in the youth market for records, alongside the increasing demand for music from a growing number of media channels, focused attention more upon the exploitation of music rights rather than on record sales. The situation regarding music rights and royalties is complicated. There are licences which cover the public performance of sound and video recordings (the royalties received by the artists vary according to the nature of the agreement between them and the recording companies concerned). These are distinct from the the copyright in the music itself. The Performing Right Society represents composers and publishers of practically all copyright music. Under the Copyright Act it administers the right to perform their works in public and the right to broadcast them. It then distributes to its members the royalties that it collects after deducting its administration costs.

When only one or two members of a band received such royalties friction often arose. The singer/songwriter of two local bands, for example, each paid fellow band members a weekly wage out of the advance from their record company and kept all royalties themselves, despite the fact that both extracted ideas and expertise from fellow members which they used and developed in their compositions. Such an arrangement often discouraged the others from investing creative input into the band's material or prompted them to leave the band. Members of another well-known local band complained bitterly when the band's songwriter received all the royalties, arguing that they were entitled to a share because it was the image they presented that sold the band's material.

The publicity over recent court cases involving rock performers and record/publishing companies had highlighted the performer's bargaining power in contractual obligations and led to a greater awareness of the legal implications of music-making as a band. On Merseyside some composers worked alone or formed songwriting partnerships instead of bands, bringing in other musicians only when they wanted to perfom or record, either before or after a contract had been signed, which gave them more control and was financially more profitable. Many band members and managers, before they had been offered a contract of any kind, discussed and organized legal matters regarding contracts and songwriting methods and products.

Kate, the manager of Up the Khyber, for example, had carefully worked out the legal and financial position of each band member according to how much he contributed towards composition. Many of the band's lyrics were written by the singer whilst the guitarist composed much of the music so any future royalties would usually be split equally between them. If the guitarist wrote some of the lyrics he would get a share of the singer's percentage. 'Being in a band', said Karen, 'means that you share everything—but not royalties, and that is the only sensible, business like way to go about it.' The band used to have a percussionist who was only given the status of 'band member' when he began to play keyboards and contribute more to the composition of the music.

In addition, bands were often advised to copyright their material at an early stage before signing any contract. They could do so by sending it to Stationers' Hall in London—except it had to be written on manuscript paper which none of the bands I met ever did. Instead, many sent tape-recordings of their material to themselves by registered post or deposited tapes with bank managers and solicitors. Members of the Jactars and Crikey it's the Cromptons! discussed the issue of copyright but never that of royalties. They were quick to point out that all of them contributed equally to compositions. Many others said the same and believed that friction over royalties could be avoided if the band's members held an equal share in the royalties. That was often not the case, however, because the creative input of individual members usually varied with each composition. Legal and financial matters were thus a frequent cause of band friction and dissolution.

The Musicians' Union played little part in the lives of most local rock bands. Musicians had to become union members if they wanted to appear on television or perform live on radio. For most, the £25 annual membership fee seemed a considerable amount and the places they performed in always paid far below union rates. Thus many saw little point in joining unless they were appearing on radio or television or signing a record contract, and most were far from doing either. Even those involved with contractual agreements rarely contacted the union for advice, usually seeking it from elsewhere. Some contacted independent solicitors who very occasionally offered legal aid, but most sought advice from other sources, whether relatives, friends, disc jockeys, or journalists. Those with experience in the music business complained that as a result bands were often misinformed and ill-advised.

PERFORMING IN PUBLIC

There were various types of places that local bands could perform in on Merseyside, some associated with a particular style of music and band. They included cafés, pubs, clubs, civic and church halls, theatres, education establishments, arts centres, hotels, and those specifically geared towards live music. The latter venues were dwindling in number, and larger venues such as the university, polytechnic, and the Royal Court Theatre generally booked non-local bands. There were a few halls or social clubs that could be hired but that was expensive and required considerable organization. When I arrived in Liverpool there were about seven main venues in the city centre for local bands (although occasionally one or two cafés and wine bars also booked bands.) One of them stopped booking rock bands because it found them unprofitable, whilst three others went bankrupt and closed. No adequate replacements had arisen by the time I left. There were also two or three outside the city centre and some of the more outlying areas such as Chester, Widnes, and St Helens had at least one main venue. Many areas, however, were lacking in such facilities.

During the 1960s there had been more venues for live music but in the 1970s many turned to disco music, which was more profitable. Suddenly clubs became big business which attracted those locally referred to as 'mickey mouse gangsters' and corrupt dealings. Stories circulated about gang violence and 'pay-offs' by club owners to gangsters and police. That continued during the time of Eric's, when live music became popular again, but while I was in Liverpool live music was said to be out of favour, which meant neither clubs nor gangsters could make much money from it. The majority of club owners therefore relied upon the sale of alcohol for profit. Few would run a club at a loss in order to promote local music as the owners of Eric's had done, and since live music no longer attracted audiences they were less willing to book bands. If they did do so it was often on slacker nights of the week in an effort to increase bar takings. Some hired a promoter of live music or rented their club one or two nights a week to a promoter who used it to put bands on.

Local bands usually got gigs through other bands and contacts in the music business, or by approaching or sending tapes to club/pub owners and promoters. It was possible to acquire an agent to negotiate and arrange gigs for a percentage of the takings but few bands, besides those that had achieved some degree of success outside Merseyside, did so, largely because there were no agencies based on Merseyside.

The Jactars and Crikey it's the Cromptons! performed in public about once a month depending upon factors such as the time of year, availability of venues, and whether they were working on new material or not. Before the performance they debated over and rehearsed a 'set' list of songs to be performed and usually attempted to recruit an audience and generate media and record company interest through radio announcements, posters, leaflets, phone calls, or word of mouth. Publicity was sometimes provided by the club/pub management (though many couldn't be relied upon to do the job properly) but more often by the band itself. Members of the Jactars and Crikey it's the Cromptons! usually had to organize all their own publicity. The most artistic member of each band (Dave from the Jactars and Huw or Tony from Crikey it's the Cromptons!) would draw a design which was then enlarged and photocopied. Twenty-five such posters might cost £3·50 and three times as much if they were printed. Leaflets were cheaper and could be distributed in cafés and pubs but rarely attracted much attention. Fly-posting was illegal but many bands did it anyway. Tog and Dave once got caught fly-posting by the police and had their names and addresses taken. Nothing came of it but the others believed they would be in trouble if caught a second time.

In the city centre posters advertising gigs were continually pasted up and new ones pasted over them within a short space of time. I was surprised to discover how much attention bands paid them. Members of the Jactars, for example, must have observed them closely for some time. They knew how long particular posters had been up for and pointed out a poster of Ryan's stuck over another band's poster because that band had in turn pasted it over one of Ryan's. Such posters had thus been strategically placed in a sort of battle for publicity.

Performances were also advertised on local radio. Roger Hill, for example, ran a weekly 'gig guide', choosing one 'gig of the week.' He once chose a gig of the Jactars and Crikey it's the Cromptons!, and on another occasion the Da Vincis, yet both still attracted only a very small audience. Performances could also be advertised in the *Liverpool Echo*, which one promoter believed a much more effective form of publicity than pasting posters up all over the city, though more expensive at £40 per advertisement.

On the day of the performance the band's gear was loaded into the vehicle they had borrowed, bought, or hired. The hire of a van for a gig within Merseyside might cost around £10 to £15. Many bands hired Bernie—quite a familiar character to many in the local music scene—to transport their gear. At the club or pub the gear was unloaded and set up along with the PA system which was hired by the band (at anything from £15 to £100) or provided by the club/pub. If several bands were performing on the same night the promoter(s) of the event might provide or arrange a 'backline' of equipment, perhaps comprising a drum kit and basic amplifiers that all the bands involved could use.

After setting up the gear, the band and the engineer at the mixing desk 'sound-checked' to set the sound levels on each instrument. They might then wait around or go to a nearby pub. Sometimes the band arranged for their performance to be recorded on a cassette machine by a friend or manager so they could listen to it critically afterwards. If the performance was well received by the audience they might perform an encore, though some bands disliked the idea of an encore or preferred to 'leave them wanting more.' After the performance the band members might mingle with their audience or watch the next band if they weren't the last or only band to perform. Later they might be paid by the manager of the venue before dismantling the gear, loading it into the van, and driving it back to the studio or building in which it was stored.

Rock bands were generally paid little for gigs, but on the whole, it was not the income from them that mattered but the publicity and promotion they offered in terms of the bands' future career. There were so many bands pursuing so few performing opportunities that just to get a gig could be reward enough. Often, however, bands ended up losing money on gigs. On average the Jactars and Crikey it's the Cromptons! managed to break even. If they made a profit they were delighted. If they made a loss each member paid an equal part of the deficit. Some bands consistently made a profit, perhaps because they had a sizeable following to swell the audience, or because their music and image suited places that paid more. (Generally such places accepted music of a more 'commercial' style.) Most bands wanted to get onto 'the college circuit' since student venues paid well and attracted sizeable audiences. A band might, for example, earn £150 for a gig at a local college of further education.

On the rare occasion when the university hired a local band, the band was paid £50 plus food and beer. The university's average payment for the more well-known, out-of-town bands was £1,500–2,000 although in 1986 one particular band was paid £5,500.

It will be shown in the following chapter that the structure of the performance and size of the audience was affected by many different factors. However, audiences for local bands were often dishearteningly small and unresponsive despite efforts made by bands to attract larger numbers. The owner of a local PA company who worked at gigs most nights of the week, said that 90 per cent of local bands generally attracted only 15–20 people. Colleagues, relatives, and friends were usually relied upon to make up the bulk of the audience. Members of other bands were often present as well, attending out of loyalty to the performing band or to keep a competitive eye on it. Media and record company personnel were sometimes invited to attend but often didn't show up. A few bands could rely upon the attendance of a regular 'following' or were able to attract an audience through their records. Naturally, the more well-known the band, the fewer problems it had recruiting an audience—although some bands performed so much that they became too familiar and uninteresting.

Largely because of the small audiences, most musicians said they were fed up with performing in Liverpool and wanted to perform elsewhere but few had the money, contacts, or organizational skills to do so. A gig in Manchester, for example, might cost around £45 or £35 plus the cost of petrol for the hire of a van alone. Thus bands performing outside Merseyside sometimes tried to organize a coach or van for their friends. The sale of tickets for the coach could cover some of the transport costs and at the same time guarantee a larger, more responsive audience. A thirty-seater coach, however, might cost £80 to hire for a gig in Manchester so the band could only cover costs if it charged about £3 per head and could fill the coach. Most bands were unable to recruit so many supporters, some of whom could not afford to see them perform outside the city when they could see them in it for much less.

One Last Fight managed to break even performing outside Merseyside but still found the audiences too small. They got the gigs by writing to clubs and sending tapes but eventually decided to hire an agent who would get them more lucrative gigs booked on a better night of the week. Having an agent, however, did not always help. The agent of one band got it a booking at a London club but the band was only paid £50 from which the agent deducted 15 per cent. Transport to London cost the band £60 so it ended up losing money.

The band expected that and decided it was worth it since A&R personnel and staff writers on the national music papers (rather than local free-lance journalists) were more likely to attend a performance in London than in Liverpool.

Trav and Dave from the Jactars tried to get a gig in Newcastle but were told that it was hard enough for local bands to get gigs there let alone those from elsewhere. When Dave T. moved to London it was hoped that he would be able to make contacts there and find gigs for Crikey it's the Cromptons! They finally did get one but through a different chain of events. After they supported the up-and-coming London band in Liverpool (the gig that was reviewed so badly), a member of the audience from London mentioned them to a friend who organized entertainment at Central London Polytechnic. That friend rang Radio One to enquire about them and was referred to Radio Merseyside where Roger Hill recommended them. Tony wanted to hire a minibus to transport friends and recoup some of the band's costs. Dave T. argued that it was too risky. He doubted that they could persuade enough people to go and thought it safer to hire a small van for £50, which, in the end, they did, thus breaking even as they were paid £50 for the gig.

A series of several consecutive performances in different locations (a 'tour') was almost impossible to organize unless the band had considerable financial backing, although there were a few opportunities for Liverpool bands to perform abroad through one or two competitions or agencies that organized 'packages' of Liverpool bands to send abroad, or exchanges with bands from particular countries. Bands with record contracts were often expected to promote their material by going on tour. It was a costly, exhausting business but through it bands raised their public profile and thus their record sales.

Some bands made a great effort to get a 'support' slot with a touring band, pestering the agents who organized the tours or the few local bands successful enough to go on tour. Often the touring band would choose a support band it knew and was friendly with, but generally a support slot was acquired through a 'buy-on' whereby the support band paid a certain amount of money to get on the tour and contributed towards fees for lighting operators, road crew, vehicle hire, hotels, etc. One band got a support slot touring Europe with a well-known band because they knew the band personally and had supported it in Liverpool. They nevertheless had to pay £5,000 for the tour, part of which was paid by a private patron but most was raised through savings and loans. Another local band got on to the British tour of a well-known band at the cost of £2,700, which was considered reasonably cheap.

When it came to live performance bands frequently suffered accident and misfortune. Vans broke down, strings snapped, the PA system was faulty, or the club was double-booked. Ryan once arranged an exchange with a band named the Gargoyles who travelled from Hull with all their equipment and arrived at the Liverpool club to discover that another band had already set up its gear. On another occasion Ryan arrived at a club with its equipment and about 50–60 supporters in tow to find the building closed.

In October 1986 the Jactars, Crikey it's the Cromptons!, the Da Vincis, and One Last Fight performed in a London pub to promote the recently released compilation album of Vulcan bands. They hired a forty-seater coach for £270 at a loss of about £50. When they arrived at the pub the promoter informed them that he couldn't pay them anything as he had paid a lot for the PA system and had booked a band from Ireland that would be 'headlining' (i.e. playing last). In addition, the audience comprised only a few people, none of whom were the invited A&R personnel, and since there were five bands to play, the first had to begin at about 9 p.m. when the audience consisted entirely of the other bands. Even their friends from the coach were absent as they were still wandering around London.

Just a few weeks previously, the Jactars, Crikey it's the Cromptons!, and the Da Vincis had had another bad experience, this time at a club in Manchester—their first gig outside Merseyside. To transport equipment for all three bands they had to hire a van and Bernie's trailer, which cost them £60. We all set off from Vulcan at about 4 p.m. but shortly afterwards Bernie's car broke down. For forty minutes we sat in a lay-by while Bernie and each band member took turns to prod and bang the engine although it was obvious that no one had any idea what might be wrong or even how an engine worked. Someone tried in vain to telephone the club in Manchester to inform the others and get them to drive back in the van and pick us up. Eventually the engine spluttered into life and Bernie decided to risk driving at a slow pace.

At the club itself events took a turn for the worse. The others had been there since 5 p.m. and were getting restless. By 9 p.m. all three bands had finished sound-checking and wandered over to a nearby pub, ate chips, and played pool. By midnight there was still no audience and we were harshly ushered from the bar by the club employees into the performance room where we sat waiting for someone to turn up. No one did. There were people in a bar downstairs but none came up. The club's manager could not have advertised the gig and the PA operator said that the previous week there *had* been a sizeable audience for a local band. By 1 a.m. the band members were too drunk to care and decided to play anyway.

Besides which, Dave T. had driven all the way from London and was unwilling to drive back that same night without having played. At 2 a.m. the manager shut the building. The PA operator felt sorry for the bands and waived his fee but each band member still had to donate £5 or more to cover the cost of transport hire.

Such experiences led some bands to avoid gigging altogether and concentrate wholly upon rehearsing and producing tapes to send to London or elsewhere. Members of the Jactars, for example, after the initial thrill and excitement of performing live had subsided as they gained in confidence, lost the sense of challenge and feeling of exhilaration aroused through their gigs. Consequently, they decided upon a 'gigging policy' whereby they would limit their gigs to those which would be beneficial in terms of money, audiences, and their future career as a band, and plan and publicize such gigs well in advance. Trav said he was just too ambitious to continue performing at the type of place they had been performing in. It was a waste of time, even though the gigs could be seen as good practice for the band. He said he had got beyond feeling confident on stage to feeling unconcerned and would rather work on new songs than continually rehearse older ones for performance. Dave agreed; they needed to perform in Liverpool city centre with better-known bands and encourage more important people to see them. At the moment they seemed to be going backwards. They started off by saying they would not play on the Wirral and their first gigs had been in Liverpool city centre, but they were now moving further into the suburbs with each performance.

In March Trav suggested that they should not do a particular performance because there was no point. Tog was the only one keen to do it. He argued that they weren't in a position to be selective about gigs and should play whenever they had the chance. He pointed out that they could break even on that particular one. Trav replied that there should be more to gigs than just breaking even and he, Gary, and Dave agreed that it just wasn't worth while performing to a really small or unappreciative audience because they ended up demoralized.

They turned down a couple of gigs and were criticized for doing so by some of the other bands at Vulcan (including Crikey it's the Cromptons!) who felt that bands should perform as much as possible in order to gain a following because in any audience there might be at least one person who really liked them. They described the Jactars as 'aloof' and 'superstarrish' but that did not perturb the band's members. They were flattered that people were bothered enough to feel so strongly about them and Trav believed that a reputation for being 'high and mighty' would do them good because it showed they were 'a band with integrity.' Tog, who had initially disagreed with the 'gigging policy', now defended it. He told Nick, the manager of Ryan, that he wasn't prepared to lose money anymore and couldn't see why they should have to 'pay to play'—though he would be prepared to do so if they were supporting a well-known band. Nick, however, believed that bands should just accept that they would sometimes lose out—it was all part of the process of trying to 'make it.' Generally, however, both the Jactars and Crikey it's the Cromptons! took whatever gigs they could get and, like most bands, could not afford to be selective. Some Party, for example, performed at pubs and clubs on the outskirts of the city even though it was 'against the band's principles' to perform in such places because they lacked prestige. They did so for the money, earning about £70 per gig.

Despite the fact that many bands on Merseyside frequently faced problems with performances, and although it was possible for a band to achieve a record contract on the basis of its demo tapes alone, the organization, preparation, and performance of gigs continued to be an important and central activity. Bands hoped that through their gigs they eventually would earn money, make contact with an audience and build up a following, attract media and record company attention, and thus achieve some kind of success; and the gig remained a crucial aspect of the ideology, folklore, and imagery of rock. But bands also 'gigged' because they valued, desired, and strove for the particular qualities that live public performance involved, and it is that aspect of performance that will be considered in the following chapter.

This chapter has focused upon the main musical activities that bands were involved with: rehearsing and recording in private and performing in public. Each required a great deal of organization and considerable investment of time and money, and each was strongly influenced by the commercial prospects and aspects of rock music. If bands wanted to earn a living from their music-making they had to perform to sizeable audiences, get press reviews and radio airplay, produce recordings of acceptable quality using instruments of acceptable quality. Consequently, bands operated under considerable commercial/financial pressures that often conflicted with, or impinged upon, their creativity. This was highlighted by the previous chapter and was illustrated here by the Jactars' argument over the recording of their demo tape where the standard of recording set by many record companies was seen by Trav as secondary to the quality of the music which is what 'really matters'.

Conflict between commerce and creativity was also revealed by the Jactars' and Crikey it's the Cromptons!' experience of press reviews. A local journalist based the strength of her praise of the Da Vincis not just upon the quality of their musical performance but upon their relative fame, i.e. their level of commercial success, saying 'They aren't big enough to rave about.' Similarly, another local journalist was unable to review the Jactars because they were so unknown. In addition, the Jactars' experience of reviews led them to conclude that whom a band knew counted far more than the quality of its music.

The commercialism of the music business also meant that many bands had to address legal issues at an early stage and legal arrangements they made often had a detrimental effect upon their creativity. In addition, money (or rather lack of money) became a pressing issue and bands' preoccupations seemed to fall into two separate and conflicting spheres: their creative music-making, and their business concerns involving financial negotiations and money-raising. Conflict between the two spheres was particularly noticeable when it came to recording. A familiar saying regarding recording was that 'time equals money'.

It is perhaps not surprising that because commercial and financial pressures upon a band conflicted with and affected its creativity, they were perceived by some as demeaning and threatening to the band and its music. Consequently, some of the attitudes and values held by members of the Jactars and Crikey it's the Cromptons! could be seen as a defensive reaction to that confrontation. For example, the Jactars' 'offhand manner' with the journalist who expressed an interest in them and their decision to be more selective about the gigs they performed, could be seen as a means of asserting or emphasizing 'artistic integrity' in the face of pressures that threatened to destroy it. Similarly, although two or three members of the Jactars and Crikey it's the Cromptons! had no objections to raising money for their band through their jobs, they did object to raising money through cabaret performance, which was seen as a form of 'prostitution'. Again this could be viewed as a defensive attitude, a delegation of their music-making to a sphere untouchable by, and removed from, the concerns and influence of money and commerce.

4

The Gig

Playing live is what it is all about.
Member of Ryan

While the last chapter was concerned with the structure and organization of bands; this chapter focuses upon bands in performance and discusses their involvement with an audience.

GIG NUMBER I.

Crikey it's the Cromptons! were to perform a gig with Fairground, another band from Vulcan. At about 6.30 p.m. the band members congregated in the office at Vulcan Studios. Tony arrived carrying a large bottle of cider and a camera which he gave me so I could photograph him during his performance. He wore a large black suit, striped shirt, and brightly coloured tie of which he seemed particularly proud. 'I collect hideous ties', he told me. The equipment was loaded into the back of a refrigerated meat van that Fairground had hired from a friend to transport them to the club, and we all climbed in after it, crammed into the jolting, steel, windowless ice box. The two bands hardly knew each other and didn't converse but Dave T., Huw, and Tony discussed amongst themselves the possibility of performing with Half Man Half Biscuit, who were currently so successful. Dave T. had been mixing their sound for them at their gigs.

The bands were performing in the Fire Station, a recently established club situated in a deserted dockland area difficult to get to but popular with people from nearby Bootle because of the discothèques both upstairs and downstairs, the pool table, large video screens, expansive bar, and modern décor. The bands unloaded their equipment at the back of the building, carried it on to the stage, and assembled it whilst the PA company set up theirs. Members of both bands had agreed that Crikey it's the Cromptons! would perform second since Trav (sharing lead guitar with Dave T. because the latter had only just joined the band) was not able to arrive until later.

Fairground began their sound-check and took so long that Crikey it's the Cromptons! were informed they couldn't have one since the club's manager wouldn't allow it after 8 p.m. This worried and annoyed Tony and Midi. 'People always mess you around in these places', muttered the latter. Dave T. assured them that Fairground would have checked that the PA was working properly and Huw pointed out that Tog would be there to supervise the mixing. Dave added that he would be free to do it himself when it was Trav's turn on lead guitar which relieved Tony and Midi. They compiled their set list, grouping the songs into two sections, those Dave could play and those Trav would stand in for.

Midi phoned his girlfriend to encourage her to attend the gig but she was unable to get a baby-sitter. 'We won't have any groupies tonight', he joked to Tony, who doubted if the girl he had met recently would turn up and rang his friend Noggin, who couldn't attend either. Tog, Gary, and Dave of the Jactars arrived straight from a rehearsal. The bar opened but Tony (who had by now finished his bottle of cider) had no money and borrowed some from Tog. He felt awful he said, and complained of pains in his knees, concluding that he was too sober. Trav arrived, followed by a friend of Midi's, the manager of Ryan, and the two Steves who lived in the flat above Tony. We all sat at tables grouped near the stage to watch Fairground perform. The room was filling up and a crowd of people gathered around the bar chatting and drinking. My companions were unimpressed by Fairground's performance and critical of it. Tony, who had been wandering around becoming increasingly drunk, informed me on his way to the stage that he was much happier now and was feeling better. 'He's off his cake', commented Dave after Tony had gone.

Crikey it's the Cromptons!' performance was not a success. To begin with, Tony was distracted by a loud buzzing noise made by the lights. It stopped when he asked for them to be turned off but then the band couldn't read their set list and the audience couldn't see the band. The band's 'sound' was also bad even though Tog was supervising the mixing. Tony's microphone kept whining and Dave T.'s guitar could hardly be heard so Tony had to ask for the volume to be raised. Most problematic was the audience. Apart from us, the place was full of those my companions referred to as 'scallies.' Many of them were drunk and high-spirited. They were dressed for a night out. The men wore smart leather jackets and the women wore bright dresses, high heels, and heavy make-up. When disco music was played immediately after Fairground's performance, the dance floor in front of the stage suddenly filled up with those women dancing exuberantly around small piles of handbags. This lively, cheerful, and mostly female gathering contrasted with ours which was almost entirely male, seated, and bored.

When Crikey it's the Cromptons! began performing the women retreated to join the men standing around the bar. The music obviously didn't appeal to them. A couple of men shouted derogatory remarks at the band. Another yelled 'Get off!', which flustered Tony who replied, 'What? Get off did you say? Do you want to come and sing yourself?' Afterwards he sang slightly out of tune and began to totter about and perform the songs in a rushed, desultory, rather shambolic fashion. Dave T.'s guitar was also slightly out of tune. After the last song Tony immediately pulled off his guitar, strode off the stage, and sat in silence while Dave T., Huw, and Midi chatted to friends. Huw thought their performance had been OK but said he couldn't really tell because he could only hear his drums. Dave T. couldn't judge how it had sounded either. The other Dave, Nick (Ryan's manager), the two Steves, and I shared a taxi back to the city centre. None had been impressed by the performance. Nick said that Crikey it's the Cromptons! were usually 'shambolic' but tonight they had surpassed themselves. Dave pointed out how much better they had been at their rehearsal earlier that day.

GIG NUMBER 2.

A month later Dave T. booked Crikey it's the Cromptons! and the Jactars a gig at Stairways, a club in which he engineered the sound for bands every Thursday. It had only recently begun to put on live bands, becoming one of the few venues for 'alternative' music on Merseyside and one of very few venues for live bands on the Wirral, attracting punks as well as devotees of heavy metal—depending upon the night of the week—and providing bands from the Wirral and 'alternative' bands with an opportunity to perform. The performance area had a bar, mirrors, raised stage, and disco lights. Upstairs was a larger bar, tables and chairs, and a video screen.

Dave T. drove Dave, Tony, and myself to the club. Trav and Tog were there when we arrived. Tog was setting up equipment. Dave T. went to help while the rest of us drank by the bar. Gary arrived. He, Dave, and Trav discussed their recent rehearsals which hadn't been going well. They went on stage to sound-check. Tony came over looking worried and miserable. He had fitted new strings on his guitar but they felt peculiar. Tog had a look at it but one of the strings snapped under his hands whereupon Tony, hands on head, turned his back in despair before inspecting the damage. Tog pointed out that the strings must be faulty or they wouldn't have snapped so easily. Trav blamed Tony for never bothering to find out which gauge string he needed but agreed that Tony could borrow his guitar for the performance. Tony became even more anxious.

Midi arrived. His new girlfriend was due at any moment and I was instructed to watch for her at the door while he was sound-checking and give her £1 for the entrance fee. There were as yet few audience members. Tony expected some of his friends to turn up and hoped that when Dave T. went to collect Huw from the Royal Court in Liverpool, where he and his friends had gone to see a well-known band perform, he and Huw would encourage other people to return with them.

While Dave T. collected Huw, Trav and Dave went to a nearby pub to see if any of their friends were there. Tony, Tog, and I remained at Stairways and visited the bar upstairs. Tog seemed offended that Trav and Dave had left without him. We were joined by Midi and friends of his, some of whom were colleagues from work. A few of Tony's friends, including Noggin, also arrived. Gary stood nearby talking to a woman—something Gary hardly ever did, commented Tog, who jokingly described how the Jactars had split into halves, one with girlfriends (Trav and Dave) and one without (Gary and himself), whereas before they had all been in the same position ('ugly and girlfriendless'). Dave T. returned with Huw and several friends of both Huw and Tony including Huw's girlfriend Alison and her sister. Trav and Dave returned from the pub and although Tog berated them in a jovial manner for going without him his tone indicated that he had in fact been quite hurt by it. Dave T. pointed out that it was almost 11.30 p.m. and the Jactars were due on stage.

Downstairs was quite a large gathering. It was an odd mixture of people: a few heavy metal fans, punks, and skinheads; Midi's colleagues, several dressed in a rather hippy style; Tony's male friends in jeans and training shoes; Huw's more fashionable friends; Dave T.'s sister and several band members from Vulcan. Each group stuck together for most of the performance. The Jactars' sound was engineered by Dave T. During their performance audience members were appreciative but remained at some distance from the band, sitting or standing beyond the expanse of floor in front of the stage.

Afterwards, the Jactars, who didn't seem particularly thrilled or disappointed with their performance, joined their friends as Half Man Half Biscuit's latest record came over on the PA. Meanwhile Tony and Dave T. changed into their stage outfits. Dave donned his usual black baggy suit and white shirt whilst Tony wore a brightly coloured shirt with a patterned, clashing tie, black, tailed jacket, pyjama bottoms, and leather flying helmet.

Crikey it's the Cromptons! went on stage. The atmosphere was good and the audience generally cheerful and responsive. Huw suggested that Tony try to encourage some dancing. Noggin introduced the band. Tony was introduced as 'Crompton Vest, ex Hitler's underpants', Huw as 'Reg Crikey on drums', Midi as 'Big Midi', and Dave T. as 'Ian Botham on guitar.' Everyone seemed to enjoy the performance. Tony's friends moved to sit nearer the stage and Noggin occasionally shouted out comments such as 'White Riot!' or 'Get a grip on yourself!' (These are titles of songs of the punk era in the late 1970s.) Someone unknown to the band also shouted something which seemed to unsettle Tony who wasn't sure if it was abusive or not, but the shouting and cheering of others relaxed and encouraged him and he began to talk more in between songs and urge people to dance.

Alison, who was drunk, was keen to dance and tried to persuade Dave to join her. Two of Midi's female friends got up to dance and when the band played its familiar cover version they were joined by another girl which encouraged a few others, including Alison and Noggin. The latter urged me to photograph him dancing. Positioning himself directly opposite Tony he began a slow, peculiar movement, sticking his legs up to each side with his hands clasped behind his back which caused Tony to laugh and step off the stage for a while to join him in his dance whilst still playing his guitar. Towards the end of the set Tony twice informed the audience that he would be auditioning for groupies afterwards and when audience members shouted for an encore, he remained shuffling around on stage still holding his guitar despite the fact that his fellow band members had left. They eventually joined him for an encore.

Afterwards they mingled with friends in the audience. Trav had been genuinely surprised and delighted by their new songs although he thought the set was too long. Tog thought the performance was 'OK' apart from the fact that Dave's guitar was too loud. I asked Tony if he had enjoyed it. 'Couldn't you fucking tell?', he replied looking extremely exuberant.

THE PERFORMANCE

The above descriptions highlight the close relationship between sound and vision during a performance and the importance of its visual aspects such as the dress and movement of the performers and the performance techniques or styles adopted, the composition, size, and appearance of the audience, and the physical (including vocal) response of audience members to the performance.

Local bands either performed in their usual clothes or changed into clothes of a similar or completely different style, sometimes with all the band's members co-ordinating colour and style. The Iconoclasts, for example, wore kilts, stripey tights, and monkey boots that had been painted or dyed to match their hair so that one member was dressed entirely in green, one in pink, one in yellow, and one in orange. Decomposed wore leather jackets sprayed with the band's name and the singer acquired tattoos which he could display during performances. The Viz Johnson Band wore sunglasses and greased back their hair, whilst the Mel-O-Tones wore T-shirts printed with a photograph of each of the Beatles above the words 'Beatle Crusher.' The manager of Up the Khyber was concerned to create a 'colonial' image for her band involving baggy trousers, braces, and shirts in safari colours with help from a friend of the bass player who was taking a course in dress design. She nagged the bands' members to set aside money for a haircut and stage outfit and organized 'band shopping trips' for the purpose of acquiring them. She was, however, largely unsuccessful, mainly because of the band's limited finances.

In addition to dress some bands made an effort to enhance the visual aspect of their performance by decorating the stage, using props, a backdrop, or instruments of a particular style or size. Tony, for example, sometimes borrowed a guitar from a member of Ryan who had painted it with a swirling, multicoloured pattern. One Last Fight constructed large stacks of speakers on stage, half of which were unnecessary or out of order and were thus just for show. Sometimes they used their band logo as a backdrop, stapling to it copies of their record sleeve. On occasion Ryan sometimes also used a backdrop—a huge sheet of white plastic with 'Ryan' painted upon it in large black letters. Alternatively, the Viz Johnson Band used beer crates and an ironing-board in place of proper instrument stands, whilst Decomposed sometimes littered the stage with cans of a particular brand of cheap lager which had become a band hallmark and was on constant order at their local off-licence. The Mel-O-Tones littered their stage with a greater variety of objects such as papier mâché masks, some of which hung from coat-hangers.

Sometimes women were also used by bands to enhance their visual image, usually as backing vocalists dressed in glamorous outfits. Keil (1966: 134) suggested that those of one particular blues performer functioned to 'heighten [his] image as the ladies' man and they offer definite visual pleasure to the men in the audience.' Such women were often treated as part of the backdrop rather than as members of the band. One musician, explaining why all his band except for the two female vocalists signed the contract with their record company, said: 'No band takes their backing singers with them all the way. They might want to change them for the next record . . . because it makes a change.'

Many bands made an effort not only to encourage their audience to dance but to be themselves more expressive and dramatic in their movement in order to convey ideas, sentiment, and emotion. Even the sight of the physical motions involved with playing an instrument could emphasize and dramatize the music heard. Bands that adopted more unusual or flamboyant stage mannerisms included the Mel-O-Tones, whose singer would sometimes bounce up and down shaking his head violently as if experiencing some sort of seizure, grasp the edge of the stage to peer into the audience before flinging himself into the audience and crawling back on to the stage. Occasionally he used props, covering his head with a mask for example and inserting his microphone into the gaping mouth. Alternatively, the bass player with the Whisky Priests always stood very still throughout the band's performances with his back turned to the audience.

Generally bands tried, or were encouraged, to incorporate more movement in their performance in order to appear energetic and enthusiastic and stimulate the audience to dance or to appreciate the music more. The singer of one band often jumped off the stage to stand directly in front of audience members and encourage them to dance. He was, however, criticized by other musicians who felt that his behaviour intimidated his audience. The drummer of another band limited himself to using a snare drum only (the part of the drum kit that usually provides the main definition of the beat) so he could dance while he played. Some bands moved spontaneously, but others carefully rehearsed and co-ordinated their movements, sometimes choreographing them for each member. During Some Party's performances the lead singer stood apart from the other band members and made dramatic, aggressive gestures with fists clenched and head thrown back. Meanwhile the bassist and guitarist played their instruments in a bouncy, relaxed manner, often walking across the stage to each other to casually chat, laugh, and exchange a few words before parting again. This looked spontaneous, but was in fact a carefully rehearsed feature of the band's performance which offset the solitude of the singer and enabled the audience to witness the rapport and friendliness between two of the band members.

This interaction of band members on stage often reflected the nature of the relationships between them and added to the intensity and enjoyment of the performance—not only for the audience but for the performers themselves. When the drummer of the Da Vincis was ousted from the band and a replacement brought in, the improvement in the social relationships within the band was reflected in the nature and competence of its stage performance. The band members looked as though they were enjoying themselves and there was more contact between them. They watched, smiled, glanced, and made faces at each other, moved more about the stage, and generally seemed more confident and relaxed.

The use of dress, stage design, and movement highlights the dramatic, theatrical aspects of the gig. Many band members made use of dramatic techniques to enhance their performance and music. Thus whilst music is used to enhance the drama in plays and films, dramatic techniques are used to enhance the music in concerts and gigs. Some band members, for example, made an effort to look enthusiastic and as though they were enjoying themselves through their facial expressions as well as their movement, even when their audience comprized only a few of people. The manager of Carry On Spying constantly urged the band's members to do so: 'If they look at you and you look like you're bored they'll think it's boring.' Bands like the Jactars and Half Man Half Biscuit, however, were against such showmanship (a member of the latter proudly declared: 'With our band there's no difference between being on stage and being in the living room') or lacked the confidence to display it themselves:

You see a lot of bands standing on stage looking sheepish, but when you think it's out of tune and you can't hear yourself then it's difficult to look confident, especially if only a few people are watching (member of the Da Vincis).

It was pointed out to me on several occasions that whilst rock musicians tended to be characterized, particularly through the media, as flamboyant and egotistical, many were in fact shy and introverted. Performing in public was a means of gaining self-confidence, self-respect, and the respect of others, and people were frequently said to have changed personality and become more outgoing through membership of a band. Others not only changed personality through performing but assumed a different persona on stage when performing—perhaps in response to the ordeal they were putting themselves through but also as a deliberate dramatic technique.

Tog had gained a lot in confidence since joining the Jactars and, like Trav, was no longer so nervous before a gig. Dave, however, remained nervous both before and during performances and didn't enjoy performing at all. Huw from Crikey it's the Cromptons! admitted to suffering occasional bouts of nerves:

Sometimes, if things go really badly, or if I particularly feel they're going badly, I get to this panic stage . . . I remember when we played in the Turk's Head . . . and it was going really badly and I started to crack up a little bit and I couldn't play properly . . . because like my hand . . . I was losing my grip all the time. It was just awful. The whole thing was falling apart and I thought . . . this sounds terrible. As it was, nobody really noticed.

Midi, on the other hand, said he was never nervous but became 'embarrassed' when he felt that the band hadn't rehearsed properly and was playing badly. Tony said he used to be 'terrified' when they first began performing but now he just got 'extremely excited.'

Performance ability and dramatic techniques were particularly noticeable in the way in which some band members addressed their audience (whether while introducing a song or otherwise) during a performance. Both members of the Reverb Brothers kept up a continual dialogue with their audience which warmed the audience to them and created an atmosphere of intimacy. One of them, for example, would jokingly berate the audience for applauding the other's song more than his. One or two punk bands made verbal abuse of the audience a part of their performance, just as the Sex Pistols, the Rolling Stones, and many other performers before them had done. To establish a rapport with an audience through dialogue required confidence and indicated the importance of personality, timing and performance skills in performers. Neil Taylor (*NME*: 9 February 1985) wrote of one performer: 'With a mere flick of his fringe he can replace lyrics with an image that exudes a confidence which captures and carries his audience', whilst Keil (1966: 173) wrote of soul:

Without a well-developed sense of timing, of how to phrase or place notes vis à vis the pulse, a sure knowledge of when to pause, where to accent, how to hold and bend a note, a word, or a limb, and so forth—without these qualities there is no soul worth mentioning.

A performance could, however, be affected by the performers' situation and mood. At one particular gig the Da Vincis and the Decemberists performed in an aggressive, exuberant, and energetic manner, exhilarating both for audience and performers, and caused by the fact that both bands had been treated badly by the gig's organizers, thus becoming angry and frustrated. They had been kept waiting for hours before they could perform and were then told to limit their set to only a few songs.

The style, vigour, and theatricality of a performance could also vary according to whether the band was a 'support' (i.e. playing first) or 'lead' band (i.e. playing last). This positioning was particularly important at gigs of better known bands, where, if an unknown band was lucky enough to play support it could profit considerably in its quest for success because of the larger audience, media, and record company attention the gig was likely to attract. However, at such gigs the role of the support bands was to 'warm up' the audience, thus whetting its appetite and building up its anticipation for the lead band whilst at the same time making sure they didn't overshadow it. They did not, therefore, have the same stage lighting or other facilities as the lead band, whose members were often annoyed when their support received a particularly favourable response from the audience, although that could sometimes spur them on to perform well themselves.

The order in which bands performed was, however, important at most gigs besides those of the more famous bands, and bands often argued over it, firstly because it supposedly reflected the popularity of each band, but also because audiences usually increased in size as the evening progressed so the last band was likely to play to more people. In addition, the audience's sense of anticipation and state of inebriation was usually greater for the performance of the last band which was likely to make it more disposed towards a favourable response.

THE AUDIENCE

As with public performances of any kind, the experience of both audience and performers was usually enhanced by the presence of many people listening and watching simultaneously. A sizeable audience could heighten aesthetic appreciation and enjoyment of the performance, as well as improve the nature of the performance itself. Members of Half Man Half Biscuit described how, suddenly faced with a much larger audience than they had been used to, their musical performance became more 'punky' (vigorous) and exhilarated them to such an extent that as soon as it was over they wanted to repeat it. But the audience did not have to be large:

There doesn't have to be a lot of people, like hundreds of people going mad. Even if there's just a few and they're really enjoying it and leaping around then it shows. And if we see that then we start enjoying it more and the music gets better. (band member).

The small size of audiences meant that bands usually knew most, if not all, their members. The presence of friends and followers could create an intimate, pleasant atmosphere but the appearance of many strangers (attending in order to see the band not just because they happened to be in the building) often heightened the band's excitement and enjoyment of the event. It could, however, occasionally antagonize loyal followers. When friends of Half Man Half Biscuit attended one of the band's gigs in Liverpool they were distressed by the large audience and media attention the band attracted due to its recent success. They told the band afterwards that things just weren't the same any more. There had been so many strangers in the audience and backstage that they had felt detached from the band.

The presence of many musicians in the audience also affected the atmosphere and behaviour at a gig since their response to the band tended to be more objective and critical. In addition, particular individuals could encourage or discourage performers. Dave, for example, was distracted by the presence of his mother and brother at one of the Jactars' gigs and worried by what they would think, particularly since Tony and Trav were obviously very drunk and lay on the stage during a rendition of 'Never Trust a Fish.'

The gender of audience members also affected the way in which a gig was experienced. The presence of many women, for instance, might change the nature of audience behaviour or that of the performance itself. Members of Some Party once described in detail the dress and physical characteristics of some females in their audience who danced in front of the stage when they played at a local college. All had been struck by the shapely figure of one particular girl and admitted to staring at her throughout the performance and playing their songs faster than usual as a result. The visual appearance of audience members could be important in other respects. Members of the Iconoclasts described how flattered they were to see women in their audience dressed in kilts similar to those they wore themselves as a declaration of loyalty and support. It had lifted their spirits and they consequently performed well.

The dancing of audience members, in addition to their appearance, could be another important feature of a performance. Generally, those bands with a regular following found that members of that following did dance. Male followers of the Farm, for example, bounced up and down, linked arms, and slapped each other on the back directly in front of the stage. Their movements encouraged others to join in. At most gigs I attended in Liverpool, however, there was no dancing at all. That may have been due to fashion—a trend

away from dance. (In the 1960s 'Mersey Beat' era there had been a
lot of dancing at gigs, much of which was intricate and complicated.)
The smallness of audiences might also have inhibited people from
dancing (at student gigs and those in outlying areas such as St Helens
there were larger audiences and more dancing) and some mentioned
that though people were reluctant to dance, if some started then
others followed. The absence of dancing might in addition reflect the
predominant maleness of the audiences. Women generally liked
dancing more than men did and frequented discothèques to do so.
(Far more women attended gigs in the 1960s.) Dancing might
sometimes even have been inhibited by the presence of musicians in
the audience who, because they viewed performances critically, were
less likely to 'lose' themselves in dance. It was also pointed out to me
on several occasions that Liverpool audiences were reputedly more
critical than audiences elsewhere, so if performers (actors, musicians,
comedians . . .) could 'win over' a Liverpool audience, they could
'win over' anyone.

Many bands, lacking a following, bemoaned the absence of dance
at their performances. A member of the Da Vincis complained that
during the eighteen months of his band's career only three people had
danced at their gigs and all had been drunk. Only twice did I witness
dancing at a performance of the Jactars, once by Trav's sister and her
friends (all three were drunk) and once at Kirkby Liberal Club when
a group of about twenty mentally handicapped people danced
vigorously for the duration of the performance.

Not all band members liked their audience to dance. Some might
have felt they were being ignored 'in favour of audience self
indulgence' (White, 1983: 176). Generally, however, bands were
delighted if audiences did so and many tried to encourage them to
and judged the performance a success if they succeeded. It communicated to them the fact that people were enjoying it:

If you can create a good atmosphere . . . then people are more likely to
dance and create their own atmosphere . . . It promotes a good feeling. It's
good for us because it makes us relax and not think we're making fools of
ourselves. We ask the audience to go to the front. Our friends do and others
follow. It's infectious. Everyone wants to enjoy themselves, they just think 'I
don't want to be the first' (Blue Nose B).

For me, when people got up to dance it meant that I was getting through . . .
In my view dance was a genuine and positive response to the music and a
way the audience could participate in the whole business of music-making
(White, 1983: 176).

There's nothing better than playing something and seeing someone tapping
their foot (The Viz Johnson Band).

Dance can thus not only integrate members of the audience but arouse affect and act as a mode of communication between audience and performers, establishing a relationship between them which heightens the sense of community and group identity and intensifies the social interaction occasioned by the musical performance. As Herman wrote of mods at the Who's gigs (1971: 30): 'It was in their dancing, in their response to their music that [they] came closest to the experience of collective excitement.'

This was most clearly revealed at gigs of bands with close followers who expressed an intense feeling of loyalty and identity with the band, a pride in being one of the original fans and never switching allegiance. If such a band released a record it sometimes, like Half Man Half Biscuit, attracted a new following to its performances. The sense of community and identity among original followers could then be disrupted, diminishing the band's symbolic potency. The band might then lose some of its original following and become a symbol for a wider community.

The Mel-O-Tones, for example, had a group of largely male followers who engaged in a particularly aggressive-looking style of dance directly in front of the stage whereby they hurled themselves in different directions so that they banged into each other or piled themselves on top of one another with arms flailing. They called it 'having a wreck'—a style of dance similar to 'rucking' or 'slam dancing'—and referred to themselves as 'our crew.' Whilst the 'crew' 'wrecked' at the front, any women present and some of the other men usually danced at their periphery in a more passive, individual, less exuberant manner. Although 'wrecking' looked a painful, antagonistic activity, it seemed, like the dancing by followers of the Farm and other bands, to provide participants with a sense of comradeship, thereby arousing and heightening emotion. It expressed male solidarity. Men helped each other out during a wreck. They picked each other up off the floor.

Shortly after the release of the Mel-O-Tones' first record some new men started to appear at gigs and join in the 'wreck.' Established followers complained of their rough behaviour and displayed scars received whilst wrecking ('It started off as a good laugh but now it's changed'). To me, however, the wrecking did not seem any more violent than before. Original followers were probably upset and disgruntled not because the newcomers were more violent but because they were unknown and invaded the sense of comradeship. An antagonistic situation thus developed.

Performers and audience alike responded not only to the sight of audience members—their number, appearance, dress, movement, and dance, but also to their mood and the sounds they made whether of clapping, laughter, chatter, shouting, verbal comments, cheers, boos, or noises of a different kind. Such sounds could lead to, 'the mutual reinforcement of the audience reaction through the feedback effect of observing (or imitating) one's neighbours' (Esslin, 1976: 80). If responses were positive, band members were encouraged in their performance, but that could be the case even if they were negative as an abusive or unfavourable audience could elicit a more powerful, perhaps angry response from the performers. It could also, on the other hand, disturb and discourage the band to the detriment of its performance.

Members of the Jactars and Crikey it's the Cromptons! varied in their attitude towards 'image' and performance. Trav said of Tony: 'He's trying to achieve a visual band and he's still got to work on that whereas we (the Jactars) are not a visual band', whilst Gary and Tony felt the Jactars should make an effort to be more 'visual', particularly regarding dress and movement. Neither Tog, Dave, nor Trav moved around much on stage. Gary thought it would improve performances if they did because 'if the audience sees movement in the band it gears them up.' Tony was critical of what he described as the Jactars' 'dead pan' stage presence, 'the way they all stand there with their heads bowed.' Sometimes, however, at one or two points in the set, Trav would play his guitar with particular energy and gusto. Bowing his head over it he would vigorously slide his left hand up and down the neck whilst strumming the strings with rapid movements of his right hand. Watching that, members of the audience became transfixed and excited, particularly Tony, who would enthuse afterwards about how wonderful it had been when Trav went 'frantic.'

   Midi and Dave T. hardly moved at all on stage. Tony, however, often spoke of 'freaking out' and going 'wild' as regards stage movement, and described how he did so at one gig:

I got the microphone, stuck it down me pants so that it looked like, you know . . . and sort of eventually pulled it up out of me pants and did an alternative sort of . . . er . . . Tom Jones, you know, swinging it from hand to hand.

But, although, like other performers, Tony had a characteristic stance and style of playing, he rarely moved to any great extent about the stage and I never saw him repeat behaviour such as that described above.

   The stage image of Crikey it's the Cromptons! changed significantly, however, after Pete joined in place of Midi. Pete moved a great deal during performances, bouncing around with a comical look on his face and taking much of the attention off Tony. He would frequently approach or stalk Huw, Tony, or Dave T., fix them with a long stare, or make a strange face or physical gesture at them. At first this distracted and unsettled the others but after a while Tony, and to a lesser extent Dave T., began to respond and the band's performances became considerably livelier and more amusing to watch. Occasionally, for example, Pete bounced over to Tony and mimicked heavy metal style movements and Tony joined in, both of them standing together swaying heads and hips in unison. Thus Pete's antics encouraged Tony to be more adventurous. During one performance he lay on the floor with his back arched as he played his guitar. Later, during a tuning break, he took a banana out of his jacket pocket (taken on stage for just such a moment) and ate it over the microphone.

The Jactars, like the Da Vincis, Blue Nose B, One Last Fight, the Decemberists, and many others, wore their usual clothes for performances. Gary described the Jactars as having a 'lads-off-the-street' image and after leaving the band he criticized his fellow band members for adopting it as part of their effort to maintain 'artistic credibility' when they should have constructed a more 'glamorous' image in order to achieve success. Tony, on the other hand, wanted Crikey it's the Cromptons! to appear 'wild' and 'over the top' in their stage dress just as he did with their movement and music. It was only he, however, who made the effort to do so. Midi never changed for performances—although he apparently once performed in a black négligé and Doc Martin boots. Huw tended to wear large patterned shirts which were perfectly presentable although Tony liked to describe them as 'the most disgusting shirts you've ever seen', and before a performance got what he described as 'a nice vicious haircut.' Dave T. wore his baggy black suit and always played with a cigarette dangling from the corner of his mouth.

Tony spent a considerable amount of time fantasizing about and planning possible stage outfits such as flippers or Union Jack boxer shorts stuffed with a courgette which he could take out and eat during the performance. 'My image', he often said, 'is to look as uncomfortable as possible', which meant wearing clothes that were 'hideous', 'weird', and 'suitably horrible', 'which don't really go together', like clashing colours, 'loud shirts' with 'horrible ties', odd socks and shoes, and an oversized suit. In reality, Tony rarely looked particularly outrageous or uncomfortable, perhaps lacking the confidence to do so. His dress did, however, vary according to the place he was performing in and the type of audience present.

During the Jactars' performances Trav only briefly introduced each song and otherwise rarely addressed the audience unless he was feeling particularly relaxed, probably due to the amount of alcohol he had consumed. Tony, on the other hand, tried to intersperse his performance with spontaneous and amusing remarks but was not always successful in doing so and his friends sometimes found his stage behaviour embarrassing and contrived and felt that in making such an effort he often went too far. Many comments and movements he made were not, in fact, spontaneous at all but had been rehearsed or thought out prior to the performance. Occasionally, when they were spontaneous (after an audience member shouted some derogatory remark for example), Tony seemed tense and nervous and he himself admitted that whenever he heard himself talk in between songs on recordings of gigs he was embarrassed at how awful he sounded. Sometimes, if provoked, his comments to the audience were almost abusive.

From the discussion of the factors involved in a gig and of the Jactars' and Crikey it's the Cromptons!' attitudes to performance, it may be easier to appreciate why the gig at the Fire Station was considered unsuccessful by Crikey it's the Cromptons! and the Jactars, whilst as far as the former was concerned, the one at Stairways was deemed successful. Musicological analysis might reveal parallel differences in the actual musical sounds produced by the performance such as variations in the timbre or inflection of the voices involved.

First of all, regarding the structure and context of the gig, although the Fire Station was an attractive and acoustically sound building it was situated in a deserted location difficult for the band's friends to reach. It also attracted the type of customer unlikely to appreciate the music and image of a band like Crikey it's the Cromptons! In addition, the gig was on a Monday, when most of their friends would have little money left over from the weekend with which to travel to see them perform and buy drinks. Finally, members of Crikey it's the Cromptons! were distressed, having arrived at the club, to find that they were not able to sound-check, and were disturbed during their performance by problems with the sound. (The acoustics of a building and the quality of the PA and its engineering were often identified as the main culprits of an unsuccessful performance.)

Relationships between the band members were good but all of them had high expectations of the gig which meant that they were tense and more likely to be disappointed and distressed if things went badly. The fact that it was also Dave T's first gig with the band may have increased tension and hindered the performance itself. In addition, Tony and Midi weren't as cheerful as usual and spoke of feeling unwell. Relations between Crikey it's the Cromptons! and the other band performing were not particularly friendly, which did not improve the atmosphere, and matters were made worse by Tony's consumption of alcohol and drugs.

Members of the audience also presented a problem for the band. Few of their friends were present. Those who were present were largely fellow musicians, who viewed the performance fairly critically and objectively, although they identified themselves with the band in opposition to the others in the building, who were socially and culturally different and were not predisposed to enjoy the music. Some of the latter were drunk and boisterous which made them antagonistic towards the band. Others paid little attention to the performance and only moved nearer the stage when Fairground finished performing and they could dance to recorded disco music played over the PA system. Consequently, relations between the band and the bulk of the audience were not good and the performance itself was not a success. Antagonistic comments from the audience were handled badly by Tony who reacted in a flustered, confrontational manner, and although friends helped out with the sound engineering during the performance, they did not respond to the music physically or vocally.

Stairways, like the Fire Station, was good for bands to perform in as regards acoustic, spatial, lighting, and bar facilities. It was also situated, as far as Crikey it's the Cromptons! and the Jactars were concerned, in a good location—an area of the Wirral easily accessible to many of their friends. It was newly established as a venue for live bands but was attracting audiences—particularly those interested in 'alternative' bands such as Crikey it's the Cromptons!—because there were so few in that area. The bands were usually booked for a Thursday, which meant that many audience members had already received their wages or Giro cheques for that week and had probably not yet spent their money. There was a £1 entrance fee but it was relatively cheap and easy for most to travel home after the gig.

This time Crikey it's the Cromptons! had plenty of time in which to sound-check. Relations between the band members were good and Dave T. was more established in the band. Tony was again nervous and apprehensive (especially after his guitar string snapped) but didn't get as drunk as he had been at the Fire Station. The audience was large and included many of the band's friends. They were divided into various groups but most were united by their relationship to the band and others were favourably disposed towards the band and its music. Several were also intoxicated and high-spirited, particularly those who had just attended the performance of a well-known band in Liverpool city centre.

In addition, there were several women present who initiated the dancing towards the end of the performance which helped break down divisions within the audience and improved the atmosphere, making it more friendly and intimate. Audience participation was particularly marked when Tony joined Noggin in a little dance in front of the stage. It symbolized the band's rapport with its audience and their shared sense of humour, further weakening the boundary between band and audience. Some of the other musicians present (with the exception of members of the Jactars, who were perhaps distracted by the disappointment of their own performance), encouraged by the presence of friends, the atmosphere, and alcohol, became less objective and critical towards the performance. The audience response was good throughout and an encore was called for.

As the audience responded well, the band's performance improved. Tony relaxed and began to address the audience in between songs. His unusual dress also made him feel more outrageous and might perhaps have increased the intimacy of the gig since those who knew him would have appreciated the humour involved or recognized it as part of Tony's idiosyncratic behaviour which they knew so well. (Tog, however, later annoyed and upset Tony, causing him to regret having dressed in such a manner, by criticizing him for being 'gimmicky', perhaps envious that things seemed to be going so well for Crikey it's the Cromptons!) Tony was also undoubtedly pleased by his impromptu dance with Noggin which he would have regarded as spontaneous.

The Jactars' performance at Stairways, on the other hand, was disappointing for themselves and members of Crikey it's the Cromptons! It was flawed and uninspired probably due to current social and artistic problems within the band indicated, perhaps, by Tog's feeling of rejection by Trav and Dave and by his comment on the two 'halves' of the band, one with girlfriends, the other without. Members of Crikey it's the Cromptons!, familiar with the Jactars and their music, though unaware of the tensions within the band, knew that the performance was not up to their usual standard.

At the Fire Station members of both the Jactars and Crikey it's the Cromptons! did not enjoy the performance of Fairground or rate it highly. None were particularly friendly or familiar with the band or its music, and as fellow musicians in a similar position as regards popularity and success, they were critical and competitive in attitude.

MUSIC IN THE RAW

It is often said that the increasing popularity of discothèques, nightclubs, and forms of recorded music such as compact discs, videos, and walkmans, threatens the continuation of live musical performance which is in 'decline.' For many in Liverpool discothèques were favoured as places in which to dance and be seen whereas live music conjured up images of small, dingy venues performed in by dreadful local bands. Recorded music is also said to condition people to appreciate highly efficient, technological production and complex structuring through devices such as layering and editing, rather than 'music in the raw.' Others have suggested that whilst not exactly replacing live performance, the development of recording techniques and the increasing consumption of recorded music has been changing the nature of live performance, making it more technological and costly with greater emphasis upon its visual aspects.

It appears to have been first the record or disc which created for rock music a concern with image beyond that already established for stage performance and spectacle . . . This 'setting' has often come subsequently to constrain performance to conform to arrangements and balance of recording, the 'record' becoming less the recollection of a performance, than the predefining 'text' *for* it. In such terms, performance can come to be largely advertisement for record, in an inversion of earlier conventions according to which performance was the primary or dominant audience relation, when songs were considered to be tested out for response after being devised in relative isolation and 'solitude' (Durant, 1984: 230).

Arguments such as these, however, tend to overlook the interrelationship between recorded and live performance: live performance does not just reflect or imitate a recording but can in turn influence the sound and structure of recordings. Some also concentrate entirely upon larger, more elaborate events though amateur, grass-roots performances remain an important training ground for new ideas and talent in all musical styles. Recordings may also stimulate and develop involvement and creativity in live performance, thereby increasing the audience for it.

There were many bands on Merseyside that preferred not to perform in public at all, but for most, live performance ('gigging') was an important and central activity. Some bands valued it over and above recorded performance, or were said to be better live than recorded, either because their music incorporated a 'raw', untamed, 'rough' quality of sound or because the visual features of their performance were particularly important. However, live performances were also valued, practised, and attended by bands on Merseyside and by their audiences for the same reasons that people universally participate in live artistic performance whether of other musical or artistic genres, or of ritual and ceremonial. Thus whilst the previous section discussed some of the factors that might determine how a gig is evaluated and experienced by audience and performers, the following discussion focuses upon particular qualities that live performance offers. Such qualities explain the popularity and universality of live performance and suggest that Liverpool's dwindling audiences could be attributed more to economic decline than to fashion or lack of interest, i.e. to the financial hardship experienced both by potential audience members which also affected performance venues and facilities, and by independent record companies that could foster and encourage live music locally.

To begin with, live performances involve a sense of occasion, necessitating preparation and organization such as buying tickets, arranging transport, setting aside money for beverages, changing clothes. The sense of anticipation and strength of commitment and concentration engendered varies according to the nature of the event, depending on factors such as the fame and reputation of the band performing and the place in which it is performing:

It's to do with what you expect. If you see local bands you tend not to expect very much. You appreciate good local bands because they are better than all the crap—but they are still not wonderful . . . What you want to see is something that you can't do (member of The Da Vincis).

Other social events and contexts such as discothèques and pubs also involve a sense of occasion and expectancy but live performance differs in that it involves the simultaneous process of production and consumption.

The different forms of aural, oral, and visual communication at a gig are related to the complex interrelationship between audience and performers. The audience responds to the performance and performers respond, in turn, to the audience and judge the effectiveness of their performance from its behaviour:

It's very complicated how your playing changes with the size and expectations of the audience. You apply your particular attitude to the notion of performance in that space and the range of musics which can come out is quite wide (Evan Parker, *NME*: 9 February 1985).

The audience is quite challenging. They put us on edge and we'll put them on edge and in doing so you create an atmosphere . . . Our reaction is to think, if they're not dancing, let's give them something more. Let's stir up other senses (the Hula, *Sounds*: 9 February 1985).

I chat to the audience in between songs. If I get a good response and know people in the audience then I have a laff with them. Otherwise I slag 'em off (lead-singer of Decomposed).

This interrelationship of audience and performers 'is one of the prime advantages of live theatre over the mechanically recorded types of drama' (Esslin, 1976: 33). It gives rose to the continual creation and re-creation of an 'atmosphere' and makes each performance immediate, direct, and accessible in impact and also spontaneous, unpredictable, and thus thrilling since the possibility of the unexpected always exists. Each performance is therefore unique:

One only has to listen to performances on an afternoon when the girls are few in number and bored, and on another occasion when there is a good turnout, an appreciative audience and an atmosphere of excitement and concern, to realize how and why two performances of the same song can be entirely different in expressive power and in form (Blacking, 1973: 71).

The uniqueness of each gig was a quality highly valued by some musicians, who proclaimed proudly that their band's performance differed each time they played.

The experience of a gig (comprising the totality of interrelated factors) is subjective and personal. The experience of audience members, for example, may differ according to whether they are outside observers (e.g. a music journalist, record company representative, or anthropologist); whether they know the band's members personally, through gigs or other contacts; or whether they are completely unfamiliar with the band, in which case their reception of the band's music is likely to be influenced by their knowledge, or lack of knowledge, of the musical codes involved. Evaluations of a gig therefore differ from participant to participant but are largely determined by the audience/performer boundary, i.e. whether the individual is a member of the band and thus primarily involved with playing (production of the music) or a member of the audience and thus primarily involved with listening (consumption of the music).

In addition, that boundary varies according to social, cultural, and conceptual factors. It has always, for example, been a focus of revolutionary aesthetics with artists like Brecht aiming to reinforce it, and the punk bands of the 1970s attempting to bridge it by activating and involving the audience in the performance. The tension, division, and power relationship between audience and performers is nevertheless usually present. 'Even when they demand audience participation,' wrote Burns (1972: 205) of actors and playwrights who attempt to demystify the audience—performer division, 'they are attempting to "theatricalize" the audience.' But in a sense *all* are performers because all create the performance:

Theirs was not the escapist appeal of previous pop stars ... for their audience were active in the creation of the event ... this dual nature of their stage performances inspired The Who's initial popularity. Not only did audiences participate through a sort of empathic communication but the group's part in the performance actually transcended the limits of the audience's likely experience (Herman, 1971: 49).

Live performance thus unites participants in common activity.

The expressive power and excitement of a live performance depends also upon the ambiguity of its symbols and images and the ability of the audience to relate them to their personal socio-cultural experiences and thus derive their own meanings from them, which is why it is often more effective when meanings and messages are not made explicit. Thus Esslin (1976) suggested of performance, and Marcuse (1979: xii) of art, that explicit political messages defeat their purpose. The symbolic nature of a performance, combined with the sense of community and solidarity it engenders and the interrelationship of its visual and physical elements (such as music, drama, rhetoric, dance and movement, costumes, settings, props, illusion) makes a performance sensual in nature. Esslin (1976: 34) referred to its 'powerful erotic component', whilst Barrault (1972: 30) wrote:

The art of theatre, addressing itself essentially to the sense of touch, is then, above all, the art of sensation. It is opposed to all intellectual preoccupation.

This interrelationship of components into the sensual whole of a performance thus encourages the suppression of critical, rational, logical thought so that imagination and emotions may be more freely expressed or unleashed and a sense of euphoria, or what has been called 'communitas' (Turner, 1977), 'transformation' (Langer, 1951; Moore and Myerhoff, 1977: 13), or catharsis can be achieved. Keil (1966: 129) described how the music, lyrics, performance techniques, and pattern of expressive symbolism utilized by blues performers in Chicago 'gives public expression to deeply private emotions' of both performers and audience creating a feeling 'of release and resiliency, even of satisfaction', which synthezises charisma, catharsis, and solidarity:

The sight and sound of a common problem being acted out, talked out, and worked out on stage promote catharsis, and the fact that all present are participating in the solution creates solidarity ... Whatever distance has existed between artist and audience to this point has been all but eliminated. [The Bluesman] and his listeners are one unit (ibid.: 137).

Band members described that state of catharsis and euphoria as a 'high' or a 'buzz':

Performance is what it's all about and what you build up to. I love it. I've never got such a high from anything in my life (member of the Da Vincis).

There's no greater buzz than playing live on stage. Sometimes when I'm doing a gig I feel like I'm going out of control (member of Jenny Lind).

As audience members, many described similar experiences:

We all share the simultaneous experience of forgetting who we are at a rock concert, losing ourselves completely when the music gets so good, and the audience are so relaxed and free and happy . . . Everybody for a second forgets completely who they are and where they are, and they don't care. They just know they are happy and that now is now and life is great. And what does it matter if you're a big star—you just know that you are one of a crowd of people. If you have experienced that enough times, it starts to become something you strive for, because it is so sweet (Pete Townshend quoted in Frith, 1983: 80).

When I used to go to gigs it used to be great to feel that you were part of a crowd that dressed the same and liked the same music. Now I'm older it's different. Now there's an atmosphere of expectancy. You know what the band is like and you expect a lot. It's all to do with adrenalin. You get a buzz out of it (member of the Da Vincis).

Once you've been to see one band live you want to go and see another (local schoolboy).

Most strove to induce the same sensation in their audience:

We still put a lot of emphasis on our live shows, on trying to act as a vehicle for people to express their rage and frustrations in a positive way (member of New Model Army, *Melody Maker*: 22 June 1985).

There's different approaches to dance music that still have the same effect . . . We try to create a trance-like state (member of Chakk, *NME*: 18 April 1986).

Such descriptions and comments depict an almost addictive state of being similar to that experienced through drugs or alcohol and, as in rituals and performances of many other groups and cultures (see Grof, 1977: 172), such substances often were taken at gigs to heighten emotions and sensations and thereby induce or enhance euphoria. If band and audience members became only slightly intoxicated it could reduce their nervousness and tension, encourage them to relax and perhaps dance, and thereby improve the performance and atmosphere. Much more intoxicated, however, and members of the audience sometimes became rowdy, aggressive, or abusive, whilst band members often found their playing ability and performance impaired. Some described an experience of panic and loss of control when drunk on stage. Many therefore refrained from drinking at all until their performance was over or, like most members of the Jactars and Crikey it's the Cromptons!, drank in moderation. Tog, for example, hated going on stage 'stone-cold sober' but disliked being 'really drunk.' To achieve a state of mind somewhere in between those two extremes meant consuming two or three pints of one particular brand of lager: 'Just enough to take the edge off so you don't begin to wonder why you're there.'

Tony, on the other hand, usually consumed such a large quantity of alcohol or drugs before a performance that he became, as his friends described it, 'off his cake.' That often amused his friends, particularly Tog, who would tell onlookers: 'Tony can play when he can't stand up. His guitar-playing ability lasts longer than his walking ability.' Tog described how Tony was so drunk at one gig he had to play while supporting himself against a pillar, whilst at another, Tony asked for two volunteers from the audience to hold him up. Tony claimed that he played better when drunk (this was vigorously denied by Huw), but occasionally admitted he had gone too far and resolved to try to moderate his consumption of alcohol and drugs. Such resolutions never lasted very long.

The use of drugs and alcohol in ritual, wrote Turner (1977), does not so much 'expand consciousness as limit and intensify awareness', and he described a similar state of being in his discussion of Csikszentmihalyis' work on 'flow' (in relation to sport) which is the 'holistic sensation present when we act with total involvement' (1977: 49). Flow involves loss of ego and:

the experience of merging action and awareness which is made possible by a centring of attention on a limited stimulus field. Consciousness must be narrowed, intensified, beamed in on a limited focus of attention. Past and future must be given up—only *now* matters (ibid.).

The striving for a sense of euphoria at live performances, whether with or without the aid of intoxicating substances, indicates this desire or need for loss of 'self' to emotions, sensations, and thoughts invoked by and through the performance that take one over, obscuring all sense of normal self with the place, time, obligations, and responsibilities that it entails.

The nature of the relationship between audience and performers affects what the former want or expect from the gig (e.g. whether they want to be entertained, impressed, challenged, stimulated) and hence the way in which they perceive and receive the music. It thus determines their receptivity to euphoria, catharsis, loss of self. If audience members are friendly with the performers they might perceive the music quite critically because they have been bound up with the various stages and processes of its production. It might, on the other hand, make their experience of the gig more intimate and enjoyable. If those audience members are also in a band their approach to the music may be even more critical, unless perhaps, the band is more famous and the gig more of an 'event.' Observers such as anthropologists and journalists, however, are necessarily more objective. Meanwhile, the experience of the performers may be affected not only by their audience but by the nature of the relationships within the band and by their emotional and financial investment in the music and its making. The fact that many took their band membership seriously, regarding it as more than just a hobby, meant that they became frustrated and depressed when their performances went badly and audiences were small, which often led to tension and friction within the band.

By surrendering oneself to 'flow' or 'communitas', a new and other self comes into being. It was mentioned earlier that some performers might also deliberately construct another 'performed' self by adopting a stage persona. This satisfied those who loved to entertain people or encourage some sort of response from them, and it provided an excuse or opportunity to behave in a more dramatic or outrageous manner. It also, however, appealed to those who found in it a challenge or release from their usual shy, retiring, or dull selves. Their nervousness often served to heighten the sense of euphoria ('flow') they experienced.

The opportunity to release tension, express emotions that are otherwise suppressed or denied, and indulge in behaviour not permissible in other contexts, is highly valued by many:

What have they come for, those people who make up the audience? They've come, first of all, to forget their daily life . . . It is a quest for purification . . . the audience comes looking for a place of dream, an ideal place. They come to dream; they come looking for the sublime (Barrault on theatre audiences, 1972: 25).

Dramatic performances have, in fact, been compared with dreams (Hadfield, 1972) because of the subliminal and instinctive, symbolic and expressive, ambiguous, irrational, and illuminative qualities that both share. Others have described gigs as akin to religious experiences with rock performers as shamans (R. Taylor, 1985), prophets or priests (Keil, 1966: 76; and Martin, 1981: 156), idols, gods, and totems (Herman, 1971: 76; and Martin, 1981: 154.)

The gigs of the Jactars and Crikey it's the Cromptons! were forms of entertainment and, some might say, escapism. (See Sharrat, 1980, on popular culture's rituals and performances as a form of escapism for the working class, and Turner, 1977: 47–48, on groups that 'escape the alienating structure of a "social system" into "communitas" or "social anti-structure"', generating 'sensorily perceptible rituals as a communitas.') They should also, however, be seen as artistic performances; creativity of a stimulating, challenging, thought-provoking kind in some ways similar to live theatre, opera, and other such events (which could also be seen as escapist), particularly since they were treated as such by the bands themselves. The Jactars and Crikey it's the Cromptons!, like many other musicians, saw their music and that of artists they admired, as something more than commercial entertainment and frequently referred to the fact that they wanted it to 'say' something. They therefore constructed it with the deliberate intention of evoking and communicating meanings and sentiments (e.g. through the ambiguity of the lyrics, the complexities of the music, or the interrelationship of the music's visual and aural elements during a gig), and often attended gigs of bands they knew or admired in the hope or expectation that they would be moved, stimulated, or impressed in some way.

By regarding and constructing their music with such intentions the music's aesthetic form became expressively symbolic and ambiguous. (Thus a road sign which is purely functional when displayed in a street becomes symbolic and meaningful when displayed on a gallery wall and is perceived as such by those who look at it and take note, for perhaps the first time, of its aesthetic qualities.) Both bands wanted their audience to drink, dance, and have a good time, but were also concerned that they (or those among them whose opinion mattered) appreciate the finer complexities and meanings in the music, recognizing in it something deeper than mere commercial formulas. (Thus the Jactars' 'gigging policy' was discussed partly because the band's members felt they had too much 'artistic integrity' and self-respect to perform to audiences that were not so appreciative.) They therefore wanted any sense of pleasure and excitement experienced by their audience to be achieved via the aesthetic qualities of the music and the performance itself, not just through dancing, alcohol, or others in the audience. (Hence Dave preferred recording to performing live partly because he felt people paid more attention to the aesthetic form of the music through the former.) The music was thus seen as the most important aspect of the performance, although the context in which the music was performed has also been emphasized because it was that which could determine the music's transformative power.

It is possible to postulate an ideal model of a gig, implicit throughout the discussion, to which participants of gigs aspired. At any gig the music, its performance, and appreciation of it, formed only part of a complex whole. The effectiveness of the music and its ability to move and stimulate both performers and audience depended upon the structuring of a multitude of interdependent factors surrounding and involved with the performance. The structure and context of a gig and the social relationships involved were thus interrelated with the artistic factors of the performance. Ideally, the balance between them was such that the aesthetic/artistic factors transcended the social relationships so that the non-rational, emotional, symbolic aspects of the gig predominated, overshadowing its more rational, pragmatic aspects. In such a situation band members and their audiences would undergo a process of transformation to reach a state of enjoyment and euphoria and a sense of harmony, unity, and identity, an experience which would overcome any existing tensions, problems, or conflicts. Marcuse termed that aspect of art 'the aesthetic dimension', the dimension where, 'art *transcends* its social determination and emancipates itself from the given universe of discourse and behaviour while preserving its overwhelming presence' (1979: 6); where subjectivity, catharsis, and 'the emergence of another reason' become possible. Bands on Merseyside, as the description and analysis of Crikey it's the Cromptons!' gig at the Fire Station demonstrates, often failed in their public performances to attain anything like that ideal model because the balance of those factors was not such that it could arise.

Like many others, members of the Jactars and Crikey it's the Cromptons! valued music-as-experience (involving participation) as opposed to music-as-commodity (involving consumption alone.) This was revealed by their emphasis upon spontaneity, originality, and communication in their gigs, their desire for a 'high', a 'buzz', or loss of self, and their use of alcohol to help precipitate it. Those qualities of performance were valued more than its mere entertaining aspects and any technical or musical skills it involved, and that was again indicated by the Jactars' 'lads-off-the-street' image (a rejection of the trappings of showmanship and a stress upon naturalness) and the emphasis they placed upon simple, cheap instruments rather than expensive, technological ones.

As indicated in Chapter 2, however, the community and solidarity the bands strove for was predominantly masculine. While women generally liked to dance, their male counterparts were reluctant to do so although some 'wrecked'—a dance form with a harsh, masculine character. Several bands incorporated overtly masculine and harsh aspects in their performance, such as abuse of the audience, and many gigs could be seen to exclude women, symbolize male solidarity, and incorporate what J. Taylor and D. Laing (1979: 45) described as the 'masturbatory imagery' of masculine rock, i.e. men watching other men in a joint celebration of masculinity. This 'narcissistic celebration of male power which structurally excludes the female spectator' (ibid.) could even be seen, perhaps, in Tony's use and intended use of banana, microphone, and courgette during his stage performance, or in Trav's 'frantic' style of guitar playing at the climax of his performance.

The complex and multi-faceted, symbolic and expressive nature of live artistic performance, its participatory and unpredictable aspects, the lure of its aesthetic dimension and the arousing intensity, transformative power, and emotiveness of the experience it can precipitate, explain its popularity not only in music but universally in other arts and contexts. It also, as Marcuse (1979) and Cohen (1974) pointed out, explains its potential and value as a political tool. The ambiguity of its symbols often determines that potential, allowing more space for subjectivity, persuasion, imagination, and the creation of meaning and metaphor. Thus although the gigs of rock bands in Liverpool reflected the historical, socio-economic reality of Liverpool life within which countless bands struggled to succeed, because of their symbolic, artistic nature they were also free of it, able to transcend it and in turn influence it, thereby incorporating both continuity and change.

5
The Deal

The struggle and hardship at the grass roots of the record industry were overshadowed by huge profits and glamour at the top which enticed thousands of bands and conditioned much of their music-making activities. The gap between the two worlds was enormous and only a very small percentage of bands ever managed to cross it. Yet there was always that element of luck, the hope of being in the right place at the right time, the belief that persistence, talent, and sound planning would win through in the end.

Knowledge of the music business and its financial and contractual operations had generally increased as the record industry had aged and matured. In Liverpool many musicians had been aware for some time of the practicalities of the business and the possibilities for success within it. The success of the Beatles and other local bands attracted to Liverpool those eager to cash in on the financial rewards its music offered. Record companies focused upon the city as a centre for the production of commercially successful bands, which gave local artists contact with the industry and greater incentive to 'make it.' Bands of the 1980s had grown up within that context, surrounded and inspired by people with experience of the music business and success within it. The city's economic decline undoubtedly fuelled ambitions and many had become more businesslike in their outlook and wary of being 'ripped off', as indicated by their legal awareness and arrangements regarding compositions. Even those bands content to just perform live in their locality tended to get sucked in by the same models of achievement that attracted and influenced others. The notion of 'making it' thus affected or preoccupied them all.

When I began frequenting the Ministry rehearsal studios the rumour spread that I was recruiting bands for CBS Records though I had been careful from the outset to explain my exact status and intentions. When my position became clearer many musicians pointed out that when they became famous I would possess valuable biographical information. They were therefore confident that they would eventually succeed, commenting that they would not be in a band at all if they didn't believe they could do so, though often adding that they also did it because they enjoyed it. One of them said, when asked if he thought his band could 'make it': 'You have to, don't you?' For many, this notion of 'making it' encapsulated a world of record sales, tours, large audiences, fans, chart success, and media appearances, i.e. fame and fortune on a national level. Others, however, just hoped to earn enough from their music to make a living. For them success represented prestige and respect for their music rather than fame and adulation on a large scale.

Whatever their desires, and despite variations in experience, class, and background, all had to encounter the same hurdles in their quest for success. The local music scene within which they operated reflected the competitive nature of the industry as a whole, involving rumour, slander, name-dropping, 'bullshitting', besieged by 'sharks', 'gangsters', 'cowboys' and 'rip-off merchants' attempting to cash in on the huge profits the industry offered. Furthermore, in order to 'make it' all had to try to reach a wider audience, which necessitated appearing on record. I never encountered a band that did not want to do so. But it was a hard task. Most bands attempted to get a contract with a record company which would provide them with the financial backing they needed or produce their records for them.

A great deal of thought, time, energy, and hard work went into bringing about such a 'deal.' Conversation and wishful thinking centred around the issue and gossip focused upon those bands that might get a deal, were just about to, or already had one. One band member, for example, experiencing problems with his car, exclaimed, 'As soon as we get signed I'm gonna set fire to this car and get a new one.' Coughing painfully, another moaned, 'Oh my God I'm dying— I don't want to die before I get signed up.' However, although many bands were well informed, organized and businesslike in their approach to the music industry, the majority were generally ignorant of the kind of tactical planning and manœuvring that might lead to a 'deal.'

IN PURSUIT OF A CONTRACT

The success of the Beatles and others, alongside the growth of the British youth market, encouraged large international record companies to set up business in Britain, invest in the development of the British record industry, and seek out British talent. In the 1970s the emergence of 'punk rock' stimulated the growth of an independent record industry to promote 'alternative' styles of music cheaper to produce than those favoured by the larger companies, and encourage and foster local talent and audiences.

From the mid-1970s, however, record sales fell. This was a consequence of the general recession in the British economy involving an increase in youth unemployment, which reduced the spending capacity of the main consumers of recorded music, and of the rise in home-taping which reflected changes in patterns of music consumption. Major record companies were pressurized to diversify and invest in other areas of entertainment and industry to keep abreast with developments in media and technology, on the assumption that, 'if a company controls every aspect of record making, then many of its costs will return as income' (Frith, 1983: 141). But the decline hit independent companies hardest since many of them had not been in business long enough to cope with such a substantial drop in sales, and many of the musical styles and imagery they fostered were adopted by larger companies that used the independents to discover talent and take the risks before appropriating, commercializing, and recontextualizing their music for a mass audience.

As the recession continued, the amount of money required to successfully produce and promote a band rose dramatically. Larger companies became more cautious and took on fewer bands, relying increasingly upon the international successes of artists who were already well established. Thus, at the expense of encouraging British music for British audiences, greater emphasis was placed upon the marketing of artists—particularly through video—and consequently upon their visual and potential international appeal. The musical product became more standardized, with commercial control of the market concentrated under a few international companies. By 1983 five of them held a 70 per cent share in both the UK and the world market; but they also manufactured records for other companies so they actually controlled almost 95 per cent of the market. All were based in London, where over 90 per cent of those employed within the UK record industry worked (Hardy, 1984).

Consequently, the type of contracts offered to bands changed. Whereas in the past companies might have taken on a band with the intention of nurturing it for a while to allow its music and image to develop, many now had little incentive to develop or even pay much attention to their relatively new, unknown artists since so much of their profit might be generated by only one or two others. Hence they were less willing to take risks, more concerned to sign bands that were already, in some sense, 'packaged', and often offered advance payment to cover the costs of just one single, on the understanding that only if that record was successful would the band's contract be renegotiated. The problem for the band if the single was a success was that it then had little time in which to produce an album to back it up.

Bands trying to get a record deal therefore had to think more in terms of the market and how they might fit into it. In Liverpool many considered carefully which particular companies to approach, distinguishing mainly between 'major' and 'independent' companies—though in reality it was sometimes difficult to do so. 'Independents' were associated with an emphasis upon live performance, 'cult followings', 'street credibility', and 'alternative' music, whilst 'majors' tended to be associated with commercial music, visual image, and thus with saleability. Most bands aimed for the latter, simply because these were generally larger and wealthier and thus afforded greater opportunity for fame and fortune. Bands like the Jactars and Crikey it's the Cromptons!, however, tended to approach independent companies, largely because their style of music would not appeal to major companies and they disliked the more commercial music those companies promoted, supporting the independents' policy of fostering alternative styles and allowing bands greater control over their material and the marketing of it. They were therefore often critical of bands producing 'commercial' music aimed at major companies. 'They're all on their bloody knees to London' was a typical comment. The distinction made between the two types of company is illustrated by the following quote:

The British music scene is divided—you've either got to be an 'underground' or indie band, or you 'sell out' to a major label. As far as we're concerned we're neither. I know that most bands, whether they're into pop or so-called underground music, want to increase the size of their audience . . . but according to the *NME* code of ethics, signing to a major entails signing your independence away (the Lucy Show, *Melody Maker*: 21 Septembeer 1985).

However, bands had to distinguish further within each category since the type of contracts and loans offered and the strategies and criteria adopted for taking on bands and choosing which records to release, varied considerably among both majors and independents. Some companies—usually independents—were more adventurous in their musical policies, for example, and some tried to predict trends in music and construct their records accordingly. Others believed prediction impossible and invested large sums of money in the production and marketing of records in the knowledge that whilst the vast majority would be unsuccessful and incur considerable losses, the success of just one could bring enough profit to cover the losses over and over. Laing (1985: 9) described this as, '"The mud against the wall approach" after the adage that if you throw enough mud against the wall, some of it will stick.'

Once bands decided which companies to approach they usually sent or took a demo tape to the company's A&R department, which was responsible for taking on new artists. A&R personnel included talent scouts who 'discovered' those artists and recommended them to their bosses who had the authority to sign them to the company. Their duties covered paperwork, listening to demo tapes, and visiting various parts of the country to see unknown acts. Much of their time was spent in recording studios, attending gigs and rehearsals, talking to bands, managers, and agents, and maintaining contacts with local music journalists and disc jockeys who could keep them informed on developments in particular areas. The music press thus assisted a record company not only through the publicity it gave the company's own artists but by providing it with information on others.

A&R personnel also monitored the activities of other record companies. Occasionally they took on a band when its contract with a rival company had run out or tried to sell another company an artist they were no longer interested in. Sometimes they tried to outbid rival companies for a band and often a 'lottery' developed whereby several companies took an interest in the same band—largely because others had and they were afraid of missing out on something. As one manager put it, 'The music business is like a poker game. If the word is out that you are an attractive proposition then all the companies want to get in on the act.' But the same thing occurred elsewhere, in football, for example. A journalist reported that often one of those companies hovering around the band might sign them just to get rid of the opposition and 'drop' them soon afterwards. It was generally believed that if a band had been dropped in such a manner, or if all the companies eventually lost interest and 'passed' on it, then the band was in a bad position since few companies would be interested in it thereafter. Consequently, bands in that position often changed their name or tried to develop a new persona.

The A&R department of one major record company employed a team of six talent scouts, assigning each a different part of the country to cover. One of them said he spent five or six nights a week attending gigs and received, on average, seventy-five demo tapes per week. To the A&R world, he said, Liverpool was the second most important place after London (with Glasgow running a close third) so he always kept a close watch on what was going on there and travelled there regularly. Its music scene changed so rapidly that he always came across new faces and bands.

The scouts that visited Liverpool tended to be young men from London in their late teens or early twenties. Generally, they only visited the city if there was a large concert involving many local bands or if they were interested in one particular band. They might visit the city several times to see that band perform and talk to its members or manager before playing their bosses a recording of the band and taking them to see it to decide whether to sign it. Many of those A&R representatives stayed at the Adelphi, Liverpool's plushest hotel. With their flexible expense accounts they might wine and dine the band in the hotel or at restaurants and bars in the city centre. To the bands they represented a successful future. One scout was told by a band member, 'You are my passport out of here.' But A&R personnel were cautious. Their future career might depend upon the success of their next signing and the music business was unpredictable and risky. Consequently, bands courted by them might initially be encouraged and excited but were usually disappointed.

Like employees in other sectors of the record industry, A&R personnel frequently changed job or company, thus reflecting the rapid fluctuations within the industry as a whole. That made it hard for bands to establish personal contact with them. Furthermore, bands and managers often discovered that when they thought they were negotiating in confidence with a particular A&R department, their business was in fact being discussed amongst A&R departments of various companies. As time passed, pressure upon the bands increased since those that had been around for a long while without being signed were said to have 'missed the boat.' Their name was familiar to the companies but no longer generated interest.

Advice and opinion on what was required in order to get a deal varied. Most were agreed that talent played only a small part and that more important was good management, a marketable image, charisma, self-confidence, hard work, and what Simon Napier-Bell (manager of Wham!) described as 'the insatiable desire to succeed— because it is those bands that will do what is necessary to succeed.' According to a local promoter bands needed:

determination, wariness of the industry, the ability to take the knocks. The music industry is a shark pool. If you can find a good raft with a good team behind you then that's sound. If it's a makeshift raft it'll go.

Like many others, John Peel said that much of it was down to 'luck', 'randomness', whom you know, and being in the right place at the right time: 'It's like saying "how do I get hit by lightning?"' (Radio 4, *Tuesday Call*: 8 April 1986.)

Pete Fulwell, manager of three successful Liverpool bands, agreed that it could happen with luck but emphasized that without proper organization and planning success would dissipate. He believed in working out 'how the system operates', deciphering the mechanisms of promotion and marketing so as to draw up a detailed 'plan of action' which bands should follow rigidly if they wanted to make a living out of it. The plan involved hard work and commitment on the part of the band (i.e. turning up for rehearsals and consistently producing songs), deciding well in advance which record company to aim for and how to cope with the quickly changing circumstances of the record industry, and compiling a set of priorities (such as when to make a single and when to make an album) and a deadline by which to achieve them.

Most bands, however, lacking the benefit of such experience and insight, perhaps lacking management of any kind, had to try to 'make it' on their own with the help of whatever literature, advice, or role models came to them via their immediate environment. Some, as mentioned earlier, presented companies with a promotional 'package' of tapes, photographs, press cuttings, biographical information, and occasionally a video, in order to show what type of band they were and how they might fit into the market. Many emphasized the visual aspects of the band and were concerned to develop a visual 'image.' The manager of one said she would have to 'sell the band' on the appearance of its lead singer whom she described as 'our most saleable product', whilst another refused to allow the keyboard player to appear in gigs, on photographs, or video until he had lost weight and stressed the importance of promotional material of good quality:

Then it doesn't matter what they look like because they look like a quality band. You can take good photos of anyone . . . It's about presenting the atmosphere of the band, not just putting make-up on them.

Whilst associations between bands could help their members obtain information and advice, most acknowledged the need for more influential 'contacts' in the music business if they wanted to 'make it' and achieve some kind of success. Many believed that those could prove as important, if not more so, than talent or planning. Consequently, there was much talk of 'making contacts', although many younger musicians were hesitant in doing so, regarding such people with reverence. Members of the Jactars were also hesitant, again perhaps because they felt that as creative people they should be concerned with the artistic aspects of music-making over and above the business aspects. Bands without managers usually relied upon their most outgoing members to make contacts and conduct other public relations work. Some tried to establish contact with music journalists, promoters, and successful local bands, as well as particular A&R persons (one manager outlined in detail his policy of flattering and indulging A&R people). The Entertainments Officer at Liverpool University described how, when he first took up the post, he had been inundated with visits from local band managers offering to take him out for drinks on the assumption that as a newcomer he would be suitably naïve and manipulable.

Many bands tried to attract the attention of record companies through their performances, inviting A&R personnel to their gigs to witness the quality of their live performance or the rapport they established with an audience. But because those people rarely turned up and seemed more likely to attend gigs on their home ground, some bands tried to perform in London or organized 'showcase' gigs, i.e. gigs staged solely for record companies. One or two clubs in London were frequently used for this purpose with bands performing in front of a small audience of A&R personnel, but in general few A&R people ever turned up and some clubs had begun to charge bands to play there. A few bands shunned gigs altogether hoping to attract attention through the quality of their recordings alone, whilst others found alternative ways such as talent competitions. One band, for example, won a local songwriting competition and came second in a contest sponsored by a local recording studio. Encouraged by one of the judges they entered a national competition in which they again came second, attracting the interest of several managers.

Some bands were ingenious in their self-promotion—even busking outside record companies and radio stations—and some could be pushy, aggressive, or manipulative. Members of one band, knowing that a rival band had attracted the interest of a well-known manager from America who was due to visit Liverpool to see it during a business trip to London, found out exactly how and when he would arrive and turned up at Speke airport to meet him. They took him to hear them rehearse and he consequently left Liverpool expressing an interest in them without having seen or heard the band he originally intended to visit.

Many bands courted publishing companies. Opinions on when to get a publishing deal and who with varied. Some approached publishing companies early on in the belief that with a publishing contract they would appear a more attractive proposition to record companies, or in the hope that the publisher would promote their material for them since it was obviously in the publisher's best interests if it was recorded and sold. Others thought it better to wait until they had a potential hit record before approaching a publisher so they would be offered a better deal. Some favoured a deal with the publishing branch of the record company they were with, or were aiming for, because if both contracts were with the same company the company might invest more into the band and its promotion, whilst others advocated a separate publishing deal in order to give the band more leverage since each company would be trying to get more money out of the other. Furthermore, if both deals were with one company and one collapsed then the other might do so as well.

A lot of bands received, at some point in their career, attention from a record, management, or publishing company. Some thought it best to keep quiet about this whilst others broadcast the news— perhaps even placing a press release in the local paper announcing their impending success—or pretended to have attracted such attention when in fact they hadn't.

Since the increasing accessibility of music-making technology had reduced the cost and mystique of the recording process, many bands were able to make records independently of the industry, financing, producing, and distributing them on their own, selling them at gigs, for example, or advertising them locally. Some did the same with their tapes. Often they were helped by independent record labels such as Liverpool's Probe Plus. Bands produced records themselves for their own satisfaction or in an effort to reach a wider audience. Many, however, saw those records as another means of attracting the attention of a record company, one more step towards a 'deal', knowing that to continue making records they would eventually need more secure financial backing. The owner of local record label Skysaw always warned bands that they would not make much money from records they had produced alone (in fact most bands made a loss) and should just regard them as a stepping-stone in their career.

Making a record independently involved recording a master tape in a studio. This was then sent to be cut, which determined its sound quality and volume (almost all cutting facilities were based in London—there were none on Merseyside), before being taken to a pressing company (again, no such facilities existed on Merseyside). The band or group of bands provided their own label and artwork, which could be printed separately or at the pressing plant. Total outlay for a 7″ single could be less than £800 for 1,000 copies provided the band(s) minimized costs by using a cheaper studio and packaging, but 12″ singles were more likely to recoup costs and were only slightly more expensive. The band(s) then had to organize distribution, publicity, and marketing of the record. If it was commercially released through an established distribution network such as the Cartel or a major distributor, they had to register with the MCPS (Mechanical Copyright Protection Society.) The distributor usually gave the band the wholesale price for the records as charged by the record shops, minus a percentage for the service (Probe charged 7½ per cent, Rough Trade charged 22½). If they were already registered with the PRS (Performing Right Society) they could claim performance rights from sales.

A few bands invested enough money to produce a master tape of a quality high enough to reach the standard of recording set by major companies—generally higher than that of independent companies—and took the tape straight to those companies in the hope that they might like it and offer the band a licensing deal whereby they would press and distribute the record for the band. (Many smaller companies had made such deals with larger companies.) That arrangement could benefit both parties. If the record was successful the company had to pay the band a higher royalty on each copy sold than if it had signed and recorded the act directly, whilst the band kept its own label, maintained greater control over its material, and proved it could do well. If the record was not a success:

It is a cheap deal—the company is spared the production costs. This is a particularly attractive way of avoiding risks in an uncertain market or with types of music a company is not used to organizing or selling (Frith, 1983: 104).

Some bands produced their own flexi-disc (a cheap record of floppy plastic). The quality of such records was not that of ordinary records but they cost less to produce. A thousand could be pressed for £200 (less studio and printing costs), but the more discs pressed, the lower the cost per disc. Some were distributed through record shops or gigs but the majority reached the public through fanzines. I did not know of any Merseyside band that produced a flexi-disc but several—including the Jactars and One Last Fight—discussed doing so and investigated the costs.

Members of the Jactars and Crikey it's the Cromptons! regularly debated the pros and cons of making a record—either a compilation record with other bands from Vulcan Studios, or one featuring their own two bands. Dave T. suggested that both bands make an album together which would cost each member a little over £100. Some of the others were in favour of the idea but Tog and Huw were dubious. Huw gave the matter much thought before deciding that it would only be worth while if it was a really good production—which would increase the cost. Tog didn't think half an album was worth the money and doubted that self-financed records were ever successful.

The idea was eventually dropped, largely because it became apparent that an album would cost more than Dave originally predicted, but also because preparations began for a compilation album of Vulcan bands.

Opinions thus varied as to whether making a record independently was worth while. Some argued that it brought bands no closer to a record contract since so many were now producing their own, but others thought a record was more impressive and received more attention than a demo tape, was more likely to be played on radio, and indicated that the band was organized and dedicated. That was verified by an A&R representative from a major record company speaking on Radio 4 (*Tuesday Call*: 8 April 1986), though she also said that evidence of local interest in the band was still more important. If, for example, the band was recommended to her by the manager of a local record shop she would be more interested in it. John Peel agreed, stressing the importance of good press reviews of the band. The cost of producing and promoting their own record was in any case too great for most bands and bank loans were difficult to acquire. Members of Blue Nose B managed to raise one only by telling the bank manager they needed it for a car. They had visited him previously with a portfolio of record sleeve designs and cost estimates but he turned them down saying it was too big a risk.

I have so far described only a few of the many plans and strategies adopted by bands in their quest for success. What follows is an account of efforts made by three particular bands in order to depict more fully the problems and issues that could be involved.

Up The Khyber

In January 1986 a talent scout from a major record company rang the Ministry rehearsal studios to inform Billy, the owner, that he and a colleague would be visiting Liverpool to hunt for interesting bands and might look in at the Ministry. Considerable excitement arose amongst the few who were told the news. An employee at the studios and manager of Rise, one of the bands that rehearsed there, immediately booked Rise for a rehearsal to coincide with the visit. Kate, manager of Up the Khyber, heard of the impending visit and surreptitiously found out when it would take place by checking the time of Rise's rehearsal in the bookings. She then, without giving the real reason for doing so, swapped the rehearsal time of her own band with one of the other bands booked for that afternoon and began to make plans for the visit, persuading the two members of Up the Khyber in employment to take that day off work.

Kate had already visited that particular record company and spoken to one of the men that was coming. He hadn't been interested in the tape she played him, saying that there was nothing new or different about the music or its romantic lyrics and that 80 per cent of the charts were love songs—if Up the Khyber wrote, for example, *gay* love songs he might be more interested. Kate therefore decided that when she met him again she would pretend to have a different band and discussed with others at the Ministry possible names for it. Jokes were made about those with homosexual connotations.

On the day of the visit excitement built up in the Ministry office. Kate waited anxiously at the window. When the two scouts were finally spotted she disappeared upstairs to inform her band (they had spent the entire afternoon rehearsing in preparation) of the arrival. The scouts were young and fashionably dressed. They discussed local bands they had seen with Billy, who asked them what they thought of Half Man Half Biscuit's recent success. One replied that Half Man Half Biscuit might be funny but were not 'Top of the Pops' material and therefore wouldn't appeal to a wider audience. He explained that his company was looking for a band that was unusual but commercial, and named, by way of example, a band with his company that had recently made a lot of money but 'without selling out in any way.' Billy and the manager of Rise then mentioned some of the bands currently rehearsing at the Ministry and the latter suggested that the scouts might like to 'drop in' on Rise's rehearsal.

Kate entered the office and greeted the scout she had met before, reminding him that she had managed the band he hated so much but informing him that she now managed a different band, adding, 'You must come up and listen to us.' He replied he didn't think they would have time whereupon Kate retorted, 'You've got to! . . . I went all the way down to London to see you and you won't even come upstairs to see us!' The scout said that he would try to later on but at the moment he needed a drink, so we adjourned to a nearby pub. Kate was in an excitable state and described to me on the way to the pub how she had hovered outside the office door for ages wondering whether to go in and introduce herself.

In the pub the manager of Rise again told one of the scouts about his band and humbly said that if they could spare the time to listen to the band for a few minutes and give him their honest opinion he would be very grateful. Meanwhile Kate discussed Up the Khyber with the other scout. Both were rather put out when the two scouts, who had heard about me from one of the other bands they visited that day, broke off their conversations to question me about my research. We returned to the Ministry. Kate went to her band, urging me to stick with the scouts while they watched Rise so that afterwards I could direct them upstairs to see Up the Khyber. As I did so one of them struck up conversation. He was, he said, new to the job, and he confided that what he hated about it was the sight of all these people 'bowing and scraping' to him, all these managers clustering around urging him to give their bands a chance. He appreciated their position because he managed a band himself but he found it very embarrassing in Liverpool because bands there had more to lose and were therefore more desperate to 'make it.'

The other scout was reluctant to see Up the Khyber but his colleague urged him to stay as they had promised. Kate was waiting at the top of the stairs. She had borrowed for the occasion two spacious, well-equipped rooms rented and renovated by another band with an advance received from a record contract. The rehearsal room could be viewed through a one-way window from an adjoining smaller room used for recording purposes. We were ushered into the latter and through the screen the talent scouts watched Up the Khyber perform two songs although they were reluctant to stay for the second, particularly since one of them now recognized the band from the tape Kate had taken him earlier. Kate stood tense and nervous while the band played and keenly pointed out that they would soon be getting a designer in to create some stage outfits. One of the scouts tapped his foot to the music and asked if those were the band's favourite songs. Eagerly Kate replied that they liked all of their songs.

After the second song the impatient scout moved towards the door muttering his thanks. Kate, visibly indignant, asked him if he didn't have any comment to make. Annoyed, he replied, 'I *still* don't like it. It's just not my kind of music. Whether or not I think a band is going to be the next biggest thing, if I don't like them I won't sign them.' He left the room but his colleague paused to comment on the excellence of the drummer and the fact that the singer needed voice training.

Kate went over everything that had happened with me in minute detail before we joined the band. She then related to them the scouts' comments and reactions, presenting them in a rather optimistic light by dwelling, for example, upon the fact that one of them asked if the band had any gigs in London, and upon the comment of the other that even if he thought a band was going to be 'the next biggest thing ...', as if he had been suggesting that Up the Khyber had that potential. The band members were, however, pretty despondent and commented bitterly on A&R people in general. Kate then expressed her annoyance that one of them should tap his foot to the music one minute and say he didn't like it the next.

The manager of Rise arrived to ask what had happened, feeling bitter himself about the scouts' reactions to Rise. Again, one of them had moved to the music as if enjoying it before stating 'I hate it.' More denigration of A&R personnel ensued but everyone began to consider the matter in a more humorous light. Billy, who also managed a band rehearsing in the building that evening, found it all very amusing and threatened to spread rumours of another A&R visit in order to boost the booking rates. Members of Rise appeared and joked and moaned about the fact that the scouts had hated them. They worked so hard on their music they said, and had performed with as much energy and enjoyment as they could muster—especially after they saw one of the men almost dance to the music. To be then dismissed in such an abrupt manner was devastating.

The following month an A&R representative from another major record company visited the Ministry to see Up the Khyber. It took Kate a great deal of effort and persistence to continually contact such people. Getting through to them on the telephone was difficult and travelling to see them in London was expensive. Again two of the band's members had been persuaded to take the day off work and again Kate was tense and excited. She had with her a hairdryer and setting gel to make sure the band members looked well coiffured and had even persuaded them to acquire and wear matching outfits with the little money they could afford. The A&R man, however, did not think the band was suitable for his company.

Another manager who frequented the Ministry was critical of Kate's management of Up the Khyber, believing that she would do better to spend money on a good demo tape instead of concentrating all her efforts upon enticing A&R personnel to rehearsals and gigs performed in shoddy venues where, since the performance was live, so many things could go wrong. That manager was also sceptical about the talents of Up the Khyber saying that Kate was trying to 'manufacture' a band, which was impossible: 'You can't polish a turd.' Kate herself was concerned to adopt what she termed a 'professional approach', and described how she recently sacked a band member despite his good looks, explaining that this was 'business' and she had acted only in the best interests of the band:

It's the same in whatever you do. You've got to be professional about it whether it's music you're involved with, a pub, or whatever. You've got to be prepared to be the boss . . . the leader, to be disliked.

Crikey It's The Cromptons!

The Jactars and Crikey it's the Cromptons! were less organized in their approach to record companies and had made few contacts, although Tog and Dave had become friendly with a young assistant producer who worked on one of Radio Merseyside's music programmes. Tony did his best to establish relations with local disc jockeys, promoters, and journalists but many were put off by what they described as his pushy manner. He and his fellow band members hoped to sign up with an independent company that would promote but not 'package' them. They had taken a demo tape to Geoff Davies at Probe but he wasn't interested. All of them were keen to 'make it' with the band. Huw said he was serious about the band largely because he couldn't think of anything else to do, and he went through phases of depression and pessimism, optimism and enthusiasm about it. His ambition was for the band to make a record and become fairly well known and respected. If it split up he intended to try to join an established band that was 'in the process of getting somewhere'. Tony also got frustrated when things went wrong with the band but was often enthusiastic and egotistical about it.

In January 1986 Midi, Tony, and Huw organized a trip to London to visit record companies and I accompanied them. We travelled down in Midi's car. None of them was familiar with London and navigating the crowded streets around Oxford Circus where many record companies were situated was difficult. They had made no appointments with any companies, which proved a major drawback. At the first company we visited the uniformed man at the reception desk informed us that we wouldn't be allowed in to see anyone without an appointment although we could leave a tape if we wished.

After the same thing happened at the next company Huw tried to telephone several companies to make appointments but was unable to get through to any. We visited more but were again turned away at reception. The others began to feel despondent and Huw worried that they were running out of tapes to distribute. At one company we met the manager of Blue Nose B who was also doing the rounds without much success, despite the fact that he had with him a record his band had recently produced on their own. At Rough Trade, the last company we visited that day, Tony informed the receptionist that they had sent the company a tape a while ago and were wondering what response it got. She contacted the A&R person who received it. He hadn't listened to it yet but promised to do so by the following day.

Tony, Huw, and Midi spent that night at the house of Midi's brother. I met them the following morning. Once again we were turned away at the door of the first company we visited. Huw, however, had managed to arrange an appointment at CBS Records and I had contacted Phil, an A&R man at London Records who was prepared to listen to Crikey it's the Cromptons!' tape and comment on it. In his office Phil played the first two songs before stopping the tape to say, 'It's not really my cup of tea to be quite honest.' He didn't think anyone else in his company would be interested either. He preferred the second song because it was more 'song-ish' but thought both songs should have been a lot 'slower' and more 'laid-back' so that their 'arrangements' and 'light and shade' were more apparent. Tony assured him that they did have other, slower songs and pointed out the humour in the lyrics, but Phil said he couldn't hear the lyrics at all, a major drawback since lyrics are important in any song. He went on to compare Tony's guitar rhythms with the style of a well-known band and told Tony that the 'range', 'colour' and 'phrasing' of his voice wasn't that good, suggesting that he took singing lessons.

Tony objected to that but asked Phil if he thought the songs were at least 'reasonably catchy.' Phil replied that he didn't and had been looking more for a 'hookier' (i.e. catchier) chorus. Tony said that they did have other good songs that weren't on the tape but was told that it was no good saying there were 'better songs at home' and that a great deal of thought should go into the tape presented to companies; the best songs should be put first and all the songs should be of the same ilk so as to represent the style of music the band was putting across. In reply, Tony said he didn't mean they had *better* songs at home but they did have more 'commercial' ones, in fact one of them was quite 'a pop song'. The songs on the tape were just the ones that he personally liked best. He invited Phil to see them play live some time and Phil agreed that it was better to see a band live.

Tony asked Phil in conclusion, if he thought Crikey it's the Cromptons! was more of an 'indie' band. Phil nodded and said the music was not really, 'major company music . . . Obviously I think John Peel would play this . . . It's not my sort of style. I like a mixture between indie and pop, that's what I look for.' He suggested that Crikey it's the Cromptons! needed an 'indie deal' to start off with and could develop interest from there. He also suggested that it might be a good idea for them to get some sort of management—'a bit of guidance'—and added that he would be pleased to listen to any more tapes they did. Midi and Huw were encouraged by his remarks and thought them quite 'fair'. Tony admitted that they had made him think more carefully about his singing and he would pay more attention to it in future. All agreed that they should send Phil another tape.

Their next appointment was with an A&R woman at CBS, one of the better-known major record companies. I expressed surprise that they were approaching such a company but Huw said he had thought it might encompass smaller, subsidiary labels. We waited in the plush foyer before being shown up to the woman's office. Crikey it's the Cromptons! had sent a tape to CBS a while ago but heard nothing. The A&R woman didn't think she would be able to find it so she listened to the tape they had brought, stopping half-way through the second song to say:

This isn't really us I'm afraid. It's interesting but it's not commercial enough . . . Being a big company we obviously have to go for things we think will sell in large volumes. Even if you had a sort of cult following and could sell about three thousand albums we basically wouldn't be interested . . . it's the nature of this company really . . . Having listened to one and a half songs I'd say you'd get more interest from independent labels . . . you'd be wasting your time going to see large labels at this stage. I think what you're doing is interesting . . . but most of the big companies are interested in things that are going to happen pretty quickly. That's just the way things are at the moment. If you had a *big* cult following with this kind of stuff then we would be interested, but if you haven't then you're a long way off.

Tony interrupted her to mention Half Man Half Biscuit and the fact that they were friends of Crikey it's the Cromptons! A few weeks earlier Dave T. had suggested that Crikey it's the Cromptons! 'jump on the back of Half Man Half Biscuit', i.e. try to use its success to further their own career. Tony had taken this up, mentioning his association with Half Man Half Biscuit on several occasions and regretting that Crikey it's the Cromptons! had never performed with them and thus didn't have posters showing both bands on the same billing. The woman didn't seem too impressed by Tony's information and said that with the type of music Crikey it's the Cromptons! played, 'you've got to have a foot in the door before a major company is going to be interested'. In other words, she explained, it would be best for the band to get on to an independent record label first because:

If you're on an independent label they [the major companies] look at you in a different way . . . You are likely to get more interest. That's just the way it works.

She asked if they gigged a lot and had a regular following, explaining:

With this type of stuff it almost has to come from the live sound . . . you build up a following, get reviews in *NME* and so on, and then you build from there. It's very hard to start with this kind of stuff completely cold . . . Get a John Peel session, try and get some press people along to see your gigs, and go to the smaller labels. I really think right now that you're wasting your time seeing the big labels.

Huw, Tony, and Midi were again quite satisfied with those remarks and were especially flattered by her comment that she personally found their music interesting, even if she didn't think it was suitable for the company she worked for.

We returned to Rough Trade, an independent company that Huw, Tony, and Midi thought more likely to appreciate their music. The A&R man there still hadn't listened to their tape but disappeared into an office to do so while we waited. He soon emerged to say, 'I wasn't particularly into any of the material I heard', and asked if that was their most recent material or if they had attempted anything since then, and if they had done much 'live work'. Tony mentioned one gig they might have and the man went on to say:

I think you've got to realize that an average A&R department gets anything up to two hundred tapes a week so something's got to be incredibly special to catch your interest . . . I go to gigs about six out of seven nights so gigs are really important. No one listens to more than two songs on a tape so those first songs have to be really special and even then we'd have to see you live before we made a decision.

The best thing to do, he added, was to give an A&R person dates of about three gigs and they would try to attend one of them. He asked if they had tried to interest any music journalists yet because, 'If you get a journalist who will champion the band that's normally the best way to start.'

Tony, Midi, and Huw were offended and disappointed by those remarks and by the manner in which they were delivered. It was getting dark and they only had time to visit Radio One before setting off for Liverpool. They deposited a tape in the foyer under a large sign requesting that all tapes and other recorded material be left at the reception desk. They were all hungry but had no money left for food. With the cost of petrol, parking, and travel on the underground to pay for, it had been an expensive trip.

A few weeks later Huw received letters from two of the companies visited. One was a standard photocopied rejection with a hand-written PS: 'Sorry you get the usual photocopied letter.' The other read: 'Sorry lads, but this is far too weird and wacky for me—but do send us any other material you would like to.'

The Jactars

The Jactars had also taken a tape to Geoff at Probe but he never contacted them afterwards and they were too shy to approach him again. In addition, they had sent a few tapes to record companies but received only two replies. One commented that their choruses weren't 'pronounced' enough, which amused them because none of their songs had choruses; the other wrote that he liked their music but he did not suggest signing them.

Recognizing that their music would not appeal to a mass audience, members of the Jactars hoped instead to be well-known, admired, and respected as an 'indie' band by a more selective audience. Trav and Dave were concerned, however, that many independent companies, in an effort to make money, now seemed interested only in bands that produced more commercial styles of music. 'It may be the case', said Trav, 'that they [the independents] are just not ready for us yet', and he predicted that the Jactars would continue as they had been for another year before they eventually 'cracked it.'

Trav and Dave agreed that they weren't ready for a record deal just yet anyway and should develop their music at their own pace without succumbing to the desire to try to 'make it' as soon as possible. Dave even suggested that it would be better if they all got jobs so that they weren't financially dependent upon the band. I pointed out that none of them earned money from the band anyway, but Dave said they relied too much upon the fact that they eventually would do so, i.e. they had become too careerist about the band, and he was sure that if the band became more of a hobby or sideline their attitude to it would change and they would become more relaxed about it and allow themselves more time in which to develop and improve their music. However, because Trav and Dave were ambitious about their music-making they got depressed when things went badly. They were sure that they would always be involved with music. Trav, for example, admitted that he had become half-resigned to the fact that he would eventually have to take a job he didn't want in order to buy himself a semi-detached house with a studio in a back room, and he fantasized about becoming 'a sort of established eccentric' widely respected for his music.

In February 1986 the Decemberists performed in London, taking a coach load of friends and relatives with them. Tog, Dave, and Trav (Gary was supposed to go but didn't show up) took this opportunity of a trip to London to visit various record companies. Karen travelled down with them and went off on her own during the day, whilst Chris (a member of the Da Vincis) and I traipsed around with them, supplied with copies of the latest demo tapes of the Jactars and the Da Vincis, an A–Z of London, and a list of record company phone numbers that Dave had acquired from the Decemberists. None of them was familiar with London and they frequently lost their way. It was also clear from the start that none was particularly good at promoting their band. All had agreed earlier that they would cope with events much better if they were drunk and they had therefore consumed a considerable quantity of wine, beer, and spirits on the coach so that before we even reached London they were already fairly inebriated. That condition worsened in London where we appeared to be touring off-licences rather than record companies.

The only A&R person Dave had managed to contact on the phone was the man from Rough Trade that Crikey it's the Cromptons! had met. He told Dave to call round with a tape. In the company's foyer he said he wanted to keep the Jactars' and the Da Vinci's tapes because he liked 'to live with a tape for a while', but he promised to send them back as soon as he could. More tapes were deposited at other companies and Chris said he was beginning to feel rather uncomfortable about taking his tape around to strangers like this— 'It's as if you're begging.'

The next address we visited turned out to be not a record company at all but a private house. Tog tried to explain to the man standing in his pyjamas in the doorway that we were looking for 'Fetish Records'. I later discovered that he only wanted to seek out Fetish Records because it was known for taking on 'electronic bands' that dressed in leather and he was curious to see what it was like but had looked it up in a book on the record industry several years out of date. We took an underground train. By this time Dave, Trav, and Tog were very drunk indeed and Trav, attempting to make cheese sandwiches out of an enormous loaf of unsliced bread balanced precariously on his lap, ended up crawling on his hands and knees in between train seats in an effort to retrieve a tub of margarine. We arrived at another company to see an A&R man that Roger Hill had recommended to Crikey it's the Cromptons! Typically, the Jactars had made no appointment and had even forgotten the man's name but asked to see whoever was available. After waiting an hour at reception they gave up and left a tape instead.

We visited another company whose A&R department had written quite favourably of the Jactars' music in response to a tape they sent. The Jactars were hesitant in mentioning the letter and tape to the receptionist. She eventually tried to contact the relevant people but they were at a meeting. By this time it was 6 p.m. and the companies were closing so we adjourned to a café where the Jactars debated whether it would have been better to have mailed the tapes to the companies instead of travelling all the way to London to visit them.

Not all the companies we visited responded. Trav received a couple of letters. One was a standard, photocopied message that read:

Thank you for sending us a sample of your music, at least one person listened to it and gave it consideration. At this time we are not able to offer you a recording or publishing contract. Don't give up hope, who knows you may write that hit album one day. (Just make sure we hear it first.) We listen to all tapes in strict order of receipt, so sorry for any delay in our reply.

The other was a brief handwritten note that read: 'Sorry, Trav, but this sounds too similar to The Smiths for me. Keep in touch.' It was only when the Da Vincis rang Rough Trade to enquire about their demo tape that the Jactars discovered that the man there had liked theirs. Despite this they were reluctant to contact him. Weeks later I finally offered to telephone on their behalf. The A&R man said he liked the Jactars' material and wondered if they had more. A few months later the Jactars sent him a more recent tape.

NEGOTIATING A CONTRACT

Many bands regarded a record contract as a pinnacle of achievement, an end to their problems, but were often unaware of how contracts, record companies, or the industry as a whole operated, which left them susceptible to the machinations of business people around them when the time came to confront those matters. Before they even began to record they had to negotiate the terms of the contract with the A&R person who discovered them, with their own solicitors, and with the record company and its solicitors. Those negotiations could take months, often dragged out by the solicitors who earned more money the longer they continued. 'The whole thing is like a big game,' said one local manager, 'with the contract being sent back and forth like a yoyo.'

It wasn't necessary for all the members of a band to sign the contract and many, for various reasons, did not. Two of the five members of Just William did not sign their band's contract. Their manager said she hadn't wanted them to because one hadn't played in a band recently which made him a risk, and the other was too fat. In other words she wanted to retain the option of sacking them. However, she also said it was in the band's best interests to have fewer members sign so that if the band was successful she could later bargain with the record company, informing them that other companies had offered the unsigned members large sums of money and in order to retain them the company would have to offer a higher price. The two unsigned members, on the other hand, explained that they hadn't signed the contract because they did not want to be 'owned' by any company and preferred to maintain their independence.

There was no such thing as a standard or normal recording agreement. Contracts with a major or large independent company set certain obligations that had to be fulfilled (e.g. a certain number and type of record to be recorded within a certain period of time) and restrictions on the band's members (e.g. upon their involvement with other companies and bands). They usually gave the company control over what would be recorded, the recording process itself, and the final product and its merchandising. In return, the band was awarded royalties discussed in terms of points. A band offered '10 points' would earn 10 per cent of the profit on each record sold, and that figure was renegotiated if the band successfully remained with the company for a long period of time. A new recording artist with a major company could expect a royalty of around 8–12 per cent, calculated on the suggested or national retail list price of that recording. Those with smaller or independent companies were usually awarded a lower rate. Out of that amount, the artists paid royalties (usually around 2–4 per cent) to their record producer. Wright (1983: 29) pointed out that:

Only relatively recently—over the last 10 or 20 years—have artists begun to receive an appreciable, and in many cases huge, percentage of the money made from a record. This may be because until then the value was thought to lie in the song itself, rather than in the artists' rendition of it. Today, however, the reverse seems to be the case.

When the contract was signed the record company gave the band a lump sum advance against future royalties which was supposed to cover the band's wages, equipment, recording and other costs, and was often tightly controlled by the company. The amount varied considerably according to the nature of the company and the number and type of record the band was required to produce over a certain period. Many bands preferred 'album deals' as opposed to 'singles deals' because they offered greater security. The band received greater investment of time and money from the company and more commitment to their promotion and development.

Recording costs were high. It might cost £60,000 to record an album, £15,000 for a video, and more on top of that for the band's expenses, the cutting and pressing of the record, and further promotion and publicity. That could amount to a total of £150,000, which was why A&R departments tended to take so long deciding whether or not to sign a band. They had to carefully weigh up their financial outlay against the talent, appearance, and general earning potential of the band they were signing:

Musicians are treated as property, each with a price, a measurable value that can be exploited, increased, realized in the marketplace . . . All A&R decisions are basically financial and the calculations have to be precisely made. Companies don't just sign a group and leave them to get on with it; they weigh the necessary investment against the possible returns. There are obvious questions to be asked: How ready is the act to record? How much rehearsal time does it need? What advance should it get for equipment? What recording costs are necessary? How much help should the company give with organizing gigs and tours and publicity? How big should its advertising budget be? The answers depend on one simple consideration: How much is the act going to earn? And this is where the problems start (Frith, 1983: 103).

Many performers, concerned mainly with the creative side of their music-making, found such calculations and demands upon their creativity hard to cope with:

The record company aren't giving me any more money yet they won't let me go until I've done another three albums . . . they ask the computer—'How much will Jerry Dammers make?' And the computer says 'nothing'—But I don't see how a computer can forecast what kind of music I'm going to make. It's ridiculous (Jerry Dammers, *Sounds*: 19 January 1985).

As one local performer put it: 'When you're young you naïvely assume that record companies are in music because they like it as opposed to tinned beans, but basically they're in it because they like tinned beans.'

Sometimes the advance received by a band seemed substantial. It was not unusual for a band to receive anything around £250,000. Just William signed a contract with a major record company in 1985 and received almost £100,000 during the first year. Many, however, found that what initially seemed a large sum, in reality paid them about the same amount they would get if they were on the dole, once rent, equipment, and other costs had been paid. In addition, many did not realize that the money was not a gift or payment but a loan they would eventually have to repay through their royalties. In fact, the company generally offered the band the most basic advance possible and might then hire expensive equipment, session musicians, and other personnel for the band's recordings, which meant that the band ended up having to pay off huge debts. The company kept a close check on the band's income and marked it off against the loan until the band had made up the amount. Once money was being made, the band was given a further loan for the next record and the whole process started again. So-called 'Pipeline royalties' could take several years to come through, keeping even a successful band reliant on further advances from the record company, and therefore under its control. In reality, most bands' records were unsuccessful, the band was unable to repay the debt, and was dropped by the company. The company then wrote off the advance as a tax loss.

Several bands were surprised, after signing a contract, to find that their lifestyle changed very little, and a few, particularly those without management to represent them, reported that they had little contact with the company that signed them. One musician explained that she hadn't realized it was up to the artist to keep in touch with the company, 'otherwise they forget about you. They expect only about 3 per cent of their acts to break into the charts so they are prepared to lose money on many others.' Knowing this, the manager of Just William travelled to London once or twice a week to visit the company her band was signed to and made a point of becoming acquainted with everyone who worked for it. She chatted with the secretaries and receptionists during their lunch breaks, developed an interest in football after discovering that one director was a football fan, went to a cricket match with another director though she disliked him, persuaded the lead singer to play with the company's cricket team, and became friendly with the accountant, dining with him and his parents on several occasions. Those tactical manœuvres did not meet with much approval from her band: 'I told them that going to a cricket match was better than putting your fist on the table,' she said, 'but they didn't understand.'

The following account briefly summarizes the experiences of that manager and her band after signing to a major record company in London.

Just William

Although Just William hadn't performed live, they attracted the attention of several record companies, largely because of John Peel's interest in them. They eventually chose to sign with RCA, partly because they liked one of its A&R men and its managing director. After six weeks and four or five meetings negotiations were completed. Later they signed a publishing deal with an American company (RCA's publishing division never contacted them). The contract with RCA stated that the band was to record three singles and an album and that the company had the option of dropping it after one album (anticipated at one year). The band's advance for that first year was £95,000. It was calculated that the album would cost £45,000 and the rest of the money would go to the band. However, the album eventually cost £80,000, £1,600 of the band's initial advance went to their solicitor, and £280 per month went on the rent of rooms at the Ministry. Recording the album took longer than expected, which allowed the company to put off their decision on whether to drop them, and the band ended up being tied to the company for a further year. In all, they received from RCA a total of £210,000.

Shortly after the contract with RCA was signed, the band's original contacts at RCA left to form an independent company, leaving the band without an A&R manager in their crucial first six months. This delayed the appointment of a producer for the album, and the first single was only ready for release fourteen months after signing the deal. The release of that single exposed flaws in the company's press and promotions departments, so much so that on release of the second single, the band paid for independent press officers and 'record pluggers' to promote their record. The band also chose a more commercial song for their second single but it was released at Christmas, a busy time for the record industry, and again didn't get much promotion. They tried to persuade RCA to finance a video but when RCA eventually did so it was too late and the record, which reached number 120 in the charts, dropped out of the charts altogether. Two more singles were released but again received no push from the company. At meetings between company and band, arranged to discuss each single, the company's managing director said they couldn't publicize the band adequately because it didn't perform live. The band's manager argued that she had problems getting the band gigs, because promoters wouldn't book the band if it didn't have much publicity and wasn't well known, and suggested that the company finance a 'support tour.' By the time the last single was released the managing director of the company had been replaced and the band's A&R man sacked. A short while later the band itself was dropped. Its album had been recorded but not released.

The Rhythm People

The Rhythm People had a one-single deal with an independent record company from which they received a £200 advance. Theirs was the only single released by that company before it went bankrupt, but although they signed up with an independent distributor the record wasn't distributed properly. Later, however, they were offered an audition with RCA. The audition went so badly that they acquired a bank loan to finance the recording of a demo tape which they sent to RCA just as the company was about to reject them. The company changed its mind.

Five months lapsed during which nothing happened though the band telephoned RCA many times. Eventually RCA gave them money to record another tape. Three more months lapsed and negotiations broke down completely, which provoked the A&R man they had been in contact with during that time to threaten to leave RCA unless they were signed. The band had by that time found an experienced manager in London who was able to recommend them to the company so negotiations began again. The band's first solicitor's bill amounted to £1,000 so they enlisted the help of a relative experienced in legal matters. Two months later the contract was finally signed. At Christmas, after another couple of months, their first single was released only to get lost amongst all the other Christmas releases. The band were annoyed with the company and felt they had been persuaded to record the wrong song. They were also frustrated by the company's rejection of many of their ideas and suggestions. By the time I met them, however, they were on better terms with RCA and were looking forward to the release of their second single.

Signing a contract made little difference to the lifestyle of these two bands. Neither had been particularly successful but neither had lost out entirely. The Rhythm People were still optimistic about their chances and the manager of Just William said she had no regrets: the band had had a nice time, bought expensive equipment, and recorded an album. They could use that recording as a demo tape to try to get another deal. When they got one she planned to buy the master tape of the album off RCA and insert in the new contract a demand for independent record pluggers and press officers. However, the band was left heavily in debt and after the disappointing experience with RCA and arguments over royalty agreements in their publishing contract, friction arose between its members. Faced with the disintegration of the band whose members were getting increasingly frustrated, disheartened, and depressed, the manager eventually quit.

The above accounts represent the viewpoint of the bands' members and managers. The record company involved would probably have a different perspective. The experiences of Just William and the Rhythm People regarding which songs they recorded, how they were recorded, and when they were released, nevertheless indicate the importance of good relations and understanding between a band and its record company, particularly with the A&R person who was responsible for supervising the band's behaviour, rehearsals, and recordings, appointing it a producer and agent, organizing the release of a record and its sleeve design, and liaising with publicity personnel on the band's behalf. The A&R

person thus acted as a link between band and company and was inevitably pressurized from both sides. Bands often chose a company through the A&R person they had contact with. It was (s)he who expressed belief in the band and pushed for it at company meetings, and problems often arose for the band if that person left their job.

The experience of both bands also highlights the way in which bands could be affected by circumstances beyond their control, such as disputes arising within and between companies they were involved with. Small companies, for example, often went bankrupt, and subsidiaries of larger companies entered into disputes with the company. Members of one band gave up their jobs to join the subsidiary of a large independent record company that split from its parent company soon afterwards, becoming bankrupt and leaving the band with no company, no jobs, and only half their recording completed. But the fortunes of bands also depended upon factors outside the company. One musician explained that his first single was released when punk was gaining popularity and because his was a very different style of music it didn't do well. Another explained that his first single was released as disco music became fashionable which meant that his company lost interest in promoting it and became preoccupied with disco artists.

Most local bands, like Just William and the Rhythm People, stayed in Liverpool after signing their contracts. However, moving to London was seen by many to be a career move. Those with as yet no contract often talked of moving there and it was generally considered a cliché for bands to do so as soon as they had a deal. It wasn't just band members who thought of and did this but local producers, promoters, and others in the music business. Generally only the wealthier or more successful bands moved to London permanently. Many of the latter found themselves pressurized to do so: they had no stable home base as they were often touring, they sometimes suffered harassment or embarrassment just walking around the streets if they stayed in Liverpool, and they had to spend time in London anyway as that was where all the business negotiations concerning their career went on between record and publishing company, agents, and media organizations. Their managers felt particularly pressurized to move in order to supervise, or keep an eye on, the activities of the companies they were involved with. For the companies themselves it might be preferable for the band or manager to be based nearby but sometimes they preferred them to be at a distance so they could get on with their job with less interference.

For those bands whose records sold well, with radio and television appearances to follow, success could completely take them over.

You can't imagine what it's like until you go through it. All your traditional environment, support system, friends etc. goes and you become involved in touring, in television and in the press, and with people who want to be associated with you just because you are famous. A lot of people get carried away by it. Women throw themselves at you. Success becomes an enormous strain on you and on your personal relationships (local manager).

It was only gradually during my stay in Liverpool that I began to appreciate the different levels of success that could be achieved. Amongst the group of bands rehearsing at Vulcan, Half Man Half Biscuit's rise to fame in the independent music scene represented a path all wished to follow. Rumours, comments, jokes, and teasing frequently alluded to their newly acquired status as 'pop stars'. During the summer a three-day concert was staged at Liverpool's Festival Gardens. Audiences were minimal until the final evening when three local bands performed to about two thousand people. Half Man Half Biscuit were the first to play, whilst China Crisis, one of Liverpool's most famous bands in recent years, played last and were paid much more.

A week later I accompanied members of China Crisis and their friends to a huge outdoor concert in Milton Keynes featuring Simple Minds, a Scottish band that had recently acquired international fame. We had 'VIP' and 'guest' passes because Simple Minds and China Crisis shared the same management company. I had spent that particular morning at Vulcan Studios watching the Jactars rehearse in a freezing cold, makeshift rehearsal room littered with bricks and rubbish. From there I had gone to the Adelphi Hotel to meet China Crisis. I had been told to make my way to the lounge of the hotel's health club. A glass wall along one side of the lounge looked on to a large indoor swimming pool surrounded by trailing plants. In the pool swam the band and their friends.

We travelled to Milton Keynes in a hired van, and the VIP stickers on it enabled us to drive up to the backstage area where the concert's promoters had set up tents and shaded tables with refreshments for the performing bands and their guests and for invited record industry and media personnel. After a while I noticed that a neighbouring tent fenced off from the others was reserved exclusively for members of Simple Minds and their entourage. I was quoted large sums of money that each member of the band was supposed to earn and the number of properties they owned in various parts of the world. Members of the vast audience (75,000–80,000 over the two days), many of whom wore Simple Minds T-Shirts, sat in the rain for hours waiting for the band to appear, having paid £13 per ticket, yet when the band finally emerged it received an exuberant, welcoming reception.

Immediately after the concert China Crisis travelled to London in a waiting van while the rest of us returned to Liverpool. They were to prepare for the recording of a new album and a lorry load of equipment had already been transported to their London hotel. After several weeks of rehearsal they would travel to Oxfordshire to record the album over a period of ten weeks at a recording studio that incorporated accommodation, sports facilities, and other luxuries at a cost of around £1,000 per day. With such models of success around them it was hardly surprising that the hundreds of unknown Liverpool bands were hit hard by failure. Older musicians in particular spent hours recounting, discussing, and musing over how close they had once come to signing 'The Deal', i.e. to 'making it', and reminisced sadly about what could or should have been if only . . . In the words of two locals involved with bands in the 1960s:

If I was eighteen or nineteen, as I was then, I could think of myself as making it today. I know I was good enough then. I envy all those people who made it. I'd love to have made it, and I think about it every day of my life (Lee Curtis quoted in Leigh, 1984: 140).

Looking back, I'm sick as a parrot that I've never made the charts. When I see some of the tripe that gets in, I'm amazed that I haven't made it somewhere. Nevermind, I've been plodding on for the last twenty years and I'm ready for the next twenty (Mike Gregory, ibid.: 144).

This chapter has discussed ways in which bands tried to make the transition from being a 'local' name to being a 'national' one, a transition that many regarded as an escape, 'a way out'. Three stages that bands were filtered through during the transition have been highlighted, each with its associated problems and conceptualizations. Bands at the first were still 'local' and unknown. Many aimed to 'make it' and sought a record contract to help them do so. A small percentage of them actually achieved a contract thus reaching the second stage, involving negotiations with the record industry. But few of those ever made it to the final stage to become successful stars of the rock music world.

'It gets easier as you go along', said Roger Eagle (Radio 4 *Dancing in the Rubble*: 29 October 1982):

but when you're starting its very, very hard. I've seen bass players who can't string a bass guitar. I've seen people who get defeated because an amp packs up or the drummer hasn't made it for the gig. I also know people who will steam over all these difficulties and just get on with it. It's a test. It's a hard school. And when you're at the bottom of the ladder trying to get a start the problems get heaped on you.

For many, a record contract represented success but in reality it was only the beginning of more problems and hurdles to overcome:

Signing a deal doesn't mean you've made it. It's one long struggle from beginning to end . . . When you've signed you are only just at the bottom rung of the ladder (local manager).

Each move away from the band's original locality marked another rung on the ladder: from music-making within a close circle of friends and relatives; to performing in front of strangers outside the locality; to London, the record industry, and contact, through recordings and the media, with a nationwide audience. In order to pass from one rung to another, bands had to negotiate the 'sharks' and confront certain 'gatekeepers' such as journalists and disc jockeys who could publicize them to a wider audience, and A&R personnel who could get them a record contract. Each stage or rung might also involve a change in attitude of bands' members towards music and music-making, representing a gradual transition from music performed largely for self-indulgence in a live, social context, to music and band as commodities to be bartered over and sold to a mass audience. That change in attitude might explain the comments of many band members on the demise of a 'community spirit' amongst bands and the increasing individualism, ambitions, and competitiveness of their members. Attitudes towards music-making also varied with the style of music the bands chose to make. That style, as suggested earlier, determined the type of place they played in and equipment and instruments they used, the type of company they attracted and approached, and consequently the amount of money they could usually expect to earn.

All bands, however, whatever music they made and whichever rung of 'the ladder' they were on, had to try to sell their music and image. All therefore experienced the conflict between creativity and commerce, the pressure to 'play the game' by, for example, adapting their music to comply with market demand (hence the distinction some made between a recording made for experimentation, i.e. for indulgence, and one made to attract a record deal, i.e. for profit). Consequently, bands adopted a set of concepts, values, meanings, and terms in their quest for success such as 'signing up', 'getting a deal', 'being dropped', and were advised to make 'contacts' which were generally considered as, if not more, important than talent or musical quality. In addition, record companies might urge bands to change their membership or image. After stating his desire to find a band that combined the unusual with the commercial and made money without selling out, Phil's first question to me concerned the physical appearance of Crikey it's the Cromptons! He was also concerned that their songs should be 'song-ish' and 'hookier'. Basically, all companies had to be concerned primarily with the saleability of their bands.

Friction between the business aspects of music-making and its creative aspects was experienced particularly strongly by bands with record contracts. After signing to a company the commercial pressures upon such bands intensified and often led to lack of understanding between band and company. The company often made direct demands and intrusions upon the band's creativity and attempted to predict and quantify it. The band was tied to the company, affected by its interests, fortunes, and activities. The lead singer/composer of Half Man Half Biscuit found the pressure of marketing upon his creativity so hard to cope with that he split the band up not long after it achieved success.

Yet commercial pressures also conflicted strongly with the values and emphases of unsigned bands like the Jactars and Crikey it's the Cromptons! that stressed the quality of their music, 'artistic integrity', and 'self-respect'. The Jactars were concerned with the creative aspects of music-making over and above the business aspects and had no manager to act as a buffer between the two spheres. Their members, like many others, bemoaned what they saw as the increasing commercialism of the rock music world:

Overwhelmingly, you have the impression that a great deal of the product that is advertised, hyped and made overly available . . . is there simply to fill a gap in the market—fodder to feed the belly of the cash cow that the mainstream music industry has become (Savage, 1984: 241).

That antagonism towards commerce was revealed in the dichotomy such musicians constructed between independent and major companies, whereby the former were seen to represent notions of respect and integrity (as well as independence of course) in contrast to those of 'selling out' and 'commercialism' which were associated with the latter and with the 'packaging' and thus the superficiality of their products. (Although Trav pointed out, disappointedly, that even independent companies seemed to be currently selling out.)

Trav and Dave were particularly concerned to achieve respect for their music in preference to fame and fortune and were anxious not to succumb to the pressure to try to 'make it' as soon as possible and to concentrate instead upon the quality of their music-making. Trav's comment that the independent companies might not be ready for the Jactars yet because they were too concerned with making money, emphasized his concern that the Jactars should not compromise or conform their music to what companies might want. Such attitudes differed from those of the manager of Up the Khyber and others who stressed a 'professional', 'businesslike' approach (which included 'sacking' members) and were concerned with the marketing and promotion of a band, emphasizing in particular its visual image and saleability.

The attitude of the Jactars and Crikey it's the Cromptons! to music and music-making is now beginning to emerge more clearly into a conceptual pattern based around the following dichotomies:

creativity	commerce
musical content/quality	image/superficiality
honest and natural	false and deceitful
artistic integrity	selling out
independent record companies	major record companies
live music for community, experimentation and indulgence	recorded music for profit and for a mass market

The businesslike attitudes, ambitions, and strategies described in this chapter could be seen to reflect a growth in commercialism, a deepening economic recession, and an accompanying rise in unemployment. However, to concentrate upon that and upon a 'climate of cultural sterility' (Savage, 1984: 241) would distort the picture and belittle the ways in which music is heard, used, and made. The music-making of bands in Liverpool, like music-making of many different kinds, was a combination of creativity and commerce, art and entertainment; music as live performance and as a recorded commodity. That so many were attracted to making music as a band and that music-making was relevant to them and to their audiences cannot be understood through social and commercial factors alone; far more important is the creative activity of music-making itself with which the following chapter is concerned.

6

Music in the Making

Music is notoriously difficult to describe and analyse. The discussion in this chapter focuses upon the ways in which it was created through composition and rehearsal. Composition could be the work of an individual or of pairs of band members, the whole band, or a combination of these. It could involve rearranging older songs, or adopting and sometimes adapting sequences of music or whole songs from other bands to reproduce as 'covers' or as part of the band's own material. Compositions could also develop from an idea, from short sequences of notes, from a lengthier and more structured sequence, or from lyrics. They could be continually recomposed or improvised upon with each performance, or relatively fixed. Generally, only one or two members of a band wrote the lyrics, one of whom was usually the vocalist who had to sing them, but many bands also discussed and altered lyrics collectively after they had been written. Thus lyrical composition could be both an individual and a collective activity.

Rehearsal, as distinct from composition, also took different forms and employed different techniques. Rehearsals could be directed towards a performance or the composition of new material. Band members occasionally rehearsed alone or in pairs but usually as a whole band, sometimes with the aid of a tape-recorder so they could practise to tapes at home. (Other forms of rehearsal were mentioned earlier, such as when band members listened to and discussed recordings of their own music or the music of others, got together to plan policies and activities, and performed in front of an audience.)

Instruments were valued not only for their sound but for their visual qualities, particularly in relation to the image the band members wanted to present. They also formed a substantial (usually the most substantial) part of a band's wealth. The importance attached to them and the dependence and affection bestowed upon them gave rise to a personalization of instruments, each being seen as having its own particular sound and identity. In addition, categories of instruments were associated with particular styles of music and their associated non-musical factors, particular geographical areas, and even particular types of people. (Stereotypes of drummers and bass players, for example, presented the first as beefy, brainless, and wild and the latter as easygoing and 'down to earth'.)

The processes of composition and rehearsal described below were those adopted by the Jactars and Crikey it's the Cromptons! The discussion focuses upon the ways in which their members conversed about and conceptualized those processes, thereby revealing their musical aesthetics. 'Aesthetics' is a Western concept usually applied to fine art. I am using the term here to refer to aural aesthetics, that is, the identification and discussion of the perceptive qualities of sound, noise, music, non-music, and to the ways in which they are recognized and valued through language and action. Such an aesthetic is culturally and socially constructed, shared by a group or groups of people but also perceived and experienced differently by individual members who have their own particular tastes, preferences, and experiences. The chapter is divided into two parts, one on the Jactars, the other on Crikey it's the Cromptons!

THE JACTARS

In Rehearsal

Dave has come up with an idea for a new song and plays it to the others on his bass. It comprises a short sequence of notes (a 'riff') which he plays over and over to enable the others to get the feel of it. Trav tries out a few chords on his guitar before playing along with Dave. Gary begins to beat out the rhythm on the rim of his snare drum and then joins in on the whole drum kit followed by Tog on keyboards. Dave repeats the riff while the others experiment with different chords and beats. They stop for Trav to check over some chords with Dave and identify which notes he has been playing. Dave suggests that Tog plays some 'deep' notes on keyboards to complement Trav's chords. Again they begin this process of repetition and experimentation using the same short riff as their base. Dave thinks the sound might be too 'dirty' and decides to drop one note of his riff in order to fit in better with what Trav is doing. He and Trav confer, watched by Gary, while Tog continues playing keyboards. They begin again, stopping for Trav to retune his guitar.

Later, Dave demonstrates a second riff he has devised to accompany the first to Trav, who watches with intense concentration. There is a thoughtful pause. For several minutes they then try out various notes and riffs to accompany the second riff before returning again to the first and the process of experimentation/improvisation based around it. Trav suggests that Tog concentrate more on the top keyboard because the sound is too 'mellow.' Tog is reluctant but Trav says it would, 'make a change and would be quite sparse as well wouldn't it? [to Dave] which would be quite interesting'. By now Trav has developed his guitar part into something completely different from that which he started off playing. Dave, echoed by Trav and Gary, complements Tog on the new keyboard sound and he and Trav agree that the composition has potential. Dave points out that because the second riff is 'harsher' it will complement the first, more 'melodic' riff. Tog wonders what would happen if they speeded it up a little. They try it for a long time before beginning to work on the second riff, breaking off for Trav and Dave to confer on what they have been playing. Dave demonstrates again how the second riff will lead into the first and Tog only now realizes that both are to form part of the same song.

Trav proposes that they practise 'the hard bit'—the change from one riff to another, and Tog suggests that Trav shout 'change' so the others know when to go into the second riff. They begin again but stop to confer about how many riffs to count before the change. Dave, Trav, and Gary watch each other while they count and occasionally Dave mouths at them 'after the next one'. They agree that it works. Dave comments approvingly on Gary's 'weird' drumming and Trav suggests that Gary lead them into the change with a drum roll.

By the next rehearsal Dave has written some lyrics. Trav tries singing them but suggests that the 'pattern' (the music) should be sorted out first. Again a long period of thought, practice and consultation (mainly between Trav and Dave) ensues. Trav suggests that one bit might sound too 'James-ish' but Dave thinks it is all right. Dave suggests a different drum beat to Gary but finds it hard to describe what he means, saying that he isn't very good at 'drum talk.' Trav suggests that they switch one riff to 3/4 time and leave the other in 4/4 which Dave says is a 'real headful'. They practise it but have problems with the counting. Dave isn't sure if he likes it or not. He can't work out why, but says, 'It's a bit too choppy like.'

During another lengthy period of concentration, discussion, and demonstration Trav and Dave agree that Tog doesn't need anything 'catchy' on the keyboards but just 'sound/noise' because the melody is coming from the bass. Trav likes one bit of the song but says another bit 'just falls into the Orange Juice guitar sort of thing'. He and Dave debate alternatives. Dave says he isn't sure if he likes where it is going or knows if it is going anywhere. Trav isn't satisfied with it either and says, 'you can imagine Big Country doing something like that.' He suggests that the other three play while he listens and decides that some of it sounds all right without him and he could just play one or two chords at various intervals. Later it is suggested that they insert a short break which would change the whole character of the piece. They practise it. Trav considers playing a short guitar riff during the break and Tog suggests that he makes it sound 'odd', in a different key. Trav tries it but isn't sure if he likes the song and asks Dave what he thinks. Dave suggests they practise it again while he tries something different and as they play he confers with Trav.

Musicianship

None of the Jactars had any kind of musical training and none could read music. Trav bought a cheap electric guitar in 1977 and taught himself to play. He learnt with a friend who visited him regularly in order to play Trav's guitar because his own had broken. Trav stressed how long it had taken him to learn and how difficult he found it. He practised by playing to records and eventually started using a chord book but it took him a couple of years before he could even put a tune together:

I think I've been going like seven years and I'm still very basic like . . . After three years I still had a very rigid sort of style of guitar playing like. I couldn't play any lead at all. I was always conscious of the fact that I wasn't coming along very well . . . But I don't think I'm ever gonna get any better than I am sort of thing which . . . well, I'm not really bothered any more like. I just sort of thrash away at the guitar like.

Later, Trav started to play an acoustic guitar (he owned one with twelve strings which he very occasionally played at gigs or rehearsals) and he helped Dave learn as well. Years afterwards, Dave began to play bass guitar with the help of 'Teach Yourself Bass' books. Although he hadn't been playing it for very long he was more confident on bass than on guitar saying: 'I quite like the guitar but I feel like I'm a very basic guitarist like, in fact depressingly basic. It's slightly embarrassing at times like.'

Gary learnt drumming through watching other drummers play. He started in 1980 and said that his drumming style had since gone through many changes and was now more 'percussive'. Like other drummers, he fixed and tuned his drums to a height and pitch that suited his individual style, altering it as that style changed and developed. He was unable to practise at home because of the noise his kit made so he stored it at Vulcan Studios using a 'practice kit' at home comprized of just 'a couple of planks arranged like a kit'.

Tog had been teaching himself bass since 1980 and keyboards since 1983. He prefered playing bass with the band because he felt superfluous stuck behind the keyboards whereas on bass he could 'really get into it.' Furthermore, although he admitted that he couldn't play bass very well he found it easier to sound competent on it, though he added that on keyboards 'at least you know you're in tune'. He mainly played what he described as 'basic three-chord stuff' on the keyboard (he couldn't play the piano) saying, 'I don't know what I'm doing half the time.' He did not contribute much to the composition of the Jactars' music. He tried songwriting with a previous band but had been unsuccessful. He was, however, interested in the more technical aspects of music-making and regularly bought the magazine *International Musician*, from which he taught himself how to engineer sound and renovate guitars.

When asked what they thought of each other's playing, members of the Jactars and Crikey it's the Cromptons! tended to distinguish between 'natural' talent and musical skills or ability. Tog described himself and Trav as 'pretty basic musicians' who would never be brilliant but also thought Trav a talented songwriter. Huw and Tony thought Trav the most talented of the Jactars: 'Trav has a natural style,' said Huw, 'his timing is not too good . . . but then a lot of people don't have good timing.' Similarly, Dave wasn't considered particularly skilled musically: 'He can't play guitar', said Tony, for example, 'Well he can play guitar but he only uses two fingers.' But Tony also commented to Midi and Huw, 'Dave's the one who gives them that certain essence isn't he? . . . Once he gets on the bass he can't put a foot wrong.' Likewise Trav commented that Dave had:

a very novel bass sort of thing . . . He doesn't play along with things but sort of plays against them . . . you could say he almost plays the bass the way he plays the guitar and the guitar the way he plays the bass . . . You see the bass isn't really, when Dave plays it, a rhythm instrument. It's usually playing out more of a tune than I'm playing on guitar.

All but Huw agreed that Gary was a 'natural drummer' with a very individual style. Trav said Gary had known what to do the moment he first sat behind the drums. Huw commented: 'I wouldn't say he was that natural myself having heard a lot of drummers. He's improved drastically though.'

Members of the Jactars often made a point of their musical incompetence and joked about it. They contrasted bands like themselves to the 'musos', i.e. those particularly concerned with musical techniques and skills. (The Ministry was associated by some that rehearsed at Vulcan with 'musos', whilst many of those at the

Ministry associated Vulcan with 'amateurish' and so-called 'alternative' bands.) Used in this sense 'muso' was usually a derogatory
term that indicated pretentiousness, although Gary, as mentioned
earlier in the discussion on stage image and performance, privately
held different views on music-making and felt that the 'very un-muso
attitude' of his fellow band members was contrived.

Tog was particularly proud of the Jactars' lack of musical ability and
stressed it frequently. He said, for example, that he always 'tried to take
as much out of a bass line as possible' (i.e. the simpler the better) and
was especially fond of one of the band's instrumental numbers because
his contribution on bass amounted to just one single note. He also liked
the fact that Trav still shouted 'change' during some songs (at
performances as well as rehearsals) in order to alert the others to switch
from one riff to another. He described it as a 'band hallmark' and was
keen to point out that in general he only knew when to change chord
when he heard Trav sing certain words of the lyrics.

Once or twice, however, other members of the Jactars and
members of Crikey it's the Cromptons! expressed quiet criticism of
Tog's attitude. Huw found it strange that Tog should be so interested
in the technical aspects of music-making rather than the more
musical aspects: 'He's more into the structure of his bass and how
many strings it has than how he plays it', said Huw, and he couldn't
understand how Tog could continually 'bang out simplistic chords'
on the keyboards without wanting to experiment and develop, for
example, some sort of melody.

The music-making of the Jactars depended upon a close partnership between Trav and Dave, who together came up with ideas,
lyrics, and compositions that were later presented to Gary and Tog to
be worked upon, re-formed, and developed. In reality, it was largely
their attitude to music and music-making that represented the band
as a whole. As the main composers they treated the music more
seriously than the other two and were more involved in its intricacies
and development and more concerned about its quality. Trav was
confident that their music was superior to that of other local bands.
He once explained that he wouldn't take up cabaret work performing
popular and familiar songs by other artists partly because it would
have a bad effect upon his own music. He described the Jactars'
material as, 'quite repetitive songs based on one idea all the way
through', but he and Dave obviously put a lot of work and planning
into the arrangement of that material and he himself pointed out that
the songs did have 'changes' within them, choosing two of them as
his favourite because they were more 'structured' than the others and
sounded as though a lot of thought had gone into them.

That emphasis upon arrangement is reflected in the above description where Trav and Dave showed concern that the keyboard sound should complement what they were playing on bass and guitar and Trav stopped playing altogether at one point because he thought it sounded just as good without him. It was also highlighted by the intricate interaction of Trav and Dave's guitar playing, which reflected a deep communication and understanding between them, and by the following discussion between Trav, Dave, and Gary concerning their process of composition:

Dave: You go for what the overall sound is and even if you just play one note that can sound very good like. Then you might feel slightly embarrassed about standing there playing one note all the time but on the other hand it adds to the whole thing . . .

Trav: Even when you're just thrashing away at one note you find you sort of just put different rhythms in like, don't you like? *[to Dave]*

Dave: Yeah . . . even if you're playing only one note you sort of concentrate more on that one note like . . . so you start doing things like making it louder on certain beats like, so you do sort of get into doing different rhythms on it like. I suppose it doesn't sound a lot like. I suppose you wouldn't really think of doing all of that on one note like.

Gary: When he [Dave] is playing one note it's like he tends to deaden it sometimes . . . *[he imitates the sound]* . . . and I come in with the high hat every so often so they go . . . *[he imitates the sound]* . . . which he [Dave] probably hasn't noticed.' *[Dave agrees he hadn't.]*

The Jactars gave themselves a great deal of time in which to construct and develop a song or instrumental piece. The process could take several months, particularly since it involved so much repetition and experimentation and there was often lengthy discussion and disagreement over factors such as timing, counting, and tuning. Their method of composition and rehearsal partly arose from, and was hampered by, their lack of musical training. Tog described it as 'battering out an idea.' Similarly, a member of the Da Vincis, a band that composed in a similar manner, described their music-making as a process of 'hit and miss' or 'trial and error.' White (1983: 144), however, pointed out in his discussion of a 'semi-professional rock group', that although:

lack of even basic training created enormously long and exhausting rehearsals . . . it also produced a tremendous amount of inventiveness. When ideas were translated, communicated and eventually played 'in' they sounded impressive.

I once asked Trav how he would define the term 'jam' that refers to the activity of jamming, i.e. improvised playing. After much hesitation and reflection he answered, 'I wonder if it has anything to do with actual jam . . . a sort of jelling together.' This seemed to me an illuminative assessment of the Jactars' process of composition and rehearsal. Trav's reference to the music (as opposed to the lyrics) as a 'pattern' also seemed apt as it implied a gradual assembly and construction of sounds and sequences to form a completed song or piece of music.

A song or instrumental piece could be judged complete once it became part of the band's 'set' of songs to be performed in front of an audience. There was little intentional improvisation during performances. But the song was never totally finished since later on one band member might, for example, devise an alternative ending which they would try and perhaps substitute for the original. In addition, sequences of chords and notes from old or incomplete songs might be revised and adapted to form a new one. Thus older songs were continually changed and developed, sometimes dropped from the set or brought back into it.

That chronological development of a song tended to influence the way in which it was aesthetically perceived and appreciated by the Jactars themselves:

When you get a new one [a song or instrumental piece] it always seems better than the last and sounds fresher so you think this is a lot better a song. But after a while it wears into the set like. I mean you become used to it yourselves. It's like getting a new record. I'll be thinking, 'This is really good like', but after a while you don't play it so often . . . I suppose you've got to keep that in mind really when you're playing because there's songs we do that we might not change like. Most of them are OK like, but . . . some things you lose interest in after a while. On the other hand, people hear them for the first time when you play it so . . . also you forget how good it is to play the older ones (Dave).

There was sometimes disagreement as to whether a song or instrumental piece was sufficiently developed to be included in the set. Trav once wanted to include a new song, stressing that it needed to be 'worked in' (to the set) and urging the others to 'take a chance on it', but Tog argued that the song was as yet not good enough.

As the Jactars' music developed, its style and character changed, a gradual transformation recognized (perhaps only partially) and discussed by the band and its audience. Tony from Crikey it's the Cromptons! said that during the lifespan of the Jactars their music had changed from a 'dirge' to a 'lighter' and more 'boppy' style before becoming a 'dirge' again. Tog thought their music had just become more 'stylized.' Trav, with agreement from Dave, believed the music had changed in accordance with his method of composing it—he used to try to write 'tunes' and use 'conventional' chords, even though he found it difficult, but tended now to come up with 'ideas' rather than tunes.

The Jactars' process of composition arose not only from musical incompetence and perhaps a conscious decision to adopt a particular style of music-making, but perhaps also from the combination of personalities within the band. As time passed, the contrasts between the Jactars and Crikey it's the Cromptons! became more obvious and it seemed increasingly probable that the different characters involved dictated to a considerable extent the way in which the music was made. Thus the generally quiet, mellow personalities in the Jactars, reflected in their hesitant, uncertain manner of speech and movement, might perhaps have determined the slow, repetitive, tentative 'jelling together' of musical components as well as the communal nature of the music's composition. This was also detectable in the attitude of Tog, Trav, and Dave to a replacement for Gary. They decided not to try to find a drummer who sounded like Gary but to let each drummer they auditioned play 'naturally' in order to see how they fitted in, and resigned themselves to the fact that the band would sound different whoever they chose but that 'different' could mean better and not necessarily worse.

The attitude of bands like the Jactars and Crikey it's the Cromptons! towards composition and rehearsal highlighted a contradiction between the strong ideals of democracy and egalitarianism they held and the individualist tendencies that existed alongside them. Their members claimed that songwriting was the combined effort of the whole band. One said: 'You can't form a band if you just want to do your own stuff because it's not democratic. You have to do other people's stuff otherwise it causes arguments and problems.' Finnegan (1986: 12) also noted this 'democratic ethos' among bands in Milton Keynes. It was, 'particularly noticeable among younger rock bands who kept insisting that they were "all equal", "there's no leader", "democracy", "we all make decisions as one" '. Those ideals, however, inhibited individuals from claiming priority in the composition process when some clearly felt justified to do so because they played a larger role in that process than their colleagues. Others, on the other hand, felt they should be allowed to contribute more towards composition. Such feelings often gave rise to tension that might be expressed during arguments or crises. Thus Trav once angrily suggested to Tog that he had no right to criticize the Jactars' music because he played such a small part in its composition, and a member of Ryan described how the band's ex-vocalist would criticize or say he disliked a song on which the band was working, and concluded that as a non-instrumentalist who wasn't involved much in the actual process of composition, such adverse comments were simply his way of 'putting his mark on it [the composition]'.

Attitudes to composition were thus bound up with notions of ownership of music. Although band members might like to claim equal contribution to composition, the legalities of songwriting had become more complex and clearly defined. The music was seen as valuable property and rights of ownership over it were often the subject of bitter dispute. Thus although the bands' democratic ideals allowed for flexibility in their composition, their members often became possessive about their contributions, which could inhibit creativity. It might be interesting to consider what would have happened as regards royalty arrangements and composition if either the Jactars or Crikey it's the Cromtons! had signed a record or publishing contract, or if Tony or Trav had left each band instead of Gary or Midi. It is probable that underlying the democracy and egalitarianism which each band either achieved or liked to think or say they were achieving, lay the unconscious or unstated assumption that Crikey it's the Cromptons! was in fact Tony's band whilst the Jactars was Trav's. Consequently, if either of them had left, the resulting crisis might have fragmented or dissolved the band or re-formed it into a completely different band with a different name. White wrote (1983: 147):

It seemed to be a convention of the more advanced semi-professional players to retain the privilege to perform numbers they had written and performed with other bands in any new band they might form. This was often an arguing point with bands which split up and reformed. When songs were a joint writing project it was difficult to assess who had the right to perform the number with a new outfit.

Lyrics

Of the Jactars' nine songs performed in their set, three of the lyrics were written by Dave and the other six by Trav. Most of them appear in the Appendix. As with most local bands, the lyrics were written separately from the music and usually outside rehearsals, either before or after the music had been composed. Both Trav and Dave put a lot of time and thought into lyrical composition and their lyrics, as well as their music, were much admired and respected by Gary, Tog, and members of Crikey it's the Cromptons!

Almost all Trav and Dave's lyrics incorporate images of pain and violence and many include themes of temptation and seduction, distrust and deceit. These often seem to involve women: 'Forced to violence against his nature I The girl didn't love him' ('Forced to Violence'); 'I can't trust you 'cause I can't trust myself' ('To My Toes'); 'Your charms are strong as stronger still ... I could be tempted' ('Things Not Seen'); 'On cold wintry evenings you can sit I And touch her I But beauty has danger I And death as its neighbour' ('Break the Skin'). Linked to these themes is a strong sense of loneliness and isolation.

It is interesting (and this will be considered in more detail later on) that both Trav and Dave's lyrics refer to 'the game': 'giving up the game'; 'This life for some I Is one big game'; 'you're new to the game'; and often incorporate contrasting words in single sentences: beauty/danger; pain/pleasure; love/loneliness; pain/kiss; comfort/hard; flowers/worms; pleasure/sin. Both also include images of the body: 'a man with no mind'; 'hand in the fire'; 'hands above your head'; 'climb your head like a climbing rose'; 'The marks on your back ... shine through your eyes'; 'loose tongue'; 'break the skin'; 'heart in your mouth'; 'brain in your chest'; 'You talk with your mouth instead of your fists I You polish your teeth with bloodstained hands'; 'nomadic eyes'; 'soiled hands no teeth.'

The way in which local band members both heard and perceived lyrics varied. Some might listen to a song and pay particular attention to the lyrics and their meaning whilst others heard them as part of the music, as sound or a voice. Such differences didn't seem to relate in any way to musical competence and skill or to the role played in both lyrical and musical composition. Members of the Jactars and Crikey it's the Cromptons! said they usually did pay attention to lyrics although Trav and Dave said it depended upon the song and the band because some bands wrote more interesting lyrics than others. Both agreed that lyrics didn't have to mean anything—'Even when David Byrne writes nonsense it sounds good', said Trav.

When it came to their own lyrics some musicians were anxious for them to be not only heard but understood and not misinterpreted and saw little point in writing them otherwise. Others, on the other hand, were content for their lyrics to be ambiguous in meaning, or overpowered and obscured by the music. Trav said initially that he thought his lyrics were 'more for effect', but then admitted:

I suppose you do want them to be heard, but I want to say more important things really ... things that haven't been said, ... it's not as if the lyrics are gonna change anything ... but you obviously think they're more important than you'll admit because they're not your ordinary love songs.

When I first met the Jactars Tog had been more flippant about the lyrics and, though he played no part in their composition, had discussed them as if they were written by the band as a whole. He joked that they were just words that 'meant nothing' but sounded 'profound', and added, 'We try not to sing about love as much as possible.'

Aesthetics

As a band the Jactars could be said to have adopted or developed a particular aural or musical aesthetic that overlaid the personal perceptions and tastes of individual members. Personal aesthetics were affected by each individual's music-making activities. Thus when Tog heard a piece of music he might listen particularly to the keyboard part, or to the drums since when he played bass he and the drummer worked in collaboration as the band's 'rhythm section.' Although such personal aesthetics were generally accepted and accommodated within the band and its collective aesthetic, they were a potential source of conflict between the band's members. Each member placed considerable emphasis upon, and frequently discussed, their own personal tastes in music. At the first rehearsal of the Jactars' I attended I was told, 'It would be interesting for you if you could see everyone's record collection.' And indeed it was.

To an outsider the Jactars might appear to share the same tastes in music. They were all familiar with particular musical styles and knowledgeably discussed amongst themselves the music and bands that formed them. At social gatherings an album might be played that had only recently been released, featuring a band they were all known to admire. The music would be discussed and debated over and it might emerge that the four of them, as well as members of Crikey it's the Cromptons!, had bought the album and were familiar with its contents. The private record collection of each member revealed, however, the contrasting history of music tastes and styles they had progressed through before joining the Jactars. Even Trav and Dave who had been close friends and music-making partners for a long time, and whose musical tastes were very similar, could point to small divergences of taste regarding what they referred to as the 'small circle' of independent bands they both admired:

I tend to go sort of from Go Betweens, Wire and that into the middle to Neil Young whereas he [Dave] goes from Go Betweens, Wire, to the other side like bands doing pretty obscure stuff (Trav).

Thus Trav envisaged the music he and Dave liked as forming a continuum of styles with those more widely acceptable at one end and the less well-known, more experimental and divergent styles at the other.

Gary and Tog, on the other hand, listened both in the past and currently to bands playing different styles of music, and Gary didn't attend the mixing of the Jactars' demo tape because he felt unable to adequately discuss the sounds they were trying to achieve. He left it to the judgement of the others, preferring what he described as a 'rockier', 'heavier' style of music involving a lot of 'distortion', and prior to joining the Jactars he had been in a band with that style. He knew it didn't accord with the tastes of Trav, Dave, and Tog but alleged that they had once enjoyed using and listening to distortion effects themselves although they wouldn't admit it now because 'it's not cool to like rock music'.

Tog often told people that his tastes encompassed all sorts of musical styles such as classical, jazz, punk, and pop, but he particularly enjoyed electronic music (especially keyboards), which was again a style of music very different from that produced by the Jactars. He had once been in a band which played keyboard-orientated music (although now, in front of the others, he referred to it as 'ultra-commercial, slick crap'). When the Jactars experienced problems composing new material Dave suggested some possible contributory factors, one of which was the difference between Tog's musical tastes and those of himself and Trav. Dave stressed how long it had taken Tog to fit into the Jactars and how little he contributed to the composition of the music. Tog had once discussed this with me, saying that although he had the opportunity to contribute more he only devised his own instrumental part, and sometimes helped with arrangement, because he couldn't compose the kind of music the Jactars played.

Consequently, Tog played a lesser role during rehearsals. While the others conferred about the music and how it should sound he, as the above description revealed, tended to continue playing his instrument, paying little attention to what was going on and making it difficult for the others to hear themselves speak. Often he lounged in a chair with his feet up and his bass resting on his knees whilst the others remained standing. Thus he generally gave the impression of being rather detached from what was going on, an impression reinforced by his posture and movement during public performances. The interaction between Trav and Dave· on stage, which was not rehearsed, was a manifestation of the close rapport between them. While playing they would watch each other intently, concentrating upon what the other was doing and occasionally smiling at each other. In between songs they often conferred and laughed with each other. Occasionally, one of them would say something to Tog or exchange a smile with him, but generally Tog seemed separate from their close interaction and often appeared to be trying to adopt a cool, detached pose.

The fact that Tog heard, experienced, and valued the Jactars' music differently from the others could also perhaps be illustrated by those of the Jactars' songs which he chose as his favourites. Whilst Trav picked the songs he thought sounded more 'structured' and well thought out, Tog described his choice as good examples of a 'short, tight pop song—the most commercial things we've ever come out with.' Similarly, Tog defined 'jam' as, 'an unstructured improvisation thing . . . trying to get things to fit in with what other people are doing', which seemed an apt representation of the process of composition and rehearsal as experienced and seen by Tog.

Tog's growing preference for playing bass rather than keyboards was also not in accordance with the preferences of the others though they rarely commented upon it. I once asked them which instrument they preferred Tog to play:

Gary: It depends upon the songs. See I play two different styles . . . With Dave on bass say, it's a bit more percussionary in a way. With Tog it's a bit more of a straight beat. It just changes the music a hell of a lot.

Trav: You see Tog's sort of bass style is playing along with the bass drum whereas Dave's is against the bass drum.

Gary: Dave's is more varied whereas Tog's is straight to the beat.

Trav: It's been a long time since we've come up with a song on keyboards so obviously we must be finding it easier with Tog on bass . . . I don't know if everyone's happy about that. Are you happy about that *[to Dave]*?

Dave said he didn't mind, but clearly their more recent material featured Tog on bass because Tog himself preferred it that way, and later the others admitted they would rather he played keyboards. Dave wanted to play more bass himself, particularly since he felt more confident on bass than on guitar.

Many bands used technical 'effects' to change or enhance in various ways the sounds they made. Trav once told me that he didn't really know anything about effects and if he tried to use them he probably wouldn't do so properly, although if he could do so he might be able to improve a few bits of the Jactars' material here and there. It was clear, however, that both Trav and Dave favoured what they described as a 'clean-cut' sound and laid far greater emphasis upon the arrangement and structure of that sound than upon the technicalities of its production or the various ways in which it could be altered through technological means.

The music-making of the Jactars could therefore, in a sense, be said to involve an aesthetic of simplicity, or, to use a term often coined by the Jactars themselves, an aesthetic of 'basic'(ness). Associated with this was the playing of certain sounds, chords, notes, sequences of notes that might contradict Western notions of harmony, melody, and music; sounds that might, in other words, be perceived as 'non-musical.' The Jactars had developed a technique whereby such sounds, chords, and sequences were integrated into a carefully structured whole. Their 'discordant', 'non-muso', 'basic' style of music was thus in reality carefully thought out, balanced, and well rehearsed. When Dave and Trav, for example, discussed how to end a new song they had been working on, Dave suggested that each could strike a few chords 'out of sync' with the other and that Trav's could be 'discordant.' They tried it out, rehearsed and developed it, and Trav was delighted with the result joking, 'Everyone will think I'm doing the wrong note.'

The deliberateness of this technique can also be illustrated by a joke the Jactars once played upon their audience. They began their set with a song they described as 'just pure noise.' They devised it at a rehearsal prior to the performance and according to Tog it worked on the principle 'that if you were getting in tune you went down or up a semitone.' In the middle of that 'noise' Trav shouted 'change' and after a few seconds of silence the 'noise' began again. In the end the real joke for the Jactars became the unexpected response of their audience, for instead of realizing the joke and sharing it with the band, they clapped in genuine appreciation at the end and Tony later congratulated the Jactars in all seriousness upon its brilliance.

Band members, like most people, found it hard to put music into words and thus describe the music they made. Dave (above), for example, had problems conveying to Gary how he wanted the drums to sound. It is perhaps because of this paucity of musical terminology that the words and means which actually were used and constructed to describe and discuss music could reveal much about the aesthetics of both playing and listening.

The Jactars' music was generally liked and respected by other musicians at Vulcan and they often compared it with music of other bands, particularly those the Jactars were known to admire. Such comparisons, however, usually gave rise to considerable debate, revealing again the individual, personal manner in which people listened to, heard, and appreciated music. When I first asked the Jactars to describe their music they said they were unable to: 'People read different things into it,' said Tog, 'You have to listen to it yourself.' All of them agreed that they would not describe their music by comparing themselves with other bands though others had compared them with many.

Despite that, I heard Tog on several occasions describe the Jactars' music to others by naming several fairly well-known bands he thought they resembled. Similarly, Trav sometimes named a few of the bands he listened to when people asked about his music. By describing themselves and others in relation to particular bands or certain categories of bands or music constructed by and for the mass media, band members (like others) avoided the problem of trying to find words that would adequately represent the music itself. The manner in which the music was described varied according to who was being addressed and how familiar they were with the styles of music being discussed. Furthermore, as Trav pointed out, there was often a difference between what bands were and what they liked to say they were.

Dave usually described the Jactars as a 'guitar band'—a factual description based upon the instruments involved but also a commonly used label applied to a certain style of band and music. (Tony also once described the Jactars as a 'guitar band' but said that unlike other guitar bands they were 'dead fresh with it . . . There's more to them.') Similarly, Tog sometimes described the Jactars as an 'indie band', a more widely used category encompassing a broader variety of music and again depicting a certain type of band (in this case one associated with the independent sector of the record industry).

The citing of bands to describe various *sounds* within a musical style was also common. Trav commented at one point in the above description that a particular sequence of music was too 'James-ish', i.e. too much in the style of the Manchester band James, thus indicating that it sounded derivative and needed to be altered. Alternatively, particular sounds and sequences of music might be described using certain adjectives or metaphors, a lot of which were common to many bands, though they might favour them differently. Dave, for example, sometimes described a piece of music or a sound as being too 'choppy', 'flat', 'dirty', or 'muddy.' The terms most frequently used by the Jactars to describe their music were 'thrashy' and 'basic.' Other descriptions revealed a liking for sharp contrasts within music and between songs. Thus 'harsh' riffs were played with 'melodic' riffs, 'mellow' songs with 'aggressive' songs, and 'discordant' notes, chords, and sounds were integrated into a more cohesive, harmonious whole. Contrasts were also, as mentioned earlier, incorporated in the lyrics.

The attitude of the Jactars to 'covers' also revealed their musical aesthetics. Bands usually covered a song because they liked and admired it (especially if it had originally been performed by a band or artist they respected and were inspired by), or because they intended to adapt or perform it as a joke. The Jactars' set included only one cover. Trav didn't think there was much point in playing covers, especially if performed as almost an exact replica of the original. If, however, the song was chosen carefully and changed in some way or converted into one's own style, he thought it could be worth while and 'great fun.' Dave agreed and, like Trav, was concerned not to follow existing trends in covers amongst both local and national bands. Trav pointed out that it was currently fashionable for certain bands to perform covers of soul music. 'That's the problem with covers,' he said, 'which ones you should do and which you shouldn't, which is hip and which isn't.' Similarly, Tog once declared, 'I hate people who cover loads of songs. I hate people who do Joy Division songs even more.'

CRIKEY IT'S THE CROMPTONS!

In Rehearsal

Dave T. has only recently joined the band in place of Trav and for the first time they rehearse in his room at Vulcan. Dave arrives and sets up his 'echo unit' (a machine that echoes sounds fed into it), guitar effects, speakers, and mixing desk which he plugs his guitar lead into. The others are thrilled with the unit and feed experimental shouts and noises into it, listening with delight to the distorted echoes that follow.

They tune up. Dave wants Tony to play him an A on his guitar. Tony asks which string it is, which causes Tog, who has come in to watch, to laugh. Tony shrugs and also laughs saying, 'I don't claim to be a musician.' He is impatient to start rehearsing and moans about how much he hates tuning and how difficult and frustrating it is. He persuades Midi to assist him. Midi eventually takes his guitar from him to tune, pointing out that Tony has put the strings in the wrong places which makes it difficult. This amuses Huw who calls Tony a 'spastic.' Tony explains that because some strings broke and wouldn't reach the pegs he had to rearrange them incorrectly. He asks Midi and Dave if they are all now in tune but they are not sure.

Trav arrives. Tony wants Dave to learn exactly what Trav has been playing on guitar, hoping he will eventually get acquainted with Trav's style of playing, so Trav has come to help Dave learn it. They begin rehearsing a song. Dave takes out a notebook in which he has been writing chords and Trav notes with admiration that he has almost filled it. The others sit and watch while Trav slowly goes over his chords and Dave notes them down. Tony says he didn't realize Trav knew Cs and As and so on. An hour later Trav leaves and they begin rehearsing another song. Tony demonstrates to Dave what Trav has been playing on lead guitar and Dave writes it down before slowly trying it out. Impatiently, Tony suggests they try it with both guitars. He wants to run through the whole song but Dave prefers to go over it bit by bit and is helped by Midi, who demonstrates how his accompaniment on bass fits in with what Trav played. Going through the song in this manner is a lengthy process and Tony gets restless. They finally run through the whole song but Dave frequently stops to consult his notebook and still has problems with Trav's style of playing.

Tony suggests they move on to the songs Dave is more familiar with. Dave says reassuringly that he will soon get the hang of things, it's just a matter of practice. They rehearse some older songs—all, particularly Dave, making frequent mistakes—before working on a song Tony describes as 'really straightforward and hideously commercial.' He shows Dave his own chords on rhythm guitar and instructs him to 'freak out' over them on lead guitar, but since Dave finds this problematic he suggests they switch so that Dave plays the chords while he 'freaks out.' Tony isn't happy with the drumbeat which he describes as 'too funky', annoying Huw who protests that he was just following Tony. Midi comments that there is nothing wrong with having a 'funky bit' and, when Tony says it isn't 'our style', mentions bands that have a variety of styles. They start again, stopping for Midi to play Dave his bass line. Karen says she hadn't realized that that was all the bass line for that song consisted of. 'It's dead simple', says Tony; 'dead basic', adds Midi.

They begin another song and Tony immediately asks Dave to take all his 'crappy effects' off. Dave frequently used 'chorus' and 'distortion' on his guitar sound and the others were always asking him not to because they preferred a 'clearer, cleaner sound.' Occasionally Dave argued that he needed distortion in order to get his notes to 'ring out.' Sometimes he turned it off only to put it on again a few minutes later. Dave now keeps his distortion off while they play the song. Tony says he likes it and wants to include it on their next demo, but Huw describes it as 'just a thrash' with nothing particularly good about it at all.

There is another break while Midi goes downstairs for some food. Meanwhile Tony plays Dave his most recent composition and Dave tries out a few guitar chords to accompany it. Tony instructs Karen (who so far hasn't been asked to sing anything) to do some heavy breathing during the song but she is too embarrassed to try. Dave gains confidence and adds more notes. At one point Tony shouts at him to hold a particular note 'because it clashes really nicely.' 'I wish I hadn't played it now', Dave laughs. Afterwards Tony tells Dave that he wants the band to sound 'professional' rather than 'amateurish' but at the moment they sound 'amateurish.'

They start to run through their set in preparation for a forthcoming gig. Tony instructs Karen to sing louder and put her mouth closer to the microphone. He asks her to scream during one song but she is reluctant. He tries to encourage her by standing beside her and screaming with her. Eventually, embarrassed and uncomfortable, she produces a little yelp on her own. Midi tells Dave that it sounds better if there is no distortion on his guitar because when he uses it he sounds different from the rest of the band—'like there's two separate bands'.

Tony wants to play some of his older songs but Huw and Midi urge him to continue practising their set for the gig. They begin another song which Tony reckons one of the record companies they had visited would like because it is one of their more commercial ones. Dave suggests they look at the books *How To Make a Hit Record* and *How To Make a Demo* because they advise all sorts of things such as how to completely redo a song and put all the 'hooks' at the beginning since A&R people only listen to the first thirty seconds. Karen questions Tony on the lyrics she has been singing asking, 'What on earth is a slippery blee?' Tony explains that it is an eel that lies on the bottom of the ocean and asks her to exaggerate the word 'blee.' Later, Tony, Huw, and Midi discuss a new cover they might do instead of their old one which Tony has grown tired of. Tony says that there are only a few bands they could do covers of anyway because only a few were 'credible' enough or 'last' long enough (i.e. perform a style of music that will not go out of fashion). He wants to 'cover' an Electric Prunes' song because they are 'ace' and everyone likes them. Huw tells him he is getting too obscure, no one knows the Electric Prunes. 'And anyway', he adds, 'if you do a cover like that you get labelled.'

A few weeks later Crikey it's the Cromptons! arrange a rehearsal from 11 a.m. to 3 p.m. but only Huw and Midi turn up on time. Tony is three-quarters of an hour late and Dave doesn't arrive until 1 p.m. It takes them a long time to set up equipment and tune instruments. Tony then turns to the new song he has written. 'This one's really ace', he says, describing just how 'brilliant' it is. 'You say that about every song, Tony', says Midi. Placing the lyrics written on a torn scrap of paper on the floor in front of him, Tony plays and sings the song to the others from beginning to end and then repeats it. Within a short space of time they devise an accompaniment but Huw breaks off to complain that Tony keeps 'changing the beat.' They start again but Huw tells Tony that he still keeps changing the beat and obviously doesn't know what he's doing. 'I'll give you a book on time signatures so you know what I'm talking about', he says and asks Tony if he knows the difference between a 4/4 beat and a 4/6. Midi thinks he does and explains it to Tony. Huw instructs Tony to count as he plays but is frustrated that even when Tony does so he still changes the beat.

Eventually they start working on the song in a more concentrated manner, short bursts of playing interspersed with brief discussion and comments. Huw points out that Tony is singing a phrase he has used before in another song but Tony denies it. Tony suggests that the drums sound a bit like Captain Beefheart but Huw says as far as he is concerned they sound more like the Go Betweens and adds that he isn't sure if he likes the song, especially the change of beat in the middle which sounds like a 'poor man's Genesis' or something Came Under Mayne (another Vulcan band) might do. Tony laughs and they continue playing, concentrating on chord changes. Tony becomes very enthusiastic and excited saying, 'I know it must be good because it's dead difficult to play.' He asks the others what they think. Huw shrugs and thinks it sounds 'a little out of control' but Midi likes it.

Tony has written another new song he wants to work on. He plays and sings it to the others and again they quickly devise an accompaniment and run through it several times. Tony particularly likes the chorus which he describes as being 'like a sort of deviant Velvets [i.e. the Velvet Underground]'. Midi thinks they sound like another band but can't think which one. Tony says it's quite an American song and a bit like 'a deviant Electric Prunes' but nevertheless 'different'. They begin it again. Tony suggests they all count to eight before changing chord which Midi finds an effort. Tony reminds Midi that he does it for another song but points out that he could listen to the vocals as well and change chord at particular words. Huw tells Tony that his voice is sounding like that of David Byrne (from Talking Heads) but Tony says he'd noticed that and was trying to change it. They work on the song for a while longer, all growing visibly more enthusiastic.

Afterwards Huw comments laughingly that it was going to be quite a 'conceptual song' and 'not exactly a hit'. Tony laughs in agreement and says it would sound really good with a saxophone and they really need a saxophonist, but Huw says they should work more on the arrangement of their material instead of worrying about how to fit in a saxophone. Tony wants to practise some of their other new songs and comments with enthusiasm, 'The songs are definitely changing chaps. There's a lot more to them and they're a lot stronger.' Huw murmurs that he isn't sure about that and Tony quietly retorts that Huw is never sure. Midi suggests they play the new song to the Jactars to see what they think. Tony agrees but is sure Dave will like it. Huw suggests that Tony alter the lyrics first as he is still sounding too much like David Byrne.

Musicianship

Crikey it's the Cromptons!, as the above description shows, employed a different style of rehearsal and composition from that of the Jactars. Tony would usually compose a whole song (comprising both lyrics and music) on his own, using acoustic guitar and cassette recorder, which he then played to the others at their next rehearsal. Within a short space of time they devised and rehearsed an accompaniment. Tony was a prolific songwriter. When I first met the band they had nineteen songs they could perform and about thirty others they had decided not to use.

Tony took the lead during rehearsals and usually had a fairly clear idea of how he wanted the song to sound, which was why Tog once commented that although the other members of Crikey it's the Cromptons! put more into the music-making than Tony gave them credit for, they were still really a 'backing band' for him. Huw wasn't happy about that and often, as the above description reveals, became annoyed with Tony, usually expressing this by criticizing aspects of the music, disagreeing with comments Tony made, or becoming sullen and uncommunicative. He often pointed out to me the 'democratic nature' of the Jactars, contrasting it to that of Crikey it's the Cromptons! He had hoped that when Dave T. joined the band things might change but Dave, like Midi, was tolerant and tended to take the role of mediator when tension between Tony and Huw became particularly noticeable.

Huw began to vocalize his criticisms more after the band visited record companies in London, perhaps because one of the A&R people they saw expressed opinions on the band's music that Huw sympathized with. In particular, Huw felt that the arrangement of the songs needed to be considered more carefully, and during the journey back from London he told Tony to look at the way in which the Jactars worked:

You don't have Trav going frantic and over-the-top and Dave doing the same. They work it out together—especially in the new songs they've been doing . . . You [Tony] don't have to play rhythm guitar all the time. Just because you write the song like that it doesn't mean it has to be that way . . . David Byrne doesn't always play guitar when he sings . . . I've told you many times that you could do a chord structure underneath or something.

I asked Tony when and how he knew whether a song was going to work out or not. He replied that he could always tell straight away as soon as they began to work on it, which led Huw to continue:

> I think it would be more accurate to say that you know when you've got it right because you're not normally listening to anyone else.

Tony: What I'm talking about is when I first walk into the room, say, with a new song, and we're just messing about with it, you can normally tell whether it's going to be a good one or a bad one. Sometimes you know it's not going to be good and then we never even try doing it.

Huw: But we disagree about that though. Sometimes I'll think a song is good but you won't give it enough time, or I'll think it's arranged wrongly and you'll just dismiss it out of hand rather than try and rearrange it.

Later Huw explained that what worried him was the way in which Tony wrote the songs. Tony composed at home using a few chords on his acoustic guitar and didn't conceptualize how the composition would sound with the whole band. When he brought a song to a rehearsal for the others to work on he continued to play it as he had done on his own instead of adapting it to form, with the rest of the band, a complete and well-arranged composition.

Huw suggested ways in which the individual personalities of band members affected their music-making. He pointed out that Crikey it's the Cromptons! moved quickly from one song to another during rehearsals and related this to Tony's rather 'frantic' character and the way he 'tends to move in different directions at once.' I only once heard Crikey it's the Cromptons! work on a song in the same manner as the Jactars. They did so because it was the first time they had started to work from scratch on a new song with Dave T. and they wanted to allow him the opportunity to get the feel of it and experiment within the structure of the song. Whenever Tony heard Dave play something he liked he yelled at him in approval.

I once asked Midi and Huw if they thought the Jactars composed more as a group than Crikey it's the Cromptons!:

Huw: I think possibly they have the same sort of ideals in music or something . . . Perhaps it's that Dave and Trav have a better understanding or because they both write the songs together so they're more like a songwriting pair.

Midi: Yeah . . . the Jactars are all into the same type of music aren't they? Whereas we're all different.

Huw: I suppose they are. I mean, I can't stand some of the music Tony likes and you're into.

Midi: I'm into seventies rock really.

Me: But you don't argue much about the music when you rehearse do you?

Midi: We have a laugh about it really.

Huw: Sometimes we do.

Midi: Yeah, sometimes we do . . . We don't really argue, it's more a difference of opinion really on what we're doing. Like yesterday, I was playing a bass line which Tony thought was far too conventional so he said to me, 'Leave that note out and that note out', and when I did it sounded far better didn't it *[to Huw]*?

Differences between tastes in music were thus stressed within Crikey it's the Cromptons! as well as the Jactars. Midi's liking of 1970s music and Cliff Richard and his outmoded style of playing bass, had become a standing joke within the band. He himself remarked good-humouredly, 'My style is sort of really dead old-fashioned, so old-fashioned no one's ever heard it before.' The different tastes of Tony and Huw were also accommodated though they could occasionally cause tension, leading Tony to deride Huw's taste and scornfully refer to it as 'middle of the road.' (Huw was also occasionally critical of Tony's musicianship.)

The music-making of Crikey it's the Cromptons! was, as with the Jactars, both hampered and enriched by such contrasting tastes, styles of playing, and by musical incompetence. When I asked them whom they watched and took their cues from whilst playing, Midi answered,

It depends on the song. It varies from song to song. Some songs I'll watch Tony, some songs I'll watch Huw . . . In 'Week Old Socks' they'll watch me because I finish it off. On 'Closet Case' I always go by the words [lyrics].

Huw, however, said that most of the time it should be he, the drummer, who gave the cues, but because Tony was inconsistent when he played, and often changed the beat and lyrics, he had to watch and wait for Tony rather than vice versa.

Tony taught himself bass and guitar at an early age but though he spent a great deal of time playing both, his musical skills were not rated highly by his fellow musicians. Tog said that Tony used to be a dreadful guitar and bass player but pointed out that he had since progressed and could now play rhythm guitar quite well. Tony believed that his guitar-playing had improved considerably; he used to play it as if it were acoustic but was now coming to terms with it as an electric instrument. Trav said that Tony still 'had to come along a lot' and wondered why he never bothered to find out the exact gauge of guitar string he wanted and as a result always bought the wrong ones. Similarly, Huw couldn't understand why Tony wasn't interested in learning musical notation or terminology and once asked him, 'How can you not want to find out what you are doing and playing?' Tony replied that he just played what sounded good, adding, 'It makes me happy.' In particular, Tony had problems tuning his guitar, often, as in the above description, having to rely upon others to do it for him. He finally bought a second-hand tuner from a member of Ryan and joked about how different the band would now sound and how they would have to rewrite all their songs.

Huw was generally considered a good drummer though he had only taken up drumming two years previously. He practised a lot at home, repeating the same basic set of exercises on a set of rubber pads in place of his drum kit which was kept at Vulcan Studios. He wanted to earn such respect for his drumming skills that he would be in constant demand with other musicians and was keen to take lessons in drumming which he felt he needed but could not afford.

Midi had taken piano lessons when younger and at the age of 13 taught himself bass and guitar. Prior to joining Crikey it's the Cromptons! he played bass, keyboards, and guitar, in addition to singing and songwriting, with several other bands. Tog described Midi as a 'bloody good bass player' and, like the others, meant that although Midi was not 'technically brilliant', he was 'extremely talented' at coming up with simple, catchy bass lines. Trav particularly liked Midi's style of bass-playing, but pointed out that Midi had been playing bass for fourteen years whereas he and Dave had been playing guitar for only six or seven so their style was still developing. He thought the other members of Crikey it's the Cromptons! also had their own individual style, but believed that in general the Jactars had 'more style', and described Crikey it's the Cromptons! as 'more straight rock musicians.'

Tony, Huw, and Midi all readily admitted to being musically incompetent but would have been equally ready to point out that musical incompetence was an integral part of their style as a band. Thus when Dave T. joined the band in place of Trav, and Pete replaced Midi, the others were presented with a problem because both Dave and Pete were said to be fairly proficient musicians and both had previously been in bands that played very different styles of music from that of Crikey it's the Cromptons! Huw and Tony were doubtful that Pete would fit in. They acknowledged that he was technically a better bass player than Midi but bemoaned the fact that because he was such a 'muso' he kept devising really complicated bass lines which they had to repeatedly urge him to 'keep simple.' They frequently mentioned how much they missed Midi and his talent for 'basic', 'spot-on' bass lines.

Pete's presence affected the band in other ways. Tony, for example, suggested at one rehearsal that they practise something different because he had problems with the song they were working on, but Pete urged him to continue working on it to try to solve the problems. Similarly, although members of Crikey it's the Cromptons! often jammed together in their own musical style, usually in a haphazard manner sometimes using well-known songs by other bands, shortly after Pete joined they jammed in a completely different style that was smoother, flowing, 'jazzy', and 'funky'. Tony could hardly contain his enthusiasm when that happened and shouted out 'This is very pleasing!' before they had even finished playing. He had obviously never experienced music-making of that kind before and said afterwards that he wanted to include it in their set. I described what had happened to a member of the Da Vincis who said that the same thing occurred in his band when they acquired a new, more experienced drummer; they had never jammed before and also became excited. The experience improved their performance and they even developed a song from a jamming session. Some time after leaving Liverpool I saw Crikey it's the Cromptons! perform again and noted that at the end of their set they played what they described to the audience as an 'experimental improvisation'.

Dave T. joined the band before Pete, and his arrival presented problems of a different kind. When members of the Jactars and Crikey it's the Cromptons! first heard that Dave was interested in joining the latter they debated at length whether or not he should be invited to do so. Tog urged them to give him a chance and pointed out that Dave had his own room and recording equipment at Vulcan Studios which the band could use if he became a member. Tony, on the other hand, was worried about Dave's style of guitar playing. According to him, Dave played 'properly' and had been influenced by styles of music which were outmoded and not in keeping with the music and influences of Crikey it's the Cromptons!

Dave had previously been in a cabaret band performing covers of reggae, soul, and songs from the 1970s and he used a range of 'effects' to change and enhance his guitar sound which neither Tony, Midi, or Huw particularly liked. Tony commented, 'We're not really a distortion band . . . it's not really our style. And all the other bands use it don't they? So that's as good a reason as any not to use it.'

Tony, Huw, and Midi all agreed that a 'flanger' and 'chorus' were too 'dated.' Huw said that all Dave needed was 'loads of reverb and a bit of distortion', thus he and the others didn't advocate cutting out effects altogether, but felt they should be used in moderation, perhaps 'just to make it [the sound] a bit more ballsy' as Tony once put it. Others assured Tony that this clash of styles could easily be accommodated and Midi commented, 'We're not gonna get another Trav are we? I think we're being too narrow-minded about it.' But Tony remained unconvinced and was worried that problems would arise and that Dave's 'proper' playing would destroy the band's 'originality'.

It was finally agreed that Dave should attend some rehearsals. Tony was determined that he should learn exactly what Trav had been playing which was why he was so anxious that Trav continue to attend rehearsals for a while to teach Dave his guitar lines and accustom Dave to his style of playing. All were impressed that though Dave, like them, could not read music, he was able to write it down in the form of dots on a six-line stave, which meant that he could learn Trav's part by transcribing it on to paper. However, teaching Dave Trav's part proved a lengthy and frustrating process and members of the Jactars began to view it critically. Tog thought it a bad idea to try to get Dave to copy Trav's style and suggested that Tony allow Dave 'more room to put his personality into the band'. Trav felt that since he and Dave had totally different styles of playing it was wrong for Dave to try to copy his:

I suppose once he [Dave] has got all the notes and that he could try and get the feel of it all, but he's going to be playing my guitar riffs in his style like, so the problem's really gonna come about when they start doing songs with Dave thinking up the guitar piece from the beginning like. I think they could have a bit of trouble there like . . . It's obvious that Dave can pick things up quickly, but whether or not *his* style is gonna be right they won't find out until they start working on a new batch of songs like. Well, by that time he'll most probably be quite well established in the band so it could all sort of fall apart a bit like.

I think they should have had a few weeks jamming around with him and seeing if his style was good enough. Because I notice one thing with Dave is he sort of does a lot of the er . . . *[Trav mimes vibrato on the guitar]* whereas I just don't do that at all. Mine's a very sort of heavy, leady sort of style like, whereas Dave's is a lot lighter. But I think . . . with Tony's sounds like, some of 'em could, with the wrong type of guitar-playing, just sort of end up being quite mediocre sort of sounds like so . . . it will be sort of interesting. 'Cos Dave would have been a teenager in the 70s so he would have been very influenced by that sort of guitar-playing, whereas with me . . . well, it's sort of the 80s really. I've been influenced by people like Neil Young 'cos he just sort of thrashes away whereas . . . I can't think who Dave would have been influenced by, but it would have been the ones who were just a bit better at playing the guitar sort of thing . . .

I think it's worth giving it a go. I don't know what they're gonna do like. It seems now that Dave is in so . . . I suppose they'll just have to make the best of him really . . . See, but this is the funny thing, Tony still seems to want to work out new songs with me, which just isn't gonna work really. 'Cos there's gotta come a point when he says, 'Right, Dave's gonna take over.' Don't know what he's gonna do about that. I think they're gonna have, you know . . . well anyway, there's a PA there and a recording studio and that.

Although Midi, Huw, and Tony were in agreement over use of effects, they disagreed over other matters such as voice. Tony agreed with Huw that he wouldn't like to compare the band's music to that of other bands because that would put the idea into people's heads when they should be forming their own opinion, but he often told people that Crikey it's the Cromptons! had been compared to Talking Heads, largely perhaps, because he admired the voice of its singer David Byrne, 'because he sort of warbles and things. Like he starts off singing deep and stretches to high notes and things which is what I do from time to time.' However, both Huw and Midi disliked the way Tony slurred the lyrics when he sang. Huw got particularly irritated when Tony distorted the words so they couldn't be understood. When Phil at London Records told Tony that his 'range' wasn't good and suggested he take singing lessons, his comments gave Huw's criticisms further fuel:

Huw: It sounds like you're punch-drunk Tony.

Midi: I think it's more frustrating hearing songs you like and you think the words are good but you can't quite catch them, so it's dead important to hear the words.

Tony: But I reckon when I listen to a song I can make out every word I'm singing.

Huw: That's because you're singing it.

Midi: Yeah, because it's only now that I'm beginning to hear your lyrics because it's only now that I know what to listen for.

Tony: I think the words to 'Philatelist' are quite clear really.

Huw: You can't tell. Unless you heard it again for the first time you wouldn't be able to tell.

Tony: I think him [the A&R man] saying I haven't got a wide range and have a monotone voice really annoyed me. I always thought Trav had a monotone voice . . .

Huw: But what you think though, Tony, isn't always right is it?

Tony: True.

Midi: It's worth listening to what he says and thinking about it.

Tony: Well what do you think [*to Midi*]?

Midi: Well I think you've got a good voice.

Tony: I wouldn't say it's monotone by any means.

Midi: I wouldn't say it's monotone no, but maybe he's got a point.

Me: Wasn't he referring to the way you were singing rather than to your actual voice?

Huw [to Tony]: You see you don't usually use your range when you sing do you?

Tony: It's only 'cos people were always telling me off at the beginning about my whooping and that.

Huw: Yeah, but it's not working, Tony. That's not the range—whooping into a high pitch. That's not having a range. In the basic body of the song that you're singing you're not using any sort of range, you're just sort of . . .

Tony: Except in 'Coldeparts' I use loads of range don't I?

Huw: Well, not over the top really . . . perhaps that song's not so bad, but some of them . . .

Huw and Midi also disagreed with Tony over volume. When the band rehearsed, Tony liked everything to be loud, particularly his own guitar and vocals. Huw thought Tony was too loud and said that half the time he couldn't even hear himself play drums. 'If we don't get a decent sound Tony's answer is to turn it up louder', said Midi, who thought it better to be too quiet than too loud. Opinions differed again on the subject of covers. Dave T. believed that the point of a cover was to do a song most people would be familiar with. Midi said in agreement that covers were included in a set purely 'to please the public'. Tony, on the other hand, wanted to cover songs he admired, presumably because such songs would also enhance the 'alternative' image and style he wanted Crikey it's the Cromptons! to present. Such songs, however, were usually relatively obscure.

In addition, Tony could be stubborn and dictatorial at rehearsals, though not in an aggressive or overbearing manner, and he tended to be emotionally unstable, passing through moods of different extremes. Midi, Dave, and Huw were sometimes annoyed by his changeable attitude to their music. One day, for example, Tony described one of their songs as 'just a bubble-gum number' but said he was currently going through a 'poppy' phase and therefore quite liked it and found it a relief from 'the heavier stuff' which he generally preferred. The following day Tony criticized that song and a number of others for being too 'poppy', 'commercial', and 'sickly', adding, 'It's my fault I suppose for writing them', and he refused to play them.

Tony also took other people's opinions on his music to heart, reflecting upon them at length. Thus when Tog commented that he had observed during a performance by Crikey it's the Cromptons! that the audience paid more attention to the faster songs than the slower ones, Tony decided that they did too many slow songs and from now on he would keep them all 'short and snappy.' The others disagreed. Huw thought they had a good balance between the slower and faster songs and that they were all 'pretty thrashy' anyway.

Lyrics

Most of Crikey it's the Cromptons!' lyrics were written by Tony. Huw had written one or two and he and Tony sometimes debated over how much he had contributed to a couple of others. Whilst Trav and Dave spent much time composing and thinking about lyrics and often experienced 'writer's block', Tony wrote his very quickly on scraps of paper or card which he then stored in a battered yellow file. To help him write them he kept what he called his 'little blue book' in which he wrote, 'things which really amuse me . . . They're really perverse things but I find them funny and so do Tog and Midi.' He offered to show them to me—'as long as you don't think any less of me as a result.' Several of Tony's lyrics appear in the Appendix.

Tony tried to write lyrics that were 'more interesting and unusual.' His desire to be different was even expressed in some of his lyrics:

> Constrictions everywhere blinding my insight
> Strings attached so hard to cut
> I've come to the conclusion that not being a run-of-the-mill-sheep
>   is a good thing
> If you want individuality you gotta pay
> What can I do will lead me to hell and back?
>
> (from 'Life's a Question Mark')

He was critical of Huw's lyrics, which he described as 'predictably boring' and 'too safe.' He disliked the fact that they rhymed and said that rhyming took the 'meat' out of songs.

The nature of Tony's lyrics varied according to fluctuations in his mood. In February, for example, he said his new songs were about, 'death, dying, how love can turn into hate, and about casual sex . . . I'm writing really miserable songs at the moment.' Karen, Tog, Trav, and Dave all commented upon how depressingly pessimistic and self-indulgent such lyrics were. Tog said that many sounded almost 'contrived' because Tony was trying too hard to sound 'hard-done-by'. Dave mentioned one particular song that made him cringe in which the line 'I'm so soft-hearted' appeared. Many of Tony's lyrics had a self-indulgent, pitiful, 'hard-done-by' tone, and the majority, unlike Trav and Dave's lyrics, were couched in the first person singular. Dave and Trav thought Tony's lyrics tended to be too autobiographical and also accused Tony of plagiarism. In turn, Tony criticized some of the Jactars' songs for sounding too morbid and miserable, 'like an electric Leonard Cohen.' Tony's more humorous lyrics, on the other hand, were popular with the others.

The differences between Trav and Dave's personalities and attitudes to lyric-writing and those of Tony were also illuminated by the manner in which they presented their lyrics to me, the way Trav and Tony sang them, and the interrelationship between lyrics and music. At first, all three were reluctant for me to read their lyrics but Tony's ego soon took over and I was presented with scraps of scribbled-on paper and allowed to sift through his lyrics file. I didn't read any of the Jactars' lyrics until the summer, when Trav presented me with their nine current songs, neatly typed on cartridge paper. When Trav sang he pronounced the words as he would do in normal speech, although he extended and stressed words here and there to give more emphasis. Tony, in contrast, greatly distorted words and used his voice in a percussive, experimental manner by trilling, whooping, screeching, and adopting a high falsetto.

Tony's lyrics encompassed a variety of themes. A few were anti-government or mourned the plight of mankind, a few were very sentimental, some were humorous and included many references to fish, one or two were about individuals Tony knew, and many (including the humorous) were about sex—several being explicitly pornographic and sadistic. (The chorus of 'Pink Cheeks' sums it up thus: 'I've got sex on my brain. I'm always the same'). Titles to the latter type included: 'Lipstick Around Your Nipples', 'Let Me Nibble Your Breasts', and 'The Smegma Song.' The lyrics featured in the Appendix were chosen because they seemed to represent major preoccupations and were amongst the best-known of the band's songs. It must be stressed that the nature of Huw's lyrics was different—one being quite feminist.

One predominant theme of Tony's lyrics is that of loneliness and isolation: 'I don't want to go out by myself' ('The Loneliness'); 'I cover my eyes now everything's gone' ('Good Old Lieutenant Lamb Liver'); 'I don't want to see' ('Nail in The Works'); 'Crawl under the carpet . . . Get under the table . . . Lock myself in my room' ('One

Death After Another'); 'If I hid in a closet . . . If I closed my eyes' ('Closet Case'). Another theme is that of deceit: 'truth . . . false . . . lies' ('One Death After Another'); 'lie' ('Week-Old Socks'); 'lies' ('I'm a Fiend For You'); 'deceitful' ('You Know Every Sin'); 'devious' ('You Devious Minx'). In 'One Death After Another' the lies are political but in other songs the deceit seems to be associated with women. Many lyrics suggest the dominance and power of women: 'The women I meet end up hurting me' ('The Loneliness'); 'Your cruel black heart eats at mine . . . Pulling at my skin . . . You took a bite at my heart' ('You Know Every Sin'); 'My life is in your hands . . . Let me out' ('Bedlam'); 'You could crush me like a flower | You know you have the power' ('I'm a Fiend For You'); 'Destructed by desire' (Surfin' Tuna Fish); 'You mess up my mind on purpose . . . You laugh at me then say you find me a bore. You confuse all conversation' ('Closet Case'); 'By the way you're a devious minx' ('You Devious Minx'); 'You're also a slag' ('Noreen').

Consequently, such lyrics reveal not only distrust of women but fear of and anger at them which might explain the images of violence and aggression against women that some of them, particularly the more pornographic ones, incorporate. A line in 'Week-Old Socks' reads, 'So I'm drunk but its no reason for abuse | You hit. I strike back', which indicates violence on the part of the writer that is a defensive reaction, and this is reflected in the following lines by Trav: 'Forced to violence against his nature | The girl didn't love him | Had to break her.' Bound up with this is also a desire for women, as illustrated by Tony's song 'All I Want is a Bundle of You.'

Tony said he had an obsession with fish and this is evident in his lyrics, many of which were about, or featured, fish. During one song Karen was required to shriek 'fishy, fishy, haddock, haddock, plaice, plaice' in the background. Another was entitled 'Starfish'. Others include lines such as 'Slap me with your frozen plaice'. 'Surfin' Tuna Fish' includes references to both fish—whereby the singer becomes a fish and develops fins—and virgins. A song Tony wrote much earlier with Noggin, Trav, and others was entitled 'Never Trust a Fish.' Tony's lyrics thus seem to associate fish with women with deceit, just as a song by Dave did:

> I caught you hook line sinker and all
> . . . .
>
> I hold the cards
> The rod and the line
> I could reel you in this time
> But I unhooked your lip and I let you swim
> You're loving the pleasure and
> you're loving the sin.

A preoccupation with fish has been shared by other bands and musicians. To mention just a few: Finnegan (1986: 20) wrote of a band from Milton Keynes named Herd of Fish 'because the band had "an obsession with fish"'. A band from Hull was called Grab Grab the Haddock. One in Birmingham was named Rumblefish. A Liverpool band in the 1970s was named Albert Dock and the Cod Warriors—featuring 'the Fish Fingerettes'. One of the Jactars' instrumental compositions was entitled 'Tadpole', whilst an album by John Lennon was named 'Shaved Fish'. Fats Waller linked fish with women in many of his songs: 'Fish is my favourite dish'; 'I like the taste of fish'; 'I want some seafood, mama'; 'You're not the only oyster in the stew.' A song by Genesis describes three man-eating fish with women's heads, and record sleeves by Roxy Music and the Damned feature photographs of women as seductive mermaids ensconced in black latex tailpieces.

Women, fish, and water have also been linked in films such as 'Splash', 'Dr No', and 'Local Hero' where the heroine of each emerges from the water and reveals fish-like characteristics. Paintings have portrayed women floating in lakes, rising out of shells, and bathing; and women appear at ships prows, carved out of wood. Some anthropological studies depict contexts where water spirits are women, and legends of fishing communities portray the ocean as a temptress, enticing fishermen away from their wives into her dangerous and mysterious waters. According to the *French Dictionary of Symbols* (1969) fish are associated, in various cultures with wealth, sexuality, and fertility. In some they may be phallic symbols. In one culture circumcision is referred to as 'le couteau coupant le poisson'. Amongst male homosexuals the word 'fish' is used widely to refer to women, as it conjures up an image of dirty, smelly creatures. Outside homosexual circles jokes and references are often made about the fishy smell of women's genitals.

Theweleit (1987) provided documentation and evidence on the association between women and water in the world's literature and paintings:

over and over again: the women-in-the-water, as a stormy, cavorting, cooling ocean, a raging stream, a waterfall; as a limitless body of water that ships pass through, with tributaries, pools, surf, and deltas; woman as the enticing (or perilous) deep, a cup of bubbling body fluids; the vagina as wave, as foam, as a dark place ringed with Pacific ridges; love as the foam from the collision of two waves, as a sea voyage, a slow ebbing, a fish-catch, a storm; love as a process that washes people up as flotsam, smoothing the sea again; where we swim in the divine song of the sea knowing no laws, one fish, two fish; where we are part of every ocean, which is part of every vagina (ibid.: 283).

He suggested that this association is a depersonalization of women, 'a specific form of oppression of women—one that has been notably underrated' (ibid.: 284). It has been used to distinguish pure from impure, bourgeois women from erotic women: 'In the eyes of men who fear streams (because they seem 'unclean') the bodies of erotic women, especially proletarian ones, become so much wet dirt' (ibid.: 421). In his autobiography, J. C. Powys wrote of his visits to Liverpool:

I lived in an atmosphere of complete freedom as far as sex was concerned . . . Perhaps they were proletarians, these wonderful Liverpool girls. Perhaps they were what all our women-folk will become in a few hundred years . . . One girl, the daughter of a seafaring family, had limbs so slippery-smooth as to be hardly human (Quoted in Shaw, 1978: 214).

The association between fish and women in the lyrics of the Jactars and Crikey it's the Cromptons!, encompassing expressions of both desire and rejection, conjures up the image of a mermaid (reinforced by the association of fish with virgins, and by a line in 'Never Trust a Fish' that reads: 'Never trust a fish that has no feet'), an image used to symbolize women as long-haired bathing beauties, innocent and desirable, but also as seductive, mysterious, fish-like creatures, dangerous and desirable.

Aesthetics

Tony once informed me that 'the whole idea of music is to turn it upside down'. Another time he described in detail how he had reformed Dave T.'s guitar-playing. According to Tony, Dave once rehearsed a song sounding like Keith Richards (from the Rolling Stones), so he instructed Dave to play the same sequence of notes but backwards, and when Dave did so it sounded much better. For another song he told Dave to intersperse some 'discordant' notes with what he had been playing, which had also been an improvement. Later, Tony explained that someone once told him that Captain Beefheart (a performer he greatly admired) used chords which he played 'the wrong way round'. Tony demonstrated the way in which the positioning of the fingers was turned back to front and said he had now adopted that style of chord-playing and had based a new song entirely upon 'discordant chords' played in that manner.

When Dave T. first joined the band, Tony described his style of playing as 'more obvious' and complained that he wanted Dave to go 'crazy' – 'only', said Tony, 'Dave has a different idea of crazy and that's where the barrier is'. Tony chose one song of Crikey it's the Cromptons! as his favourite because it had a 'really mental' ending, and when the Jactars played the joke on their audience described in Part 1, Tony took the song seriously and liked it so much because it was 'a barrage of noise'. When he was about to play the others a new song he had composed, he nearly always said he would 'give it a quick blast', and when rehearsing with a saxophonist, Tony asked Midi what key one of their songs was in before instructing the saxophonist, 'Just freak out in the key of E then.' The saxophonist told Tony that he liked their music because all the songs were based upon minor sixths and sevenths. When Dave T. later pointed out that he had yet to see Tony play one major chord, Tony proudly replied that he did in fact play one in 'Week-Old Socks'—which was why, said Dave, Tony didn't like that song. Similarly, when Pete told Tony that he liked the 'musical anarchy' of Crikey it's the Cromptons! Tony was delighted with that description.

Tony's musical aesthetics were revealed in greater depth during the mixing of Crikey it's the Cromptons!' demo tape. He instructed the engineer to make his guitar sound 'chunky', 'resonant', 'upfront', 'dead punchy', and not too 'tinny', 'wimpy', or 'velvety'. When I first asked him to describe his music he immediately replied, 'uptempo, discordant, jazzy, frantic, pop'. He also described his paintings as 'frantic'. He painted colourful, abstract pictures that often portrayed fish, monsters, and phallic symbolism.

Tony's urge to be eccentric, to 'freak out' and create musical 'anarchy', music that was as loud as possible, 'crazy', 'mental', 'upside-down', 'back-to-front', and 'discordant', revealed his desire to break out of structure and order and produce something spontaneous, something seen as being in some way 'natural' because it was regarded as 'raw', 'wild', chaotic and emotional, beyond rational, sane thought and behaviour, something almost uncontrollable and therefore exciting. (Attali, 1985: 142, on the jazz term 'to freak freely', which means to improvise, noted: 'A freak is also a monster, a marginal. To improvise, to compose, is thus related to the idea of the assumption of differences, of the rediscovery and blossoming of the body.') This was also revealed in Tony's attitude to stage image and performance described earlier, where he expressed a desire to 'clash' and go 'over the top' and 'wild' in his dress whilst 'freaking out' with his movement. Other members of Crikey it's the Cromptons! and members of the Jactars to some extent shared Tony's musical aesthetics. The preference of both bands for a 'clean-cut' sound indicates again the desire for natural, unadulterated sound, something honest and genuine, a purity of expression.

Trav (who distinguished between what band members liked to think their music sounded like and what it actually sounded like) once commented, 'I think I know what Tony is *trying* to be but I don't know what he really is.' Tog, Dave, and Gary nodded in agreement and decided that although Tony desired a sort of 'manic', 'frantic' sound, he didn't manage to achieve it. Trav thought Tony came closest in 'Starfish', which also happened to be Tony's favourite song. Similarly, when Tony played Midi a tape of music by himself and Dave from the Jactars, describing it as 'really wild', Midi commented that it wasn't particularly wild at all. Interestingly, when I asked Tony to suggest why a 'jam' was so named he replied that it was 'because people tend to jam in as many things as they can'.

I asked Dave T. and Pete, who were less likely than the others to share Tony's musical aesthetics, what they thought of Crikey it's the Cromptons!' music. Pete said he liked some of it and generally enjoyed playing it because it was so different from what he played with his other band and because he could work out his aggressions through it. Dave T. said he didn't really think about it but just liked to play.

Although I have contrasted Crikey it's the Cromptons!' process of composition and rehearsal with that of the Jactars, both bands generally shared a similar musical aesthetic. In the Jactars this was largely dictated by Trav and Dave, whilst in Crikey it's the Cromptons! much of it came from Tony. Thus the four main themes implicit in the music-making of the Jactars: emphasis upon natural talent, simple and clean sound, originality, and musical incompetence as style, were all shared by Crikey it's the Cromptons! Members of the latter also emphasized and distinguished 'natural' talent from musical skills and ability, and preferred music that sounded 'simple', 'clean', 'clear', 'fresh', and 'basic' as opposed to that which was full of 'crappy effects' like 'distortion' and sounded 'choppy', 'flat', 'dirty', 'muddy', and 'crap'. (This clean/dirty dichotomy is a familiar one. In this particular context it should be distinguished from that which Keil mentioned, 1966: 157, in his discussion on Chicago Blues fans where 'clean' generally referred to that which was 'new' or modern whilst 'dirty' referred to that which was 'old'.) Sounds with a masculine, aggressive quality were also favoured—such as 'upfront', 'chunky', 'punchy', 'ballsy', and 'thrashy', as opposed to sounds that were 'tinny', 'wimpy', 'velvety', 'poppy', 'sickly', 'commercial', and 'slick'. Both bands favoured 'noise' of some kind and incorporated it in their music (Trav and Dave, for example, wanted 'noise' on the keyboards to contrast with the melody on the bass whilst Tony loved loud, 'pure noise').

Both bands also stressed unconventionality and originality and worried about sounding 'derivative'. They therefore tended to avoid 'covers' and 'rhyming' (which Tony thought 'predictably boring and safe'), and the Jactars never used choruses. Both had also adopted a style of musical incompetence in contrast to bands they scorned for being 'commercial' and 'musos'. For Tony that style meant the incorporation of 'clashing', 'deviant', 'upside-down', 'back-to-front' elements, and he favoured music that sounded 'mental', 'crazy', 'frantic', and 'wild' but at the same time 'professional', not 'amateurish'. For the Jactars it meant incorporating dissonance and contrasts in their music and musical elements that sounded 'weird' or 'odd'. In addition, the two bands shared certain lyrical themes— those of violence and pain, loneliness and isolation, distrust and deceit. The lyrics of both linked deceit with women and fish and expressed the dominance and power of women and thus fear of them, anger at them, and occasionally a sense of violence towards them.

These themes indicate a desire to produce music that is spontaneous, natural, unadulterated, and therefore honest, genuine, and pure. (This emphasis upon spontaneity and naturalness was also revealed earlier by, for example, the Jactars' 'lads-off-the-street' image and the emphasis of both them and Crikey it's the Cromptons! upon unrehearsed, uncontrived movements and comments on stage—although Tony's weren't always as spontaneous as they might have appeared.) Such music was associated with masculine qualities and opposed to that which was technical and commercial; distorted, derivative, and affected; full of 'hooks', rhymes, and choruses, and associated with dirt and rather soft, feminine qualities. It is possible to link the latter music, the lyrical themes of deceit and anger, and themes expressed in previous chapters where honesty was associated with music of quality, creativity, and artistic integrity, whilst deceit was associated with superficial music, with 'selling out' and commerce. The process of 'selling out', i.e. succumbing to the pressures of commercialism, was referred to earlier as 'playing the game' and both Trav and Dave referred to the 'game' (though in different contexts) in their lyrics on temptation, seduction, alienation, and deceit. Furthermore, the conflict discussed in previous chapters, between democratic ideals and the legal requirements of commercialism, has been reinforced.

It must be emphasized that the musical aesthetics of the Jactars and Crikey it's the Cromptons! which encompassed these themes, oppositions, and distinctions, was thoroughly relativistic. Tensions and contradictions regarding the personal aesthetics, attitudes, and ambitions of the four members of the Jactars have been discussed, yet compared to Crikey it's the Cromptons! the Jactars appeared 'democratic' and uniform in their tastes and personalities. Both bands, however, shared certain musical and lyrical themes and thus an aesthetic, and both opposed bands that embodied a contrasting aesthetic, identifying themselves with a category of bands they admired and respected which some might label 'indie' or 'alternative'. Thus to place the music-making of the Jactars and Crikey it's the Cromptons! within a wider perspective, the following chapter develops the discussion further by analysing their processes of composition and the aesthetics that lay behind them, in relation to rock music as a genre.

7

Style and Meaning in the Music

MUSIC OF ORDERLY DISORDER

This chapter considers the music-making of the Jactars and Crikey it's the Cromptons! within the wider context of rock music and music in general, thus highlighting its cultural, social, and historical specificity.

The aesthetics and ideology involved in the production of the Jactars' and Crikey it's the Cromptons!' music had been particularly influenced by British and American punk styles of the 1970s. The 'do-it-yourself' message of punk, which has been well documented elsewhere (see Frith, 1983, and Laing, 1985, for example), encouraged many people, including members of the Jactars and Crikey it's the Cromptons!, to form bands. Trav, Gary, and Dave began making music together in the late 1970s at the age of 13–14 years, when punk was at its height. Later they joined Tony and others and experimented in Trav or Tony's house with various sounds using hairdryers, hoovers, cardboard boxes, bottles, typewriters, in addition to more conventional instruments. As far as the music itself was concerned, punk:

meant an attitude towards musical performance which emphasized directness and repetition (to use more than three chords was self-indulgence) at the expense of technical virtuosity (p.14) . . . a challenge to the orthodoxy of 'artistic excellence' in punk's choice of musical style; and the aggressive injection of new subject matter into the lyrics of popular songs, some of which broke existing taboos (Laing, 1985: 12).

Williams (*NME*: 26 January 1986) wrote of the:

undying punk principle that musical ability not only tends to be *boring* when possessed by skinny white boys but can be a downright hindrance if one wishes to communicate ideas that are fresher than last February's free-range eggs.

Members of the Jactars and Crikey it's the Cromptons! had clearly adopted that challenge to technical and musical virtuosity, believing that 'musos' who trained themselves in, and often became obsessed with, musical and technical skills had, in doing so, lost the right attitude (as had those bands that used backing tapes at their performances instead of live musicians). They had lost, as one person put it, 'that feel'. Similarly, White (1983: 197) wrote that amongst jazz musicians: 'there is a distinction drawn between feel and technique. Those who have great technique sometimes place less emphasis on 'feel' whereas those who have limited technique sometimes place greater value on the feel of the music.' A musician who rehearsed at the Ministry said that he and other bands at the Ministry believed in 'musicianship' and hadn't time for Half Man Half Biscuit and 'their friends'. As far as he was concerned that was not music and those bands would vanish in a few months whereas bands like his continually worked hard and achieved something musically.

When Tog and Tony formed the short-lived Vegetable Smutt Kraft Band, Tog decided to play lead guitar though he knew nothing about it and couldn't play it, 'which', he explained, 'is the kind of sound we are after'. He and the others readily proclaimed their musical incompetence, as did many bands influenced by punk. ('Virtuosity kills the simple spontaneity of rock'n'roll'—the Inca Babies, *Sounds*: 5 January 1985.) When the Iconoclasts first began performing, the bass player would give her bass to the band's roadie to tune. The first time he did so he tuned all four strings which, she informed him, was unnecessary because she only used one of them. Such bands appear to have adopted an aesthetic of musical incompetence. However, this did not involve incompetence as such, but on the one hand the competent contrivance of it, and on the other, the skillful construction of a complex whole from an assortment of simple and incompetently played (whether intentionally or unintentionally) sounds, chords, and notes. Such bands therefore adopted an aesthetic which often required considerable care and skill to embody in their music. Thus Tony admired a song by a well-known band which he described as 'just two chords', whilst Tog derogatively named another band at Vulcan 'three-chord wonders', and jokingly asked if it was true that they had come up with another chord that week. Clearly the first band was appreciated for expressing an aesthetic of simplicity (or incompetence) whilst the second was criticized for being musically incompetent.

The musical aesthetics of the Jactars and Crikey it's the Cromptons! was thus expressed in various guises in the music of other bands and could even be seen to encompass rock music as a whole as well as trends or genres within other art forms. Cooper (1982: 77) wrote of Echo and the Bunnymen:

None of the three were musicians and to this day they have difficulty tuning guitars and find it impossible to play with other people . . . The Bunnymen's success is the chemistry of three people from the same background finding a common music because they didn't play well enough to know the clichés . . . The Bunnymen's virginity, their lack of experience, is their essence.

At a 1986 conference of the International Association for the Study of Popular Music, a member of a band named Talulah Gosh claimed that his band and a small group of similar bands dealt, like punk, with music as noise and instruments as objects. They produced 'poppy', 'lyrical', 'tuneful' songs but he explained that their melody and lyrics were contradicted and subverted ('attacked' as he phrased it) by the manner in which the instruments were played, for although the band's members could play their instruments 'properly', they used them in a 'non-instrumental' way. He cited a band that took that style to an extreme making what he described as, 'pure noise with songs . . . it's about noise yet at the same time it's about music'. Similarly, a member of the Shop Assistants was quoted as saying:

We usually manage to get out of tune at the same time . . . I like the idea of having extremes. On the one hand there's the guitars going wild, and accompanying that there's Alex's vocals, highlighting the tunes that run through our songs. Only now do people realize that it's possible to have noise and still have tunes in there as well—before it's always been regarded as only possible to have one or the other, but not both (*NME*: 17 August 1985).

The relationship between musical elements such as music and lyrics can thus be complex. They act and react upon each other or independently of each other. When I asked Ryan's vocalist what the band's lyrics were about he answered that they were all about love, whereupon the guitarist proudly declared that his chords were 'all about hate'.

In the 1960s the Who treated instruments as objects by smashing them up during performances. 'I smash guitars', said Pete Townshend, 'because I like them. I usually smash a guitar when it's at its best' (Herman, 1971: 45). This was explained as an attack on commodities which were seen to come between audiences, performers, and the music. 'If I stood on stage worrying about the price of a guitar then I'm not really playing music. I'm getting involved in material values' (ibid.: 52). According to Herman, the Who wanted their music to appear: 'constrained and orderly yet frantic, with instrumental lines that intervene with such complexity that they give every appearance of chaos; what Townshend elsewhere called an "orderly disorder"' (ibid.: 58). Turner (1983: 118) wrote, 'it takes a great amount of order to produce "a sweet disorder", a great deal of structuring to create a sacred play-space and time for anti-structure'.

The guitar-smashing and 'orderly disorder' or the Who are examples of what Martin (1981), following Turner, called the 'symbols of anti-structure' which pervaded popular culture in the 1960s:

The arts and the Underground were the primary milieux in which the cultural vocabulary of liminality was developed during the 1950s and 1960s—ambiguity, taboo breaking, anti-structure—in short, the symbolism of ecstatic disorder (ibid.: 137).

This was particularly characteristic of rock, a youth music that embodied rebellion. By seeking to invert, subvert, turn 'upside-down' musical conventions and treat instruments illegitimately, Tony, the Jactars, and Talulah Gosh were thus following in the footsteps of other artists from the Sex Pistols, the Flying Lizards, and the Who to the Surrealists and Dadaists who originated at the time of the First World War and whose spirit came to pervade art, popular music, and popular culture in general (Russolo's 1913 manifesto was entitled 'The Art of Noise' and Satie, one of the predecessors of the Dada group, incorporated mechanical instruments such as typewriters in his music and was attacked by the press for doing so). Anti-structural symbolism in rock music thus became, as in other musical genres, art forms, and various political movements, a taken for granted style displaying rules and predictable patterns, i.e. structure. In reality, any musical form would be unintelligible without structure.

Inversion and disorder were also emphasized in the Jactars' and Crikey it's the Cromptons!' performances, in their rejection, for example, of some of the traditional forms of rock showmanship such as elaborate stage dress or contrived, rehearsed movements, and in Tony's striving to 'freak out' and be 'wild' and 'over the top' in his stage dress and movement which involved wearing 'clashing' colours and looking as 'uncomfortable as possible' in odd socks or oversized suits. In the adoption of such styles both bands again followed the attitudes of many others before them:

There is a beautiful photograph of the Comets with the bassist lying on his back with his feet in the air balancing his instrument, wearing ostentatiously odd socks. This is the first installment of the body symbolism of anti-structure (Martin, 1981: 164).

The lyrical themes of the Jactars and Crikey it's the Cromptons! (including those of violence and pain; loneliness, alienation, and helplessness, as though one were 'a dead leaf' floating in 'a fast stream'—from 'Tongue'; and of women as deceitful temptresses) again reflected those prevalent in other styles of rock music. Rock's ideology has been specifically directed towards youth and rebellion and throughout its history lyrics have expressed aggression, romance, sexuality (largely male sexuality), and misogyny. According to Laing (1985), for example, punk lyrics involved, on the whole, those same themes, but because punk was designed to shock, violent themes were particularly stressed and sexuality represented in a more aggressive manner:

The Stranglers' songs . . . have scenarios of pornographic fantasies, with strongly sadistic overtones, and elsewhere that group and the early Adam and the Ants produced litanies of detailed violent acts: 'I'll sew up your mouth', 'You kicked my cheekbones in', 'Smack your face', 'Treat you rough', 'Beat you till you drop' (ibid.: 76).

Many rock lyrics express the younger generation's sense of alienation, frustration with their elders and the world at large, and their worries about their future. Such lyrics often exhibit, therefore, a sense of hostility or a depressing, pessimistic tone highlighted by Julie Burchill in a review of the Jesus And Mary Chain (*NME*: 23 February 1985):

Horrible nasty sound for big baby boys to sit around feeling depressed and important to. Funny, isn't it, how many people—particularly those in beat combos—feel important, the stuff of zeitgeist, blitzkrieg and history, when they're down in the dumps, and feel trivial, not 'real', when they're happy.

The above themes are often characteristic of song texts outside rock music since, as Merriam (1964: 46) pointed out, the language in song texts is 'often more permissive than in ordinary discourse', which gives composers licence to express themselves in a manner inappropriate in everyday language. Lyrics can often, therefore, reveal psychological processes and 'deep-seated values and goals stated only with the greatest reluctance in normal discourse' (ibid.). Analysis of them can thus illuminate both 'ideal and real behaviour'. Expressions and styles of enunciation in song texts are also often different from those of everyday speech. In rock music, for example, words are frequently distorted and accents changed.

The ideology of rock music, as opposed to pop, has generally incorporated the belief that lyricists should write what they really feel or think as if to do so is to be natural and genuine and to do otherwise to be contrived or false: 'Rock . . . carries intimations of sincerity, authenticity, art . . . These intimations have been muffled since rock became the record industry, but it is the possibilities, the promises that matter . . .' (Frith, 1983: 11). Thus many lyrics are deeply personal expressions of their composers who are often self-conscious about them. Tony said that some of his lyrics were perhaps too personal, and Trav said he never showed his lyrics to people and worried about people reading them. Consequently, band members who did not contribute towards lyrical composition often didn't know the lyrics or were unaware of their meaning. Tog, for example, said that of all the Jactars' songs he only knew some of the words to one of them. He rarely listened to the lyrics when he was playing because he was usually concentrating upon the drum beat—though he sometimes listened to them on recordings. Similarly, the lyrics of One Last Fight and the Da Vincis were written by the vocalists and their meaning was cryptic and personal to them. The other band members appreciated that and although they didn't understand the lyrics they admired them and found them interesting. Nevertheless the lyrics were written on their behalf and did express their own feelings in one way or another.

Consequently, interpretations of lyrics could, even within a band, vary considerably, as revealed by the following quote in which members of the same band discuss one of the band's songs entitled 'Perfect Circle', the lyrics of which had been written by Michael, their lead vocalist:

'Peter always tells this story about how "Perfect Circle" was inspired by a bunch of young boys playing baseball', says Michael. 'To me, it was about my ex-girlfriend. A lot of times they [the other band members] won't see the words until we record the song; a lot of times they won't want to.' 'We're just like anyone else', said Peter. 'We try and interpret them personally but actually we know Michael, so barring maybe three songs over our recording career I know what they're about because I know the girl or the person, or the time and the place. But I think one would get the emotion anyway, whether or not one knew the particular circumstances. He writes in a pretty oblique manner, and that's OK' (*NME*: 6 July 1985).

The nature of such lyrics is thus paradoxical in that whilst their intended meaning and its interpretation can be highly personal and individual, they are also written on behalf of the band as a whole and for public performance. (This public/private dualism can also be seen as characteristic of music on its own: 'Because of its lack of word or pictorial imagery, music seems to be the most inward of the arts. But it is also the most immediately social, in the awareness of kinship it evokes among a body of listeners, without impediments of any kind'—Finkelstein, 1976: 14.) Lienhardt (1985: 144) highlighted the dualism between the public and private nature of lyrics in his discussion of African songs which are:

contrary to what was once supposed about their anonymous, communal 'folk' origins, usually assigned to their individual composers, who hold the copyright, as it were, and they contain images and illusions which are incomprehensible . . . without a knowledge of intimate local and personal experience of the composer himself. In this respect, like much of the best poetry, they make the private self public, while retaining a sense of privileged admittance to its privacy.

The private nature of lyrics *is* therefore expressed in the context of a performance but can also be obscured through distorted enunciation and accent. Lyrics may thus be incomprehensible or misunderstood by audiences, but at the same time accepted as part of the band's general style. Their intelligibility may be considered unimportant as long as the audience knows what the song is supposed to be about and as long as the music conveys and supports that meaning. Audience members might also impose upon lyrics their own meanings and interpretations. Their lyrical content might be taken to address them, conveying collective sentiments and acting as a form of psychological expression and release for them as well as for the composer(s) and performers. The lyrics may not intentionally express meanings and sentiments relevant to audience members, but by expressing the personal, individual experiences of their composer they might also reflect aspects of the composer's social and cultural environment which may be shared by the audience.

From its beginnings, rock music has involved repetitive, predictable, and simple beats, rhythms, melodies, and lyrics, accompanied by certain sounds and styles that have often been 'conventionally unaesthetic or dissonant' (Durant, 1984: 180). Rhythm and volume have been emphasized as well as aggressive, arrhythmical noise, and themes discussed above such as rebellion have been consistently played upon. Because rock has been primarily aimed at youth and marketed as such it has often, as Burchill and Parsons (1978) pointed out, promoted an 'illusion of youth rebellion' or, as Martin put it, 'The semblance and symbol of revolt without its reality . . . Thus rock is the ritual gesture of liminality not a first instalment of revolt: the image and not the substance' (ibid.: 167). 'The teenage world of rock and roll', wrote Kerridge (1984), 'provided a door through which youngsters who might otherwise have been respectable could now enter the underworld.' Similarly, Clover (1985) and Burchall (1965) have pointed to the 'myth of rock'n'roll and the revolution'. This rebellious image of rock with its accompanying symbols of disorder and anti-structure has often led to its being associated with working-class youth in particular. Many have been keen, for example, to point to the working-class roots of punk (e.g. Marsh, 1977). Yet that is another illusion. In reality, anti-structural symbolism in 1960s art, as Martin pointed out, appealed particularly to middle-class bohemians, and punk symbolism of the 1970s did much the same. It was not even the case that punk's musicians were predominantly working class as Laing (1985: 122) has shown.

The stance taken against technology by members of the Jactars and Crikey it's the Cromptons! was also a long-standing anti-structural device brought to the fore yet again by punk. Technology stood in the way of their ideal of honest music-making. The problem, however, was how to maintain and project that honesty whilst recording: in other words, how to use advanced technology to produce music that sounded 'raw' and expressed an aesthetic of simplicity opposed to technology. They, like others, wanted to capture the essence of live performance on recordings. Thus Tony was critical of his band's first demo tape because it sounded 'too controlled and contained', and contrasted it with a recording of one of their live performances which had more 'vitality and power'. He and other musicians thought their bands sounded better live than recorded because they sought to achieve that 'rawness' of sound as part of their musical style. (Many also preferred live performance because of its visual aspects.) Tony also described one or two of his songs as 'live' songs as opposed to those that sounded better recorded.

It was, however, difficult, if not impossible, to reproduce the live sound on a recording. One sound engineer bemoaned those bands who came to a studio wanting to sound live:

They just presume that you can plug in and play as usual and get a live effect. They don't realize that playing live and recording are two completely different things. To begin with, you don't have the same volume that you get when you play live. You also lose the visual effect which amounts to over 50 per cent of the live experience.

Achieving that 'live effect' thus required considerable skill and a suitably chosen studio and engineer. To help them decide which studio to record in musicians listened carefully and critically to recordings of other bands. For most, their choice was restricted by limited finances although, as mentioned earlier, bands like the Jactars might use simpler studios for ideological as well as financial reasons. They and others, however, often found that simpler equipment did not necessarily produce the raw sound desired. Huw, for example, pointed out that their demo tape sounded too 'contained' only because they couldn't afford a good quality recording and an engineer skilled enough to mix it properly.

Thus whilst technology (including instruments as well as recording equipment) was seen as a constraint, its creative, beneficial potential was also recognized (particularly by bands making different styles of music from that of the Jactars and Crikey it's the Cromptons! and expressing a different attitude towards technology), as shown by the following quote from a band named Wire, admired by both the Jactars and Crikey it's the Cromptons!:

It became clear very quickly . . . that we had to separate the two processes of playing live and making a record. Live the idea is still very much that of the guitar-based group; on record we found it was necessary to embrace current technology . . . We started by constructing the pieces in the familiar way but then as we got more familiar with the technology, we got excited by the possibility of fusing the two. If it sounds technological then good, but behind it all the playing is still there. What it allows you to do is to take the best parts of performance and utilise those to build up the ideal copy (*NME*: 18 April 1983).

The medium of their art was only one of many constraints put upon the music-making of the Jactars and Crikey it's the Cromptons! and other bands. In addition there was its commercial nature. Most band members made a distinction between 'commercial' and 'non-commercial' or 'alternative' music, which often led to argument and discussion on the definition of 'commercial' music. Tony, for example, described his music as 'alternative' and 'non-commercial' and often derogatively referred to 'commercial' music as 'pop' or 'bubble-gum music' played on *Top of the Pops* and Radio One. Huw pointed out that Tony had written some songs which were 'catchy' and hence commercial. Tog, in support of Huw, reckoned that any of Crikey it's the Cromptons!' songs could, with 'hype' (i.e. publicity and financial backing), be pushed to the top of the charts, and added, to annoy Tony, that it would be harder to do that with the Jactars' music which was definitely less 'commercial' than Crikey it's the Cromptons!'

Whether their music was defined as 'commercial' or 'non-commercial' most bands wanted to appear on record and 'make it' in some way, which meant that they usually had to deal with those institutions involved with the mass production and commercialization of music. To sell their products such institutions categorized and labelled music into certain styles or genres. Thus the music industry to a certain extent prescribed the music heard by the general public because many bands orientated themselves, their music, and their image towards those categories in an effort to achieve success. Geoff Davies believed that music should reflect its performers' thoughts and feelings because that was what art and entertainment ought to be about. He bemoaned the fact that musicians were now 'calculating how to jump on the band wagon and which type of song has a good chance of getting into the charts . . . Anyone who does this is merely a business man as far as I'm concerned.' No band, he said, should have to make compromises to try to sell records: 'If you've got something in your head that you think is great there are always other people who will like it because nobody is alone.'

Whether bands conformed to commercial categories and labels or reacted against them, they still used them as a reference point and were generally unable to seclude their music-making from commercial considerations. There were so many bands competing for success that many succumbed to the pressure to produce music directed in one way or another at particular record companies. A clear example of how this could happen was the reaction of Crikey it's the Cromptons! to the comments of A&R people they saw in London. Huw agreed with some of them, trying to persuade Tony to change his music-making accordingly, and all of them began to think more carefully about their songs and their appeal to record companies. Dave T. even suggested they look at the books *How to Make a Hit Record* and *How to Make a Demo*, and Tony wondered whether they should 'completely sell out' and make 'commercial music' in order to get a deal and then revert back to their original style to record a 'way out' album. For a while he considered their 'more commercial' songs quite favourably and produced two songs he thought one of the companies they visited might like.

Other bands allowed their music to be far more constrained by commercial considerations. At many rehearsals I attended musicians avoided experimentation during music-making, preferring to play safe in case record companies wouldn't like it. Roger Hill described described this as 'the subservience of imagination to production'. Leigh (1984: 100) wrote of Liverpool bands in the 1960s:

Groups lost their individuality as they tried to emulate the successful sounds of others. They knew that there was big money at stake and yet this was their undoing. They became greedy . . .

The members of one local band who wrote strongly political lyrics, were constantly pressurized by their manager and others to sacrifice their principles and tone down their lyrics to make them more acceptable. Some bands, after months or years of failing to achieve a record deal, completely rewrote their songs in an effort to make them more 'catchy' and acceptable. Those under contract to a record company usually released their most 'commercial' song as a single, particularly if a previous record had been unsuccessful. Often they were pressurized to do so by record company personnel. Also important (as illustrated in Chapter 5) was whether that particular style of music was currently in vogue.

Thus most bands were involved with the continual re-formation and adaptation of their music in order to satisfy not only themselves but their audience, whether it be the friends, relatives, and locals who attended their live performances, the unknown potential audience they hoped to eventually reach through their records, or the particular record company or A&R person who might make that possible.

CULT OF ORIGINALITY

The Jactars and Crikey it's the Cromptons! described themselves as 'alternative' and didn't like to be 'labelled' or categorized. They wanted, like other bands I met, to appear unique and make music that was 'different'. Their quest for originality could perhaps be placed within a general cult of originality that has influenced all arts this century. Despite that, most bands were also keen to acknowledge their musical 'influences', i.e. particular bands they admired that had influenced them.

Considerable emphasis was placed upon deciphering the influences of bands, and band members often proudly displayed their ability to detect, identify, and trace them in their music. If certain influences were attributed to a band with which its members disagreed, or when its music was described as 'derivative', it was usually seen as a great insult. When one club owner returned Crikey it's the Cromptons!' demo tape to them saying they were too 'derivative', the band's members were outraged, particularly Tony, who often declared that his main aim was to make music that was 'really different' and once told me how anxious he became when his voice was compared to that of others because he so badly wanted to be unique. Afterwards, he spent hours arguing with others at Vulcan about whether his music was in fact derivative. The manager of Ryan compared it to the music of Talking Heads and to one of that band's songs in particular. To prove his point he played a recording of the song to Tony, who was forced to admit that there were certain similarities. They also discussed the music of One Last Fight. A member of Ryan said it sounded like that of the Cure but Tony disagreed and pointed to one particular sequence of music which he described as a 'rip-off of the Virgin Prunes'. He mentioned this to members of One Last Fight but they said they had never heard of the Virgin Prunes. Tony was determined to play them a recording by the band so they could hear the similarity for themselves.

Members of the Jactars also spent much time discussing, identifying, tracing, and arguing about influences of other bands and acknowledging and denying those attributed to their own. When Roger Hill broadcast their advertisement for a drummer on Radio Merseyside and described them as sounding like the Smiths, a well-known Manchester band, they were shocked and upset. Trav reflected pessimistically,

whatever you do you're just going to get categorized. The Jactars have been put in the Smiths' category. No matter what you do, if you have a bass and two guitars you get compared to other bands of that nature.

The problem was not only that people listened to music in such a subjective, individual manner that they heard and appreciated the same piece of music differently, but that whilst acknowledging their 'influences' and perhaps admitting that it was difficult (if not impossible) to be totally original because everyone had been influenced by somebody, many bands nevertheless wanted to create their own distinctive style of music and be appreciated for doing so. There seemed to be a feeling that to do so was to be not only original and creative but honest and genuine. Thus a member of the Da Vincis described the music of One Last Fight as 'false', explaining that he found it 'contrived . . . like lots of bands put together'. The quest for originality was clearly revealed in the earlier descriptions of the Jactars' and Crikey it's the Cromptons!' music-making where the bands' members pointed out that a sequence of music, a sound, a style of playing or singing, or even a whole song, sounded too much like that of another band and it was altered appropriately.

However, although it was common for bands to unconsciously mimic the music of other bands, many *consciously* borrowed from or adapted the music of others to incorporate it in their own and claim it as their own. If the Jactars or Crikey it's the Cromptons! did that then I was not aware of it (though Tony once told me he had 'ripped off', i.e. stolen someone else's guitar rhythms), but it was apparent amongst some other bands. Such 'borrowing' was not a random or haphazard process but involved a certain amount of skill, subtlety, and etiquette. Two members of Carry On Spying, for example, described how they had listened to a record by a well-known band and heard a bass line they particularly liked, deciding to use it themselves. However, the bass line sounded familiar and they realized that it was similar to that of another band they knew that also rehearsed at the Ministry and for that reason they couldn't use it: 'It's too close to the knuckle', said one, 'to use stuff from another Liverpool band.' Bands rehearsing in the Ministry regularly gathered in the office to chat and joke and often accused each other of stealing sequences of music which might have been overheard at rehearsals or performances. Generally such accusations were made in a light-hearted, jovial manner, but occasionally the rivalry between partic-ular bands made them more serious.

The fear of having one's music 'stolen' and the stress upon originality contributed to what could be described as a mystification of the processes of music-making (reminiscent in a way of Pete McLaine's comment on Mersey Beat bands in the 1960s: 'Everything was so secret in those days because so many groups were rehashing old songs. The KGB or the CIA couldn't have been more secretive'—Leigh, 1984: 78). Some bands, for example, kept their performance techniques secret and were reluctant to discuss them with outsiders. (Such mystification also occurs in other performance arts—see Burns, 1972: 155, for example, on acting.) Similarly, trumpet players in New Orleans have been described as covering their hands with hankerchiefs when playing so as to shield their fingering from the view and mimicry of others. Bands didn't usually like being watched at rehearsals. When I first began to attend rehearsals of Up the Khyber the band's manager regarded me suspiciously and wanted my assurance that I would never reveal to others my observations about the band and the way it operated. Sometimes band members referred jokingly to such secrecy. A member of Rise, for example, once referred to a musical technique or style of his band during conversation with members of Up the Khyber. The technique surprised the latter, which led the member of Rise to comment that he was giving away all Rise's 'secrets' and should keep quiet.

Copying or 'borrowing' another band's music was acceptable if acknowledged and presented in the form of a cover. Thus members of the Jactars and Crikey it's the Cromptons! attended a performance of a band that had recently acquired notoriety in the independent music scene and were appalled that their songs were 'complete rip-offs' of various other bands. Tog thought it would have been much better if they had just done covers. 'In fact,' he added, 'as cover versions they would have been really good.' A local cabaret performer, however, said that cabaret, involving the reproduction of familiar songs, had become a 'dirty word' among rock musicians and was viewed derogatively. This was illustrated earlier by Trav's attitude to cabaret and covers. Most rock bands started off playing and rehearsing covers but progressed on to their own material. Thereafter many were against performing a lot of covers because they felt that to do so showed a lack of creativity and initiative. 'It's very easy to copy someone', said a member of one, 'but it's the hardest thing to be original.' Midi was shown earlier to regard the performance of covers as an indulgence that pleased audiences but some musicians didn't like the idea of 'playing entirely for an audience' and saw covers as 'entertainment' and thus demeaning, as opposed to the creation and performance of original material which was integral to a band's self-respect.

The covers performed by bands like the Jactars and Crikey it's the Cromptons! were often viewed as a relaxing diversion from their own material, as with the latter's version of the well-known song 'Waiting for my Man' which they usually performed at the end of their set or as an encore if one was demanded. With such covers emphasis was again, as mentioned earlier, placed upon originality and creativity. Yet because the Jactars and Crikey it's the Cromptons! chose to cover songs of bands they admired that often made music of a style similar to their own, their covers might also be seen as a declaration of allegiance and thus a conveyor of identity. Members of another band said they only did covers 'for a laugh':

We do one which is very tongue-in-cheek, done very differently . . . taking the piss out of it. You find a lot of bands doing covers of bands that sound like them whereas we do . . . a very different type of music that they [the audience] don't expect us to do so they know we are really doing it for a laugh.

The injection of humour into the music, performance, and general image of a band was common practice. The lyrics of Crikey it's the Cromptons!, for example, were largely based upon Tony's individual sense of humour which his co-band members to some extent shared. That same sense of humour was also expressed in Crikey it's the Cromptons!' music, stage dress and performance, poster designs, name, and song titles. Tony sang songs about fish playing a guitar with a plastic fish dangling from its neck, posters advertising one gig featured a drawing by Huw of a mutated fish-like creature with 'let them eat plankton' printed underneath, and, discussing his stage image, Tony would fantasize about performing with a frozen haddock strapped to his forehead.

Other local ('wacky') bands displaying humour in their music-making included: Half Man Half Biscuit, whose lyrics about television personalities amused listeners nationwide; the Mel-O-Tones, who had an unusual stage image and produced their own comic entitled 'Trash Can' featuring members of the band and their friends in cartoon form; and the Veggie Band, whose members were proclaimed 'born-again veggies' and included Colin Cucumber and Barry Beetroot. Many bands incorporated humour in more subtle ways. Lyrics, for example, might contain references or jokes recognizable as such only to the band's members and close friends. Musical jokes might also be included, such as the Jactars' instrumental number of 'pure noise', Crikey it's the Cromptons!' ending of one song during a performance in 'tongue-in-cheek', 'heavy metal' style, and their inclusion of some drunken yodelling on a demo tape recorded in a studio late one night. Such humorous elements brought band members and associates closer together as participants in a shared code and were thus an important part of the band's image and identity.

Earlier, the strong sense of identity conveyed by a band's name was mentioned, representing the band as a thing in itself, over and above its individual members and somehow defining them. That could also be said of the music, which was not conceptualized as an expression of its four or five *individual* makers but as an expression of the band as a whole, over and above the individuals that comprized it. Again this was an important aspect of each member's identity and was bound up with the bands' 'democratic ethos' discussed earlier. A member of the Da Vincis said that all bands comprized members with different tastes in music which was usually reflected in their music. However, he continued, 'sometimes it can all come together and you can produce something that is an expression of the whole band'. Similarly, a member of Blue Nose B said of his band: 'We all have different music tastes but we've moulded ourselves into our own sound', whilst Pete Best said of the Beatles, 'We had a group sound. It wasn't just one person' (Davies, 1986: 30).

Thus bands, like instruments, rooms, studios, and engineers, were said to have their own particular 'sound' which comprized their music and musical style, the specific instruments that made it, and the way it was presented through their 'set'. Much attention and discussion focused upon that sound because it was seen to express and convey the band's identity. Thus Tony wanted Dave to turn off the guitar 'effects' he was using saying 'We're not really a distortion band', and members of Carry On Spying, after someone pointed out that all their songs sounded different and some sounded like those of other bands, completely rewrote many of them. They agreed there was a danger the songs might all end up sounding similar but said that at least they would have their own distinctive sound.

In general, that sound was conceptualized as a fixed, unchanging identity, but it was also considered important that a band should develop and progress through time and be *heard* to do so. Its new songs should thus be seen as a move forward, either because they improved upon older songs or because they represented a change of style or emphasis. Ideally the sound thus retained its essential characteristics whilst continually changing and, in a sense, developing with the band members themselves. 'If you don't progress you regress', said one local journalist, criticizing a famous local band for not developing its style over the years. Similarly, the Jactars' new demo tape was criticized by some of their friends as a 'backwards step' because the new song on it sounded just like their old ones: 'At least Crikey it's the Cromptons! are progressing in their stuff', said Tony.

That emphasis upon development reflected the rapid fluctuations of trends and styles in the national music scene which encouraged the quest for change and originality, for hitting the right 'formula' at the right time. Bands were expected to continually compose new material. One man, for example, proudly declared of his band, 'We're not afraid to drop or change songs.' Hence the existence of the process described in the previous chapter whereby new songs were composed while older ones were rehearsed and continually recomposed for performance as a set. Those new songs were gradually introduced ('worked in') to the set whilst older ones were dropped and later revived or fondly played and remembered within the privacy of the band as 'old faves'. A local band named Wake Up Africa was described by members of Crikey it's the Cromptons! and their associates as 'professional', but they criticized that professionalism as a sort of 'selling out'. Wake Up Africa had been together for six years and were still performing songs they had played at the start of their career. In other words, they had worked on the same few songs until they had honed them down to perfection, a policy regarded by others as unadventurous.

Although I have suggested that the band and its sound existed as a thing in itself over and above the individual personalities that comprized and produced it, those individuals were obviously important components and appreciated as such. Through them the character and image of the band was constructed and developed; thus when its membership was threatened, or when someone left the band, a crisis arose because the band's sound and identity was under threat.

MASS CULTURE AND IDENTITY

The construction of identity through tastes in music was important not only for the band as a whole but for the individual, as revealed in the previous chapter. Considerable emphasis was placed upon the music tastes of each band member, with Trav envisaging the music he and Dave liked as forming a continuum of styles as if that represented the range and extent of their personalities. Concern was shown that such individual preferences should not conflict with or interfere with the band's sound. Members of Some Party once explained that the differences between their tastes in music never became particularly problematic because if a member's influences began to emerge in his playing 'we pull him in line'. It is thus important to note the way in which particular musical styles, forms, and even a particular sound (whether of an instrument, voice, technological device, or band) could be invested with so much social and cultural significance.

As mass culture rock music is received via all sorts of channels and in all sorts of situations. Its commercial nature means that it involves continual promotion and marketing of new styles and trends by the record industry in order to make its companies as much money as possible. That sense of change and movement is, as we have seen, incorporated in the ideology of rock:

Rock was always meant to be illusory and ephemeral, such stuff as dreams are made of; barely existing as a definable whole at all and then always in a state of eternal and perpetual flux, constantly being either consumed or renewed within the flutter of an eyelid; a place in which a three-minute song could encompass infinity or nothing at all, where ideally everything should exist just long enough to die, being transient in order to flare with life for an instant forever remembered on record—rather than splutter for an age. It should always be young and never old. Uncompromised by experience and unbridled by routine, not existing long enough to receive the withering touch of either (Tony from Sigue Sigue Sputnik, *Melody Maker*: 24 August 1985).

Thus rock music is contemporary and immediate. Records evoke particular periods of time with their own particular styles, images, and happenings. Individual songs can have a personal relevance in that they relate to one point in an individual's life and conjure up associated feelings, experiences, and relationships, but they can also evoke communal feelings and experiences and they play upon a sense of community in their audience and in a way give rise to it. (For discussion on how pop songs play on a sense of community with others and create an 'illusion' of community see Laing, 1969; Frith, 1983 and 1981; Williams, 1976; Riesman, 1957; and Sartre, 1976.) There is a sense that all have experienced the same music, progressing through and growing up with the same bands and musical styles, and thus share a similar history.

This contemporary, temporary, temporal nature of rock music also means that individuals experience a feeling of having grown out of particular styles so that looking back at music one listened to in previous years is like looking at old photographs of oneself with a feeling of embarrassment at how one used to look. Members of the Jactars, Crikey it's the Cromptons!, and other bands spent many hours reminiscing and laughing self-consciously about bands and songs they used to listen to and like, listing them in chronological order and associating them with their age and activities at that particular time. Each band and musical style was recognized as the product of a specific period and appreciated as such. Thus when Tog played me a recording by a band he and Midi had previously been in, I was told to bear in mind the fact that the music 'is good for what it is . . . It's good for 1980.'

Rock music is striking, however, not only for its encompassing, communal nature, but for its diversity and the way in which its styles and sounds are adopted and used to construct and identify various groups and even geographical areas. The appropriation of sounds and styles by various subcultures, for example, and the way in which such styles to a certain extent create those subcultures, has been well documented elsewhere (see Hebdige, 1979; Willis, 1978; and other studies produced at the Centre for Contemporary Cultural Studies at Birmingham University). Here it is perhaps interesting to note how the process relates to rock bands. It was shown earlier that the incorporation of individual music tastes into the construction of a band's sound, which was often claimed by the band to be both original and 'different', could prove difficult if those tastes were particularly diverse or conflicting. Thus advertisements placed by bands looking for new members usually proclaimed which musical groups and styles the band liked or was influenced by in order to attract appropriately like-minded applicants. (Lonely hearts advert-isements also proclaim musical tastes, i.e. they are a basis upon which friendships are formed.)

As part of a nationwide *audience* for recorded and commercial music, each individual or band could thus be associated with a particular taste group constructed through musical styles promoted and marketed by the record industry. In addition, as rock music *makers* there was a sense in which each member participated in that construction of style, taste, and meaning in rock culture, and perceived themselves as doing so, which was part of the attraction and excitement of being in a band. The messages and meanings of those particular styles were continually contested and debated, which meant that their producers, performers, and listeners felt a sense of involvement within the debate.

Music, in other words, is a shared code, and appreciation of it depends both upon an understanding of that code and a willingness to understand it. Rock music has been regarded as youth music not simply because of the intrinsic nature of the music itself and the way it has been associated with youth and profitably marketed as such, but because the existence of the so-called 'generation gap' has made the older generation unwilling to learn or appreciate the codes involved and the younger generation more anxious to appropriate them exclusively as its own. Rock music is thus a boundary marker that gives rise to strong feelings of allegiance and identity involving all sorts of non-musical factors.

MUSIC

In order to appreciate why people formed and maintained rock bands it is important to consider not just the appeal and attraction of *rock* music, but also that of music and music-making in its own right.

Band members delighted in the *physical* activity of producing noises and sounds. Some expressed a personal dislike of the music their band produced but nevertheless loved playing it. In turn, the music itself could arouse a physical response which is often the main intention of some musical forms. Many styles of rock music, for example, are constructed to encourage people to dance and feel energetic, sensual, or romantic: 'it is music to slop beer to, wave arms, punch fists, shout along and sweat to', proclaimed the reviewer of one gig (*NME*: 23 July 1985). Such physical movement can, as suggested earlier, play an important role during live performances by acting as a visual element of the music, conveying and generating emotion. Thus pleasure can be aroused by music alone—by the repetitious, predictable, familiar characteristics of well-known pop songs perhaps, as well as by the cacophony, bustle, and spectacle of a live performance. Frith (1983: 206), *New Society* (9 December 1984), and Martin (1981: 154) have all pointed out that the essence of rock is 'fun' or 'play'. It makes people feel good. Music is also experienced physically within the body. Sounds are absorbed by the body and resonate within it.

Yet music is used not only to arouse pleasure but to convey and stimulate a variety of other emotions and give emotional release. Lullabies, for example, are constructed to sooth and lull the emotions whilst other musical forms are used to calm and heal or arouse and heighten spiritual feelings, as with religious musics. Music can also provide or encourage the opportunity to 'let off steam' and perhaps express violence or hostility of some kind as revealed by the way in which musicians sometimes use their instruments almost as an extension of themselves and as a means through which to express their feelings. Thus Pete said he could 'work out' his aggressions with Crikey it's the Cromptons! and Tony strummed his guitar in a petulant manner when he got frustrated. The arousal of certain emotions and excitement can in turn affect the music and the performance of it as indicated in Chapter 4.

The physical, emotional, and pleasurable quality of music and music-making cannot be experienced in quite the same way through any other form of social or creative and artistic activity, which is why music is so popular and valued so highly. McGregor (1983: 81) summed it up thus:

Pop is energy. Rock is energy. Movement is energy. We are all energy, we are part of the Heraclitean stream, we are moving in blowfly trajectories from creation to death and as we hurtle along this invisible airborne stream we try to conjure up images, symbols, correlatives which correspond to this sense of speed, tragedy and joy and we create music.

The power and intensity of feeling in music and other creative art forms have been variously attributed: to their ambiguous nature which can articulate a variety of shifting feelings and meanings (Langer, 1951: 206); to the fact that art creates a moment of 'universal humanity' (Brecht, quoted in Fischer, 1963) and 'expands human kinship' (Finkelstein, 1976: 109); to the 'magic' inherent in art, the merging of the self with the whole which makes all art 'necessary' (Fischer); to the 'liminality' and 'communitas' in the arts and in ritual (Turner, 1969); and similarly, to the fact that while 'history develops, art stands still' (E. M. Forster, quoted in Blacking, 1981: 138). Music can thus externalize the internal, communicating things otherwise uncommunicable. It has power and autonomy, creating its own space and time where all kinds of dreams, emotions, and thoughts are possible.

Music communicates messages through its musical structures, verbal texts, symbolic forms, and through the emotions they arouse. Thus music is ideal for making meaning. It is used as a framework to express and convey memories, sentiments, and ideals; ideas, values, and arguments. Music is therefore, in a sense, 'good to think' (Lévi-Strauss, 1970). These are not just individual, subjective expressions and creations but reflect aspects of the society and culture within which the music is made. Music may be described as a series of 'human images' and 'portraits' (Finkelstein, 1976: 10), 'tonal expressions of human experience' (Blacking, 1973: 31), or 'humanly organized sound' (ibid.: 32). It is therefore 'an ideal field for the study of relationships between patterns of social interaction and the invention of cultural form' (Blacking, 1979: 3).

Consequently, techniques, styles, contexts, forms, and functions of music and music-making vary according to culture and society. The process of composition and rehearsal within a rock band was developed and learned together by all the band's members and was thus suited to, and affected by, their particular personalities and relationships between them. But it was also culturally conditioned, affected by: those members' aesthetics, values, attitudes and outlook, musical training and skills, and their legal status within the band; the band format and the instruments and technology used; the style of music made and styles and trends of music produced by other bands; and by the particular market and audience aimed at. Herman (1971: 15), for example, illustrated how the process could be affected by economic trends by describing how the ease with which electric guitars could be purchased on credit in the early 1960s encouraged the development of 'small guitar-based bands.'

Descriptions, definitions, and categorizations of music are also culturally conditioned, as is the way in which music is valued, appreciated, and responded to. It may be valued as an art and a source of aesthetic pleasure, for its spiritual, symbolic, or philosophical qualities, or for the possibilities it opens up for social interaction. The way that rock music has been viewed in Western societies has to some extent determined its rebellious nature and the power of its symbolism. Cultural attitudes towards particular geographical areas are also relevant, such as the way in which Liverpool has been regarded as a centre for the production of rock music.

Thus different societies and cultures and the various social, cultural, geographical, and age groups within them adopt their own musical forms and styles and react against or respond to each other's. They also hold their own particular criteria of musicianship and excellence; concepts about music, music-making, musicians, and relationships between performers and audience; and emotional and other responses to music. Movement to music, for example, varies from individual to individual, but differences between members of different cultures can be more striking since although physical movement is universally generated by music, the particular forms and styles that movement takes are culturally specific. Thus the same piece of music can encourage completely different kinds of physical responses within different cultures.

Throughout this book culture and society have been seen not only to be reflected in music but also affected by music. People make music but: 'there is also a sense in which music makes man, releasing creative energy, expanding consciousness and influencing subsequent decision-making and cultural invention' (Blacking, 1979: 3). Music thus exists as a thing in itself irreducible to its specific situation, makers, and score or to the more general social, cultural, and economic context within which it was produced. Marcuse (1977: 72) suggested, not only of music but of art in general, that it 'breaks open a dimension inaccessible to other experience' through its transformation of content into form. As suggested earlier, it is this quality that gives music its political and symbolic power and throughout history music has been used for political and ideological purposes with much effect.

In a controversial but thought-provoking argument Attali (1985) described music as a 'battlefield' and discussed the political power of 'noise'. He examined distinctions between music and noise, harmony and dissonance, and ultimately, order and disorder, and the way in which they reflect the social structure. Relations between harmony and music express social, hierarchical differences: 'music . . . creates order . . . Internal and external noises do violence to the code and to the network' (ibid.: 30). As a threat to the social order noise is hedged with rules and legislation that seek to control it:

noise had always been experienced as destruction, disorder, dirt, pollution, an aggression against the code-structuring messages. In all cultures it is associated with the idea of the weapon, blasphemy, plague (ibid.: 27).

Noise or music can thus destroy or replace a social order. This idea, as Attali admits, is not new. A. Jackson wrote (1969: 296):

Rhythmical sounds are predominantly man-made and are readily identifiable with social order, whereas din or arrhythmical noise is more typical of breaking of man-made order . . . As Douglas (1966: 94) says, 'ritual recognizes the potency of disorder' for 'disorder spoils the pattern' yet its potential for patterning is indefinite. Therefore breaks in the pattern of events may be reflected in disordered arrhythmical sounds while a taking up of a rhythmical beat again reasserts human control over events—but even that is speculative.

Hebdige (1979), in his study of subcultural styles, used the word 'noise' to 'describe the challenge to symbolic order that such styles are seen to constitute' (p.132), whilst Tagg (1979) demonstrated the way in which atonal music is used in film to express danger or threat.

'Noise carries order within itself' wrote Attali (ibid.: 33). Here again therefore, we see order in disorder, structure in anti-structure: 'What is noise to the old order is harmony to the new' (ibid.: 35). Attali's main preoccupation was the effect of money upon this battle, the increased commoditization of music that selects and isolates the musician: 'Money enters the picture and widens the rupture music contains within itself' (ibid.: 30). It therefore intensifies the power struggle between what counts as noise and order.

Basically, what members of the Jactars and Crikey it's the Cromptons! most enjoyed doing was making music. This was clearly revealed by their gig in Manchester (Chapter 4) where, in the early hours of the morning, after being treated badly by the club's managers, severely disappointed at the absence of an audience, they performed to and for each other through sheer enjoyment of music-making and its social benefits. However, in order to play music and attempt to make a living from it, the Jactars and Crikey it's the Cromptons! were required to become involved in, and preoccupied with, matters such as organizing gigs, raising finances, hiring and buying transport and equipment, renting rehearsal space, recording demo tapes, and arranging publicity. Their music-making was constricted by commercialism. It determined where and when they could perform, who would attend their performances and hear their music, the way their music was located and valued, and the way it was supposed to be structured and seen to progress with time and with current trends.

Members of the Jactars and Crikey it's the Cromptons! were not explicitly political or idealistic. They scorned 'commercial' music but did not (unlike other bands such as some of those labelled 'art', 'progressive', or 'experimental') articulate any coherent, considered views or philosophy on commerce and creativity or even on what they meant or were trying to achieve in the music they made (although individually Trav and Dave had clearly considered such issues). They did not, therefore, propound upon the evils of commerce. However, in the making of their music the Jactars and Crikey it's the Cromptons! not only explicitly but implicitly and unintentionally reflected, expressed, and confronted aspects of their surrounding environment and their feelings about it. They did so through the styles of music they chose to make and listen to—which embodied a certain ideology in rock, i.e. that of 'authenticity'; through their lyrics and musical sounds; and through their attitudes to the marketing of the music. This was particularly noticeable in the lyrics on deceit and isolation, the incorporation of elements of disorder (noise) in the music's order, and the creation of musical 'purity' and 'honesty' by stripping the music of its 'impure' commercial trappings. The music's hidden distinctions between purity and impurity, honesty and deceit, reality and artifice, expressed the contradiction and tension constructed by our culture between art and entertainment, creativity and commerce, culture as a collective, creative expression and culture as a commodity. Thus although their music was made outside of the market-place it reflected the contradictions and alienation of commerce and of modern industrial capitalism in general.

The same contradictions and tensions have been revealed and explored in the music and culture of groups from the same or different periods and genres. Willis (1978), for example, writing about the 'cultural politics' of motorbike boys and hippies in the 1970s, described the way that each group took commodities like motorbikes and records from their environment and used them in their own distinctive and politically significant way that was a 'striking back at the heart of the commodity form and its detailed domination of everyday life (171) . . . an unequal struggle against the unrecognized or misunderstood determining social and economic structures around them' (ibid.: 181), an attempt to find 'meaning and potential' amongst the 'worst productions out of the dead hand of the market'. Their cultural activity, like that of the Jactars and Crikey it's the Cromptons!, therefore showed 'a creative response to modern conditions' (ibid.: 174).

Beethoven composed his music at the time when music first became commoditized and Finkelstein (1976: 54) wrote that Beethoven showed:

a squeamishness about his dealings in money matters, as if it were not fitting for an artist to drive a bargain. But in moving from aristocratic patronage to the marketplace Beethoven had to handle the marketplace on its own terms.

Like the Jactars, Crikey it's the Cromptons!, and musicians of other genres and eras, Finkelstein suggested that Beethoven expressed that problem through deliberate use of 'dissonance', 'new chords', and 'dramatic oppositions', 'in the face of an audience that presumably wanted only sweet sounds' (ibid.: 58). Thus his music was also seen by some at the time as: 'a kind of individual "defiance of society"' (ibid.: 58). Finkelstein (ibid.: 97) suggested that Schoenberg and Stravinsky's 'atonal', 'dissonant' music also expressed the composers' 'alienation' and the constrictions of the market-place.

Durant (1984: 76) wrote of 'dissonance' and Attali (1985: 33) of 'noise', that it signified 'censorship and rarity': 'Concerted attempts to develop atonal music can come to appear in such terms a counterpart to a larger cultural decline into a meaninglessness for the individual of the modern world' (Durant, ibid.).

the very absence of meaning in pure noise or in the meaningless repetition of a message, by unchanneling auditory sensations, frees the· listener's imagination. The absence of meaning is in this case the presence of all meanings, absolute ambiguity, a construction outside meaning. This presence of noise makes sense, makes meaning. It makes possible the creation of a new order on another level of organization, of a new code in another network (Attali, ibid.: 84).

Conflict between creativity and commerce is widely felt. Those involved in different occupations, arts, and cultures experience the same pressure to 'sell out'. Regarding popular music, for example, Becker (1963) described the way in which the conflict was experienced by American jazz musicians of the 1940s, giving rise to the development of 'deviant' jazz groups that constructed a distinction between 'hipness' and 'squareness' which reflected the commercial pressures they were under and was developed in order to try to minimize them. Harker (1980) examined the contradictions and pressures of rock music as a commercial form in relation to the lyrics of particular rock stars such as Bob Dylan and John Lennon, which reflected the dilemma of their position, trapped in between commercial pressures and attractions and the need to express integrity and counter-cultural or revolutionary sentiments and messages. Similarly, Coffman (1972) considered some ways in which that conflict of roles was expressed and resolved by other rock stars and by their audiences (again in the performers' lyrics, but also in the development of a 'cult press' through which their audience could keep track of their experiences and activities); whilst Laing (1985), Frith (1980), and others have studied that conflict within the context of the 'punk' movement.

Why is it, however, that some groups either explicitly or implicitly express cultural opposition or resistance to hegemony whilst others do not? Although Liverpool bands like the Jactars and Crikey it's the Cromptons! responded to commercialism by expressing its alienating effects in their music, other bands took on commercial values and ambitions and constructed their music accordingly. The increasingly capitalistic attitude and outlook of such bands and their effect upon rock music in general were commented upon by many (see Thrills, *NME*: 23 February 1985, and Savage, 1984: 241, for example). That difference in attitude cannot be explained as a simple reflection of the different degrees of oppression, marginalization, and dissatisfaction experienced by such groups or bands, although inevitably music-making, including the making of meaning in and through music and the realization of the potential of music, music-making, and other forms of creativity, reflects, and is conditioned by, class, as is leisure in general.

Middle-class education and models of thought often emphasize the benefits and possibilities of originality and creativity, so that experimentation and the expression of ideas and meanings in the arts is encouraged. Those influenced by such models are likely to have access to a variety of arts and styles through all sorts of media channels and environments. In addition, they may be provided with, or encouraged to take, the leisure in which to further their aspirations of performing, playing, creating. Some might be able to do so with the financial assistance and encouragement of their parents. Growing up with a middle-class model of success and conception of how to succeed might thus encourage a relaxed, open-minded approach to music-making and its possibilities. Those provided with such a model, whilst not necessarily encouraged to struggle against, or even question, dominant ideologies, might at least be more likely to be made aware of their existence than are others who presume that is as things are or should be.

Many band members in Liverpool had not had access to such models of thought and creativity. Some said that at school they were made to feel pretentious if they expressed interest in creativity of any sort. In such a context joining a band was seen as a creative and 'different' thing to do and many of those who did so distinguished themselves from those they called 'scallies'. They wanted, said one man explaining why he and his friends joined bands at school, to show that they were just as important as everyone else, and were unable to state or demonstrate that through other means of expression. Peers who showed hostility to that chosen form of expression and creativity did so, he said, because they felt threatened or undermined by it. It did seem as though many such bands viewed their creative efforts differently and sought to achieve different things through them. In general, their members could not afford to spend such a lot of time and financial resources, let alone emotional investment, upon their band and still see it as a hobby or leisure activity, or an art form with which they could experiment and allow themselves the time to develop.

Although not all members of the Jactars and Crikey it's the Cromptons! could be described as middle class, several of them had grown up in a more middle-class environment with access to various channels of thought, creativity, and music-making that might have been denied them had they been from another area or gone to different schools. Encouraged by that and by punk (which, as suggested earlier, involved such thinking and attitudes) they sought to experiment with their music-making and express originality in their music, and had the time, leisure, and space in which to do so. The form and structure of their music and its underlying concepts and meanings reflected this. In contrast, members of several other bands who had originated from less privileged areas of Liverpool, sought ideals of professionalism in their music-making and wanted to entertain with their music and achieve respect for their musical ability. They also attempted, as the Jactars, Crikey it's the Cromptons!, and others phrased it, to 'play the game', and in doing so achieve fame and fortune on a commercial, mass cultural level.

This chapter has emphasized a continuity of ideas and structures throughout musical styles and genres. It has demonstrated, for example, that many other musicians besides the Jactars and Crikey it's the Cromptons! have sought to make music that reflects an aesthetic of simplicity and dissonance, of competent incompetence, 'orderly disorder'. As in the previous chapter, it was suggested that such music was seen by its makers to be natural, pure, spontaneous, and thus honest—hence Cooper's reference to Echo and The Bunnymen's lack of musical expertise as their 'virginity'. In addition, conflict between creativity and commerce has again been highlighted in expressions of anti-commercialism by bands like the Jactars and Crikey it's the Cromptons! (such as in their term 'selling out'), the Who (who felt that instruments as commodities stood between them, their music, and audience), and punk and hippy bands that 'assume an opposition between art and business, between honesty and bureaucracy' (Frith, 1980: 57).

The rebellious attitude of such bands, their challenge to technical and musical proficiency and their stress upon honest, meaningful music and lyrics, illustrates their role in what Frith (1980, 1981, 1983, and 1986) has described as the recurring ideology of folk in rock (as opposed to pop), involving a concept of 'authenticity' opposed to commerce and technology which are seen as 'false'. This ideology, Frith pointed out, developed through romanticism, the folk tradition, and the mass culture debate of the 1920s and 1930s.

The belief in a continuing struggle between music and commerce is the core of rock ideology . . . The assumption is that rock music is good music only when it is not mass culture, when it is an art form or a folk sound (Frith, 1983: 40) . . . mass media critics . . . contrast mass and community, fragmented consumption and collective creation, alienation and solidarity, passivity and activity (ibid.: 48).

Frith (1986) highlighted three ways in which opposition to technology has been expressed: technology is opposed to nature and seen as 'unnatural', to community in that it is said to alienate performers from their audiences, and to art:

The continuing core of rock ideology is that raw sounds are more authentic than cooked sounds . . . A plays to B and the less technology lies between them the closer they are, the more honest their relationship and the fewer the opportunities for manipulation and falsehoods . . . if good music is . . . honest and sincere, bad music is false—and technological changes increase the opportunities for fakery (1986: 266).

However, Frith also (ibid.: 269) mentioned the way in which, paradoxically, 'technological developments have made the rock concept of authenticity possible', which the experiences of the Jactars and Crikey it's the Cromptons! verify: Records have made the music available, and technology can be used in unconventional ways and can benefit or stimulate creativity.

The value placed by bands like the Jactars and Crikey it's the Cromptons! upon authenticity, honesty, and spontaneity in music-making, in opposition to technology and commerce, was also indicated by their quest for originality and distinctiveness. That often involved a personalization of music and music-making through humour, and an emphasis upon creativity, self-expression, and identity. It reflected again the belief that music should be a genuine and natural expression of the emotions, thoughts, and intentions of its makers:

Our music comes from the soul. It's what you would play if you came from a working-class background in Liverpool. Pete Wylie's songs [a well-known rock performer from Liverpool] reflect his upbringing whereas It's Immaterial's [a well-known band from Liverpool] reflect nothing. They know nothing about being on the dole (Blue Nose B).

We are growing, the music it comes from our feelings together and from a natural empathy between us. We play and it comes out, we release it, it is a part of us that we cannot explain, we do not know where it comes from, it is natural (member of New Order, quoted by Edge, 1984: 77).

Authenticity was also emphasized by the desire to create a sound to represent the band which was seen as somehow natural, changing and growing with the band and its members. 'We've moulded ourselves into our own sound', said a member of Blue Nose B.

The expression of and emphasis on such attitudes and values surrounding the notion of authenticity indicates a quest for meaning, a desire to create something meaningful and thereby achieve integrity and self-respect. This was reflected in the mystification of music-making, involving an attitude of secrecy towards composition and performance, and the distortion of lyrics and accents, which heightened the sense of importance involved, as perhaps, did the exclusion of women from music-making. The music-making was thus a male activity, bounded by secrecy, rituals, and masculine values. Morbid, depressing lyrics were associated earlier with the desire to feel 'important'. The existential, pessimistic nature of Tony,

Trav, and Dave's lyrics might again indicate a desire for meaning, reality, and honesty in music-making.

Finally, the quest for meaning was also reflected in the scorn bands like the Jactars and Crikey it's the Cromptons! directed against 'cabaret' music which was seen as meaningless and demeaning, as 'entertainment', a form of 'prostitution'. It is interesting that in general women in Liverpool favoured music that was danceable or romantic in tone. Such music was usually regarded as more commercial than 'rock' and thus associated more strongly with 'entertainment'.

8

The Threat of Women

In drawing together the various themes that have been highlighted so far, this chapter discusses their practical implications regarding the functioning and development of a band, focusing in particular (and largely from the perspective of the men involved) upon the way in which they relate to women, or rather, to the absence of women.

The music and music-making favoured by the Jactars and Crikey it's the Cromptons! was honest and clean; natural, simple, and 'virginal'; but also exciting, alternative, important, and meaningful. Music and music-making of this nature was opposed to that which was dishonest and derivative; dirty and distorted; technical and affected; boring, meaningless, commercial, and soft. The latter was also associated with 'playing the game', 'selling out', and with 'prostitution' (also referred to as 'on the game'). Implicit in this distinction is a notion of purity and impurity and an opposition between that which is real and genuine and that which is just 'a game'. The former has been associated with masculinity and democracy whilst women and femininity have been associated with the latter. This is tantamount to suggesting that women were seen in some way as polluting.

THE ABSENCE OF WOMEN

Women and Rock

When I first began my research I was particularly determined not to ignore women who, in several earlier studies of youth and popular culture, had been treated as socially insignificant, peripheral, stereotyped, or even invisible. I thought it likely that women in mixed social groupings would be subordinate to activities and styles determined by men, but was concerned to look out for ways in which some of them might play a more active or aggressive role than might be expected, or might manipulate male forms and styles to their own advantage. I was astonished, however, to find an overwhelming absence of women in the rock music scene on Merseyside, not only in the bands themselves but in their audiences and many of their social activities.

In general, women are more restricted than men physically and socially by institutions which channel them into marriage and impose upon them moral codes and sexual taboos. Women on Merseyside therefore had different leisure opportunities from those of men and more domestic commitments, and often lacked the access, encouragement, and freedom to indulge in a world of music-making. Those who did become involved tended to be less confident or ambitious about their music-making than their male counterparts. At a local school I visited the younger girls did express interest in playing instruments, and community arts workers told me that girls often participated actively in music workshops. Evidently, however, from the age of 14 onwards something seemed to discourage them from pursuing such interests. It was perhaps what McRobbie (1978) termed 'the Culture of Femininity' that took over so that they became preoccupied with courtship, marriage, and motherhood and adopted different interests from those of boys, such as dancing which, as McRobbie (1984), Frith (1983), and Chambers (1985) pointed out, is one of the few sources of acceptable sexual expression open to girls.

The 'Culture of Femininity' is reinforced by the media which promote unrealistic images of women and of women's dependence upon men. Rock music, for example, is central to youth's social activities and thus plays an important role in the construction and discourse of gender and sexuality. Boys are encouraged to take an interest in the actual making of the music. Young men in Liverpool showed great delight in the simple fact of making noise (as illustrated by the reaction of members of Crikey it's the Cromptons! to Dave T.'s echo unit) and many expressed a general confidence and exhibitionism in their performance of music. Women, on the other hand, are not encouraged to take an interest in the technicalities of sound production and generally lack the confidence to do so. Thus girls' magazines rarely review records or inspire their readers to learn to play instruments or take music seriously. Readers are encouraged instead to concern themselves with the physical appearance of rock performers and with their personalities. This differs considerably from the contents of music journals such as *New Musical Express*, *Melody Maker*, and *Sounds*, all of which have an overwhelmingly male readership (see Frith and McRobbie, 1978: 8).

Gender differences are constructed, maintained, and negotiated not only by the way in which rock music is *used* but by the actual musical styles and their marketing. Frith and McRobbie (1978) emphasized this by contrasting two extremes: 'teenybop' involving soft, feminine male idols of the 'boy next door' type who appeal to young girls in particular, and 'cock rock' involving masculine, phallic, aggressive lyrics and imagery and an emphasis upon live as opposed to recorded performance. Meade (1972) pointed out 'the myths of female inferiority' proclaimed by rock lyrics and described 'the exploitation and dehumanisation of women' in the rock scene both on and off stage, whilst Shepherd (1987) discussed the way in which 'male hegemony' operates not just through lyrics and musical styles but through the actual vocal techniques and sounds produced and adopted by both male and female performers. Sexuality, as portrayed through rock music, has thus been predominantly masculine. Women's perspectives/'voices' have only occasionally been heard— through female singer-songwriters, for example, who express through their music the feminist concept of 'personal politics'.

Punk rock *did* inspire many women to make music because it demystified the process of music-making as a band and promoted lack of musical expertise as an advantage instead of a hindrance. Female punk performers often challenged traditional romantic conventions and styles, including that of the passive female singer and entertainer. However, punk was still an expression of masculinity and aggression (Laing, 1985, for example, has written on naming and phallic symbolism in punk), and although a movement named 'Rock Against Sexism' emerged from it which aimed to promote more positive images of women in rock and encourage women to form bands and play instruments, the movement disintegrated, perhaps reflecting the splintering and diffusion of the women's movement itself.

Punk might have challenged images of women in popular music but it did little to change their career opportunities. Steward and Garratt (1984) presented a positive account of women in rock, focusing upon the few women working in the typically male domains of the music business such as studio engineering and record production. However, in the record industry men still usually occupy every important role while women are restricted to lower, non-creative jobs. As performers women still tend to be packaged as traditional, stereotyped, male images of women (though there are obviously several well-known exceptions, such as Madonna, upon whom most of the feminist writing on rock music seems to be currently focused) and few are instrumentalists. In order to gain control over their music and image many women have to work outside of the male-dominated rock industry in the independent sector or on their own. In doing so they miss out on wider audiences. The sexism of rock music content and practice is reflected by controllers of TV and radio in the images and material they choose to present, and it permeates the whole ideology of rock, with women of very diverse styles being lumped together and labelled as 'women in rock', when often the only thing they have in common is their gender, or being written out of rock history altogether just as with different musical genres, art forms, and many other histories written by men (see Placksin, 1985, for example, on women in jazz, and Steward and Garratt, 1984, and Greta Kent, 1983, on women-only bands of various musical styles).

My impression is that although women are, in general, notably absent from rock music, that absence was particularly noticeable in Liverpool. While living there I acted as secretary for the Sefton Area Musicians and Bands Association. Of the fourteen bands in the association, totalling sixty-six performers, only one member was female (a vocalist). A compilation album of local bands released around that time and funded by Liverpool City Council was entitled 'Jobs For the Boys'. When a local female performer tried to raise funding for one entitled 'Jobs For the Girls' none was forthcoming, but in any case she had trouble finding enough female artists to fill the album, and when a local community centre decided to stage an event entitled 'Women and Music', they too had difficulty finding local all-women groups or even an organizer for the event. The latter, along with the main performers, were eventually recruited from outside Merseyside. In 1989 I conducted a survey of the local music industries for Liverpool City Council. 252 people running businesses or services within the various industries were consulted. Only 18 of them were women.

A Community Arts apprentice in St Helens found that the music workshops she was involved with were all-male. Girls from the local community told her that they didn't participate in the workshops because they were criticized and called 'slags' for wanting to do something that was mainly a boy's activity and received verbal and physical abuse from the boys. She consequently set up an 'all-girls' night at the community centre, but the boys objected, threw bricks through the windows, waited for the girls outside and threatened them with violence. The girls wrote and recorded a rap song about that situation and it was broadcast over loudspeakers to the whole estate. It was only then that the girls were granted status and respect from the boys.

Liverpool and Merseyside might have been quite extreme in this respect because gender differences, particularly amongst the working classes, were marked. There was some segregation of men and women's cultural and social activities (on a Friday or Saturday night the city centre would be frequented by large single-sex groups on their way to or from a club or bar), and a tension between the sexes often emerged. Many male band members showed lack of respect, liking, and understanding of their female peers. That was directed against local women in particular. Women elsewhere—in London for example—were said to be more 'liberal' and 'intelligent'.

Lane (1987) suggested that the 'masculine' character of Liverpool arose from its role as a port. 'A reputation for adventurousness', "heroic" drinking exploits and sexual "conquests" were a critical part of a sailor's credentials and gave him the reputation of being a "real man"' (ibid.: 101 and 102). This production of an image and an ideal of a desirable, free-wheeling life of adventure and independence was significant. Furthermore, port activity depended upon casual labour. That insecurity in the employment of the men of the family meant that work done by the women was very important: 'The organization and management of survival was, of course, done by women. Teenage boys and men, for their part, could escape to the ships' (ibid.: 96–7). Consequently, women were usually the focus of domestic life. Band members tended to refer to home as 'me mum's' even when both parents lived there. Many men had no work by which to assume their role as providers and, even if they had, that work often bestowed lower status than did the world of football and music to which many had turned. Consequently, football and music had become a male domain.

The absence of women might have been further enforced by the fact that many local bands, following on from the Beatles and others, emphasized music-making as a business and a career, which made the desire to make it a more exclusively male preserve that much stronger. Finally, the lack of active student involvement in the local music scene might also indicate why women seemed so conspicuous in their absence, as the activities and music tastes of female students tended to be more compatible with those of their male peers.

As a woman myself, I was unable to become 'one of the lads' and initially my presence might have made some people uneasy. It is possible, however, that a male researcher might not have been tolerated for so long or might have been regarded as more intrusive or suspicious. Consequently, certain information might have been withheld from him whereas it might have been presumed that as a woman I was too naïve to abuse or misuse it. Nevertheless, my activities obviously conflicted with those normally expected of a woman. I attended gigs alone, expressed interest in the technicalities of music-making and in the attitudes and concerns of those who made it, and contradicted in other respects most women many of the band members were familiar with.

The women who *were* involved in the Liverpool music scene were mostly backing singers and non-instrumentalists. They formed a sort of floating population since they did not play as great a role in the bands or music scene as did the men, and generally allocated less time and commitment to music-making. Even female instrumentalists usually found that they were not treated as equal members of the band by their male counterparts and were ignored during conversations and decision-making. In addition, they often encountered distrust, at both a personal and professional level, from women as well as from men. One musician was certain that her performance was viewed more critically and judged more harshly when her audience could see she was a woman and admitted that she did the same herself when she saw other female musicians. 'You just assume they are there to add glamour and not for their performance abilities.' A local band manager also expressed suspicion of girls in bands because he suspected they were there merely to enhance the visual image of the band and add 'sex appeal'.

Thus many men did not want such women in their band because they saw them as inferior musicians and the women had to work much harder than their male counterparts in order to prove themselves. Outside performances they were often mistaken for girlfriends of male band members and, since the performance circuit was controlled by men, it was difficult for women to organize things themselves. One musician described how she had approached the manager of a venue to discuss arrangements for her performance and he had insisted upon addressing his remarks to her boyfriend who accompanied her, even though the latter pointed out that it had nothing to do with him but was her affair.

Distrust of women musicians was also expressed by record industry personnel. Two such musicians who worked alone said that A&R men they spoke to did not like the idea of women in control of their own music-making and suggested that they would be better off working with someone else, or presumed that they were just temporarily dabbling in music and would soon give up and settle down into domesticity. Furthermore, men in the music business tended to view women performers in sexual, marketable terms. Even a band such as the Iconoclasts, a local punk band playing a loud, forceful style of music with a corresponding visual image, that used to be all-female but now had one male member, found that they were not taken seriously by men they had to deal with and were, as they put it, 'classed as pairs of tits on stage'. They were consequently persuaded to take on a manager to represent them. In addition, they had to cope with abuse from largely male audiences and had composed a song entitled 'Perverts' to dedicate to whoever happened to be shouting the abuse. The one man in the band also had to put up with much teasing and joking, particularly from male colleagues at work.

Women performers such as those tended to be treated as a gimmick. The Iconoclasts were seen as a novelty and thus a saleable product. Consequently, when We've Got A Fuzzbox And We're Gonna Use It, an all-women band similar in style, achieved national success, it was said by others and by the Iconoclasts themselves that now the Iconoclasts would never make it, as if, as a gimmick, once it had been done it could not be repeated:

It may sound cruel, but within the confines of the American music we all once went potty over, The Bangles have outgrown their use. A bit like our very own Slits in fact—another band who never realized that being an all-girl group is a notoriously dodgy gimmick to base a career on (Mat Smith, *Melody Maker*: 15 March 1986).

Similarly, the Jactars once considered getting a female drummer because they were currently in vogue within the circle of bands they admired and would also have 'novelty value', whilst the manager of Ryan, commenting on all the well-known bands with female backing vocalists, said: 'It's a bit of a cliché having a female singer in a band.' In 1989, at a seminar on the music business organized by the Musicians' Union and held in Liverpool, the head of A&R at London Records commented, after discussing the success of solo performers such as Michelle Shocked and Tanita Tikaram, 'The trouble really at the moment is that there is a glut of female singer-songwriters.'

As pointed out earlier, local audiences for rock bands also tended to be overwhelmingly male. Male band members socialized together because they had a lot in common and because their band membership took much of their time so many had few female friends to attend their performances. The maleness of their gigs probably deterred more women from attending, as did the nature and location of the venues in which so many gigs were performed.

There were few independent or successful women in Liverpool's music scene. Penny and Kate who managed Just William and Up the Khyber, became involved largely in order to help their ambitious boyfriends who had formed the bands they managed, but Penny disliked the way that people always categorized them as such: 'She manages a band because her boyfriend's the singer.' Neither woman was ambitious for herself though each was very capable and intelligent. Both described problems they encountered with men in the music business but mentioned that they had also been able to use their femininity to their advantage.

Penny described some of the ways in which a woman could assert herself and her opinions in the music scene. Her involvement with it had, she said, given her, 'a peculiar tolerance of sexism and a lesson in "gamesmanship"'. Her attempts to 'interfere' musically were staged in a deliberately confrontational manner. She emphasized her influence over her boyfriend and, since respect for her opinions was never going to be a realistic option, resorted to 'childish, foot-stamping histrionics'. She developed as a result: 'a completely split personality: a woman certain of her ideas and aims but unsure of her role, becoming even more extreme in order to get her ideas across.' She also found the need to 'distance (myself) from other women in the music scene who were so despised'. Consequently, she became critical of them.

Women as Intruders

Women were not simply absent from the music scene but were *actively* excluded. Some girlfriends did help with the organization of a band and attended performances, but many were discouraged or barred from membership of bands or from the band's rehearsals, recordings, performances, and other social activities. Initially it might have been an ego boost for a band member to have his girlfriend present. Often, however, she would tire of it and so would he and the other band members and her presence would no longer be tolerated. Various explanations for this were proffered by the men. Generally they liked to be 'with the lads'. This was by no means peculiar to Liverpool or to rock musicians. Wilmer (1987: 195) wrote on black American jazz performers:

A number of musicians' wives are actually involved in their work through soliciting and arranging gigs for them, answering their mail, completing their tax returns, compiling publicity and aiding their application for grants, as well as encouraging them to create even in their darkest moments. Yet the idea of a wife or any woman being involved to the extent of following them on gigs or turning up at rehearsals is generally considered restricting. These are times when they want to relax in an all-male environment.

The five members of one particular band got on well with each other, frequently enjoying what they called 'having a laff', particularly on a Saturday night when they went clubbing. Their girlfriends stayed at home. I only met one of the women once. Individually, a band member might occasionally refer to another's 'girlfriend', but when the men were together their girlfriends were rarely mentioned. Months later I discovered that three of those 'girlfriends' were in fact wives and mothers. The drummer became a father around the time I first met the band yet I had heard nothing of it.

It was clear, after discussing this with members of that band and others, that marriage and fatherhood did not suit the image many bands wished to present. One said of a fellow band member that he didn't like people to know he had a wife and child and was embarrassed when they found out. Davies (1985) and Leigh (1984) pointed out a similar sense of embarrassment experienced by John Lennon and other Liverpool musicians during the 1960s. An unmarried member of the above-mentioned band expressed hostility towards the wives of his colleagues and saw them as little as possible. The wives rarely went out with the band or attended performances and he felt it would not be fair if they did otherwise; neither he nor the others would put up with it. His unmarried colleague once got annoyed when the drummer cancelled a rehearsal because he had to stay at home and babysit. He said that he wouldn't mind other excuses but hated something like that—'It's just not on.' Similarly, Wilmer (1987: 193) wrote:

the musician who puts his wife and family before the music has always tended to be rejected by the subculture. The group itself frequently takes the place of the conventional family, especially when there is little work to be had and the musicians come together often to play and develop a corporate philosophy.

Wilmer quoted the wife of such a musician who said: 'You must realize that the music is first and a woman is next. He's not going to give up the music for a woman, but he could give up the woman for the music' (ibid.: 194).

On several occasions I was informed that two things split up a band: women and money. Many reminded me of the breakup of the Beatles, attributing it to Yoko Ono's relationship with John Lennon, and at the time the media also blamed the splitting up of the Beatles on the women in their lives (see Davies, 1985: 279 and 436). Some band members adamantly declared, 'We're not gonna let girls split us up', or banned women from rehearsals because 'We take it dead serious.' Many complained that women were a distraction at rehearsals because they created tension within the band and pressurized the band's members to talk to them or take them home. They were also said to object to their boyfriends spending so much time with the band. One musician described how his girlfriend of four years, fed up with the amount of time he spent with his band, asked him which was more important, her or the band. He replied that the band was and she moved out. A local manager believed that men tended in any case to get on better with each other than with women which was why all-male bands survived longer than bands of both sexes. Another man declared assertively, 'No beef [i.e. women] in this band!', and described how the band had just 'sacked' its female member because she created 'sexual tensions' among the other male members. A member of East Of Eden said that he either went out with the band or with his girlfriend but never mixed the two: 'You have a different time with girls than with blokes. Girls get offended by our jokes.' A fellow member nodded in agreement saying, 'It doesn't mix', whilst a third commented: 'The best way to split up a band is to get girlfriends involved.'

Paradoxically, many band members suggested that others joined bands for the sole purpose of enhancing their image and thereby attracting women. Few knew of any so-called 'groupies', but several said the fact that they were in a band did make them more attractive to women. It was hard to verify this amongst the bands I knew best but the more famous or commercial bands, and those with particularly handsome members, did attract women, as did bands that played music of a cabaret style, presumably because the nature of that music and the venues in which it was performed were more attractive to women. Some members of those cabaret bands described how women 'threw' themselves at them at gigs and said they could have gone home with a different woman each night if they wished. In fact, the rate of divorce amongst them seemed significantly high.

It is ironic that the success of many bands, especially those that performed more commercial styles of music and aimed for major record companies and chart success, depended upon their appeal to women, who form the bulk of young record buyers. Typically it was the men who were the performers, the stars, whilst women were their admirers. Thus members of Some Party spoke one afternoon of their exclusion of girlfriends from rehearsals and performances, yet that same evening performed in a local school to an audience of screaming teenage girls. The adoration embarrassed them yet they realized that their future depended upon it.

One of the local women who managed her boyfriend's band pointed out that there were very few 'ways in' to the music scene for a woman, and being a girlfriend was still the easiest. In addition, she suggested two factors that made a rock musician such an appealing boyfriend. Firstly there was the 'glamour' factor:

The girlfriend basks in the reflected glory of her boyfriend. She wants other people to be envious of her. However, for this to work she needs opportunities to show him off. If she's excluded too much from the band's activities she'll become resentful and see the band as 'competition'. She'll interfere, she'll make demands . . . and she'll constantly engineer situations so that her boyfriend is being tested in his loyalty to her versus the band. The band becomes 'the other woman'. It's the reason women are attracted initially to band members and then seem to be so destructive to a band.

Secondly, there was the 'creative' factor—'the thinking woman's version of glamour': The woman is tolerant of her boyfriend's faults which are often put down to artistic temperament. Furthermore, 'writing a song about you, or for you, is worth a whole year's supply of flowers'.

It is also ironic that when musicians were questioned about their musical experiences with regard to their childhood and family life, the hidden importance of the women in their lives was often revealed. Usually it was the mothers that encouraged their sons' musical activities, perhaps taking them to music lessons at an early age and paying for lessons and instruments, providing them with the physical space to rehearse in within the home, or passing on to them enthusiasm for music, and music traditions. It was often the mothers, grand-mothers, and aunts, who played the piano within the home, remember-ing song lyrics and encouraging singing within a family context.

TENSION AND CRISIS

This section documents three changes in membership involving the Jactars and Crikey it's the Cromptons! in order to demonstrate one way in which the exclusion of women by band members from the band and its music-making world might operate in practice. All three situations constituted periods of uncertainty or crisis for the bands and each, in one way or another, involved women.

Crisis Number 1

The Jactars, as mentioned earlier, were considered a mild-mannered, close-knit, harmonious group and one of those least expected to split up. Yet at the beginning of June 1986 Gary left the band, much to the surprise of his fellow members, Crikey it's the Cromptons!, and other bands at Vulcan Studios. However, although Gary's departure appeared sudden and unexpected, it became increasingly clear that it resulted from a combination of social and artistic factors which had created underlying tensions within the band.

The Jactars' method of composition and rehearsal necessitated, as described in Chapter 6, close contact and understanding between all four members but it was particularly dependent upon the friendship and partnership of Trav and Dave. In January Dave moved over to Liverpool and a few months later his work on a Community Programme Scheme increased from one to three days a week. He began to socialize more with colleagues from work and returned to West Kirby less. Meanwhile Trav was spending more time with Karen and never visited Dave, so the two of them saw less of each other. In the spring Tog also moved to Liverpool. Neither he, nor Dave, nor Gary had a telephone now so communication between themselves and Trav became a problem. From February onwards the band experienced difficulties composing new material, a creative block that became more and more frustrating, and rehearsals became less frequent.

During this time Gary became depressed due to domestic and financial problems and Tog and Trav argued about which sound engineer to use for the band's next recording. After the argument Dave confided his belief that problems were brewing up in the band. He said that there were a number of factors involved and the argument over the recording was just a part of it. He emphasized that it was a matter of 'musical direction' rather than of social causes and, as pointed out in Chapter 6, indicated that the real problem concerned Tog and the difference between Tog's musical views and ideas and those of Trav and himself. Unlike Dave and Trav, Tog also lacked ambition and wasn't too concerned about whether the band would 'make it' or not. He had never contributed much to the composition of the music but had, since joining the band, gained a great deal in confidence, particularly through working in the office at Vulcan Studios. Consequently, he now commented more freely during rehearsals, as illustrated by the argument over the sound engineer.

Trav's attitude, according to Dave, was that since Tog didn't contribute much to the composition of the music he had no right to determine where or how it should be recorded. When Tog insisted on playing bass for a new song, arguing that keyboards wouldn't be appropriate, Trav remarked: 'Isn't it about time you came up with your own songs, Tog, instead of criticizing other people's?' Dave believed that the buildup of such friction was the main cause of the band's recent creative block. The recording of the demo tape in mid-May was a subdued affair and no one seemed enthusiastic about the results. Gary didn't even turn up for the final 'mix'. During May the band hardly rehearsed at all.

When I mentioned the lack of communication within the band to Gary after he had left he agreed that it had been one of the main reasons for his leaving. Recently, he said, 'the atmosphere at rehearsals could be cut with a knife'. The social aspect of the band was shattered and there had been no enjoyment in it any more. He also said that although he appreciated the music the band made it didn't accord with his own personal tastes, and whilst he thought the band had 'a formula' and might 'make it' if they worked hard, he didn't think the others had the right 'professional' approach. He believed that a band should make some effort to present a glamorous, marketable image and he personally would aim for major record companies and 'big money'. He realized that the Jactars were trying to maintain artistic credibility but said, 'like it or not it's a business'.

Trav and Dave were annoyed with Gary for leaving. Dave worried about what the band would do without a drummer, frustrated that they should experience such a set-back just when other bands at Vulcan appeared to be 'getting somewhere'. Trav was more optimistic and thought it just as well that 'bad blood' had been eliminated. Gary had not been enthusiastic recently so the band would be better off without him. His departure might also bring the remaining three of them closer together. Trav and Dave were keen to discover Gary's reasons for leaving. They knew that his musical tastes were different from theirs but were surprized to learn the extent of that difference. Both believed that Gary left because he had started to go out with Nula, an ex-girlfriend of Trav's. Trav suggested that Gary's main reason for joining a band in the first place had been to get a girlfriend so he now had no reason to be in one any more. Both were dubious when they heard that Gary intended to spend the summer working in a slate mine before trying his luck at acting and believed that his main motive was to impress Nula. Later I suggested to Gary that many might join a band in order to attract a girlfriend. He agreed that might be the case but did not believe it would be effective.

Gary intended to continue playing drums and perhaps join a more 'rocky' band, but said he would take his time and wouldn't advertise himself. A few weeks later, however, a notice appeared on the board in the Vulcan office advertising for a bass player to join Gary and a guitarist. In September Tony reported that Gary wanted to rejoin the Jactars. The Jactars decided against it since Gary had let them down so badly.

Around the time of Gary's departure Tog and members of Crikey it's the Cromptons! began to comment more upon Trav's relationship with Karen. Tog mentioned how rarely he saw Trav nowadays and attributed it to Trav's involvement with Karen saying, 'He's still obsessed with her, to the point of not socializing with Dave, which I think is a mistake.' Karen and Trav did join the others at parties, gigs, clubs, and pubs, and Karen attended some rehearsals, but the two of them often sat together, removed from the others. Criticism of this grew stronger during the summer. The others were annoyed when Trav missed social occasions to stay at home with Karen or when he and Karen left them early to get the last train home. Tony expressed disgust at the way 'Karen has completely taken over Trav's life', and was appalled that Trav should have allowed himself to be 'closeted off' from the others.

Huw said that they were becoming increasingly annoyed that Trav no longer socialized or got drunk with them and also blamed this upon his involvement with Karen, saying that he and Dave (both of whom had just split up with their girlfriends) had been plotting ways of getting Karen away from Trav. Huw believed that Karen, although not averse to drinking herself, objected to Trav getting drunk and described how disappointing the evening of Trav's birthday had been because Karen had been there which meant that the others had hardly spoken to Trav at all.

Similar situations arose in other bands. Members of East Of Eden, for example, explained that the singer of the band didn't socialize with them because his girlfriend didn't want him to. On the one hand, she liked the idea of being the girlfriend of the singer of a band, but on the other she felt threatened by it because she worried what would happen to her if he became famous. The other band members resented her and were particularly annoyed when at one of their performances the singer had felt pressurized to dedicate one of *their* songs to her.

When I asked Trav if he thought his relationship with Karen had in any way affected his involvement with the Jactars he thought about it for a while and decided that generally it hadn't, although he did add that, if anything, it meant he no longer spent hour upon hour strumming his guitar on his own during the day. Later, however, during another conversation, he did comment that he no longer socialized with the others as much as he used to and supposed that might have something to do with Karen. He agreed that socializing with fellow band members was important for the success of the creative process.

Obviously a number of social and artistic factors could be seen to have caused this crisis in the Jactars. Social factors included: the lack of communication between the band members which was partly due to the geographical movement of some of them, Trav's relationship with Karen, and Dave's job commitments; Tog's gain in confidence and the consequent friction between him and Trav; Gary's domestic and financial problems, his and Tog's ambitions for the band which contrasted with those of Trav and Dave, and his desire for a girlfriend. Artistic factors included the method of composition and rehearsal adopted by the Jactars which necessitated close contact and understanding between all members; Gary and Tog's musical aesthetics which differed from those of Trav and Dave; and finally, Tog's musical skills and his preference for playing bass rather than keyboards. None of those factors could be pinpointed as an overriding cause and many could have been either causes or effects of the friction within the band. Yet during conversations after Gary's departure it was those factors involving women that were particularly emphasized.

Crisis Number 2

Karen had sung with other bands before joining Crikey it's the Cromptons! but still lacked confidence and was understandably embarrassed to perform some of the lyrics and noises that Tony presented her with. She was thus usually inaudible at rehearsals and performances. In addition, she was not treated as an equal member of the band by the others and was generally ignored. At rehearsals she often sat in a corner reading a book whilst the others continued regardless. She rarely interrupted to ask what she should do and it is probable that a man in a similar position would have been less willing to sit in silence and, moreover, that the band would not have allowed him to do so. Karen was also not invited to accompany the others on a visit to record companies in London despite the fact that they invited me shortly after meeting me for the first time. It was only once, after Tony praised her latest public performance with the band, that I heard Karen participate as a member of the band by suggesting which particular songs they might rehearse. Karen began to attend fewer rehearsals and performances but the others rarely seemed to note or comment upon her absence.

Tony frequently talked about replacing Karen. He liked her, he said, but she was a terrible backing vocalist and he would prefer someone who was louder with more confidence and exuberance, someone who would 'dance around and go crazy on the singing'. He also wanted someone who looked good—not that Karen looked bad he added, but she didn't really have the right image. The new singer had, of course, to be female, said Tony when I asked, and he wanted her to wear 'skimpy dresses'. At the end of March Kathy, sister of Dave T., turned up at a rehearsal dressed in stilettos and tight jeans. She had been at a recent gig of Crikey it's the Cromptons! when it had been suggested (debatably by her or by Tony) that she sing with the band. Tony had urged her to attend the next rehearsal.

For the first time in a while Karen also turned up. It was a rather awkward situation, but Karen appeared calm and the others were distracted by the presence of a potential new saxophone player so Karen and Kathy were left sitting with nothing to do for most of the time—except when Tony persuaded first Kathy and later Karen to fetch him some beer from a local off-licence. Kathy's presence was not commented upon until Dave T. arrived and asked Tony, in Karen's absence, whether it was all right with Karen that Kathy was there. Tony, looking slightly uncomfortable, assured Dave that it was fine and that basically they could only have one backing vocalist so the best one would remain. Kathy interrupted to say that she didn't want to push anyone out, and Tony, inhibited by the others, tried to convey to her what he felt about Karen as a backing vocalist, concluding, 'Quite honestly, you look more the part.' Kathy retorted that that was all very well but she couldn't sing, whereupon Tony said he was sure she could, adding, 'Basically, you've got to be very mercenary about this sort of thing.' Midi commented that he didn't see why they couldn't have two backing singers. Tony appealed to Huw but the latter shrugged and replied that it had nothing to do with him.

They continued rehearsing while Kathy and Karen sat patiently waiting to be told what to do. Eventually, they were given microphones and Kathy was instructed to follow Karen's lead. She proved just as inaudible and hesitant in her singing as Karen but they didn't have much to sing and later, when Trav came in to watch, Karen mouthed 'I'm bored' at him. After the rehearsal, on the way to the pub, I questioned Huw and Midi about the situation. Midi thought Kathy would be good for the band but hoped it would be all right with Karen. He thought Karen had been improving and could improve further with encouragement from the more flamboyant Kathy. Huw agreed that Karen was still weak but worried that Kathy was too unreliable. He said that the problem with bringing friends (like Karen) into a band was that you couldn't ask them to leave. He was glad to leave it all to Tony.

At the next rehearsal I spoke to Karen, who was obviously upset by Kathy's arrival but good-natured about it, despite the fact that her last public performance with the band had gone so well that she had gained confidence, resolving to make more of an effort. She pointed out that there wasn't enough work for one backing vocalist let alone two, but said she would see how it went. I asked her why she didn't try to expand her singing role and she replied that she had mentioned it to Tony once or twice when he was really drunk. Kathy did not appear at this rehearsal and nor did Dave T. so there was very little practice and everyone became despondent. After several hours Karen, who had been sitting in a corner reading a book, still wet with rain after her long journey to the studio, asked Tony (without hint of sarcasm), 'Is it all right if I go now?'

In April Tony brusquely informed the others that Karen was no longer in the band and had been 'sacked'. Midi objected but Tony insisted that Karen was too 'static'. He couldn't get along with her when she was in the band and thus couldn't get on with Trav either. Karen assured Tony that she would try much harder and attended one more rehearsal before Tony declared that she was now definitely out of the band. He'd had a word with Trav and told him Karen wasn't in the band any more so that was that. As Kathy seemed to have given up attending rehearsals (she had only ever been to two) Tony suggested they advertise for a new backing vocalist but Huw said they had enough to work on as it was.

Midi was sad Karen was no longer with the band because he really liked her. He pointed out, however, that it wasn't really her type of music and that her voice was suited to a more 'melodic' style. He also, quoting Mick Jagger, said that 90 per cent of rock'n'roll came from below the waist: 'In other words, rock'n'roll is a very sexual thing and Karen is not a very sexual person.' An additional remark prompted Tony to state that what Karen needed was 'a good raping'.

Karen was ejected from Crikey it's the Cromptons! despite the fact that she was friendly with the other members, socialized with them, and frequently got drunk with them. Again, her departure resulted from a combination of social and artistic factors. As one woman amongst many men she lacked confidence and encouragement, was often excluded from participating in and discussing band affairs, and was appraised in terms of her sexuality and image in addition to musical ability. As Trav's girlfriend she was also felt to threaten the friendship between the men. Tony, for example, felt that her relationship with Trav affected his own relationship with him, perhaps partly because Trav was sympathetic to Karen's position in the band.

Coincidentally, as Karen's career with Crikey it's the Cromptons! was ending, the Da Vincis were parting company with Faith, their drummer. They criticized her drumming skills but it was clear that she and the singer/founder of the band were also at odds for social reasons. In addition, Faith didn't drink and did not therefore join the others in the pub after rehearsals. When they found a male replacement the atmosphere within the band changed and they all began to socialize together more and enjoy themselves more. Consequently, they reported a great improvement in their music and their performance of it.

Crisis Number 3

In July Midi started seeing a woman he soon became serious about. In his usual jovial manner he talked of moving in with her, buying her a ring, and marrying her. That same month Tony anxiously reported that Karen had told him that Midi's new girlfriend seemed to have completely taken him over and, if she wanted to, could probably stop him playing in the band.

A few days later Midi left the band. He rang Tog at Vulcan to inform him of his decision and then rang Huw. He explained that he had a lot of commitments at the moment, including babysitting for his girlfriend's son while she was at work. He sounded definite so Huw did not try to dissuade him but visited Tony to break the news. They were all shocked. It seemed to have come completely 'out of the blue'. Midi had never given any indication that he was about to quit and seemed as keen as ever to remain with the band. His departure was a real set-back to the band, especially as it coincided with Dave T.'s move to London and they would thus have little rehearsal time in which to initiate a new bass player. 'Something like this', said Huw, 'brings you to a total halt.' However, much to the annoyance of the Jactars who still hadn't found a permanent drummer, Crikey it's the Cromptons! had, within the space of a few days, acquired Pete (boyfriend of Dave T.'s sister Kathy) as bass player.

Tony was particularly upset by Midi's departure. He felt very close to Midi and enjoyed his company. He telephoned him to persuade him to stay but according to Tony 'he was a different Midi'. Tony suggested they go for a drink sometime but although Midi agreed Tony said he 'sounded as though he didn't really mean it'. The others shook their heads over the matter. Tog reported that it had been entirely Midi's decision and that his girlfriend in fact urged him not to leave the band in case he regretted it. Both Tog and Tony were sure that Midi would regret it, that it would be one of the biggest mistakes he had ever made. All agreed that Midi left because at the age of 28 he felt he should be married and settled down, and that was verified by Midi himself who told Dave T. when Dave rang him to ask about his decision to quit, that basically he just wanted to look after his girlfriend's son in the house he and she were now renting and eventually get a good job. Tony couldn't understand this and said that Midi had been so much a part of Crikey it's the Cromptons! he was irreplaceable. He and the others continued to talk about Midi with fondness and began to reminisce about him and his idiosyncrasies. Meanwhile, none of them heard from Midi besides Karen who worked with him. She and Trav reported that Midi had changed and they didn't get on with him so well any more. He had become 'domestic' and 'different'. Pete stayed with the band though at first they missed Midi's characteristic bass lines and worried that Pete would not fit in musically or with the band's image.

One noticeable consequence of Midi's departure was that Tony in particular occasionally directed rather angry remarks at women, particularly at girlfriends of other band members. He expressed disgust, for example, at how Trav was 'under Karen's thumb', and later worried that Kathy might interfere with the band and with Pete's involvement in it. Something would have to be done about it, he said, 'We'll have to try and get rid of her.' Later he commented that girlfriends were 'bad news for bands'.

The causes of Midi's departure were obviously his relationship with a new girlfriend and his accompanying motivations to 'settle down' and get a 'proper' job.

THE FISSILE STRUCTURE OF BANDS

Crises often arose in bands. Men joined bands for the social and artistic factors involved, but under pressure those factors could conflict, giving rise to certain tensions and contradictions that gave the band its fissile nature and surfaced during arguments and rifts. Thus the professed democratic, egalitarian nature of bands like the Jactars and Crikey it's the Cromptons! concealed the fact that within them the contrasting musical aesthetics and influences of their members, as well as their assessment of each other's musical abilities, often conflicted with the bonds of friendship between them. The personal ambitions of individual band members also conflicted with collective ambitions as those individuals exploited their membership of the band to achieve their own ends whilst at the same time working for the good of the band as a whole. In addition, although members of a band might, as with the Jactars, claim collective composition of their music and organization of the band, in reality their individual contributions varied. Thus at a time of stress Gary and Tog's lack of contribution was emphasized. Such frictions and tensions overlaid, and could result from, the nature of the social relationships existing within the band incorporating clashes of personality, lack of communication, or personal problems and grievances outside the band.

The social and artistic factors involved in the life of the band were thus interrelated, shaping and affecting each other. Each time someone explained to me why a fellow musician or manager had left the band or had been 'sacked' their explanation encompassed both social and artistic reasons. Members of East Of Eden, for example, said they 'sacked' their bass player because his tastes in music differed from theirs, he wasn't as committed to the future of the band as they were, and he didn't socialize with them as much as they felt he should. The manager of another band, explaining why she 'sacked' the band's drummer, said that his drumming was not good enough, he smoked too much, and he was too friendly with another member of the band of whom she wasn't particularly fond. Between the two of them, she explained, they would get one-fifth of the band's royalties even though they didn't write any of the songs. She sacked one of them in the knowledge that the other would then probably leave the band of his own accord. Davies (1985: 211) wrote of the sacking of Pete Best from the Beatles and assessments of his drumming skills:

What makes or doesn't make a good drummer is hard to define, but as a personality there is some evidence to suggest that Pete had not fitted in . . . Pete presumed he was a proper part of the group, after so long, and was naturally surprized when the end came . . . The Beatles themselves did feel a bit guilty, but they say that it was a joint decision . . . They'd never felt that Pete was one of them and it was only a matter of time.

In the three cases discussed above the same set of 'redressive mechanisms' (Turner, 1957) were put into action to try to resolve the problems or crises that had arisen. For example, when it came to finding a replacement for the departed member, in each case the bands resorted to the network of mutual obligation and support within which they were involved. Thus Dave T.'s friend Pete was brought in to replace Midi and Huw stood in for Gary. Although the latter was supposed to be a temporary arrangement and the Jactars worried initially about whether Huw's drumming style would be appropriate, he stayed with the band and everyone was happy that he should continue to do so. This was despite the fact that the Jactars had auditioned other drummers whom they didn't know as well and had found one or two whose musical skills and style they were quite pleased with.

Secondly, after each crisis there was a reassertion of the desire to 'make it' and new plans were made for the band. This united the band's members by emphasizing their common plight and goals. In addition, both Midi and Gary were said to have changed personality after leaving their band, whilst Karen was usually referred to in the context of her relationship with Trav and was said to dominate him and seclude him from the others. Gary was seen only occasionally after he left the band and the others reported that he had changed and had acquired 'weird' ideas about music. For the first time they commented that he still owed one of them some money (which he had been lent a long time previously) and had never put as much effort into the band as themselves, being lazy, for example, about putting away equipment. Such accusations and comments served to estrange the departed further from the band and thus justify their departure from it, which again helped to unite the remaining members. The collective activity of music-making also served to heal rifts and frictions. Thus music, as Turner suggested of ritual (1957: 302), 'contrives to stimulate in its members sentiments of . . . unity, of general belonging together, which transcend the irreparable divisions and conflicts of interests in the social structure'.

Finally, in all three situations women (Karen and the girlfriends of Gary and Midi) were both directly and indirectly identified as the *main* cause of schism or friction and thus used as scapegoats, given the role of villain and blamed for the tensions and crises that had arisen. That occurred because the women were marginal or outsiders and because they were a channel or means through which men might leave the band and they therefore threatened the unity of the male group. For the same reason women in many other cultures and societies are also blamed for misfortunes that occur. In many African patrilineal societies, for example, it is familiar practice to use women as a scapegoat, by accusing them of practising witchcraft, in order to maintain the solidarity of the men of the lineage.

This notion of women as a threat to male groups and their creativity is not new. Frith (1983) pointed out that beatnik ideology equated creativity with unconventionality. Women and domesticity were associated with convention and thus seen to threaten men's creativity and independence. Keil (1966) suggested that the show of solidarity among male blues performers in America might indicate, among other things: 'a hardening of the battle lines—the men mustering their forces so as to slug it out on equal terms with the women'. And Frith and McRobbie (1978) noted the way in which some rock lyrics reveal a deep fear of women.

Many men in Liverpool immersed themselves in a world of music, partly in search of identity, fulfilment, and a sense of purpose, and partly in retreat from their domestic and economic environment, both of which were usually outside their control. In doing so they sought the support and companionship of other men. The same could also be said of some sports, such as football which was very popular in Liverpool. Men's loyalties (besides to their mothers) were to their band, their team, their mates. Girlfriends didn't fit into that and to reject the band's social life for a girlfriend was regarded as an act of treachery. Dunning (1986) studied rugby as a 'male preserve' in relation to the 'production and reproduction of masculine identity', developed in response to the increasing threat of women: 'A principal recurrent aspect of rugby songs consists in the fact that they embody a hostile, brutal but, at the same time fearful attitude towards women and the sexual act . . .' (ibid: 84).

It is clear that in some sports, as well as in rock music, women are likely to be feared as intruders into male solidarity and the sports' symbolic forms are likely to convey that fear of, and hostility towards, women. Hargreaves (1986: 111) pointed out that sport is 'much more significant, with respect to the production and reproduction of masculine identity', than Dunning and others suggest, with the 'ideological dimension' being crucial. Hargreaves wrote of the symbolism of male power, activity, and beauty that, 'present the male models as virile, and an object of emulation for men and desire for women.' Thus both sport and rock music offered young men, amongst other things, a respectable fantasy incorporating images of masculinity and power.

In the security of their male groups, and perhaps under the matronly eye of a manager, band members in Liverpool indulged in acts of self-display, exhibitionism, and courtship directed at women yet conducted under the cover of a misogynist language and ideology incorporating comments, metaphors, lyrics, and styles of performance. This expression of male solidarity and narcissism, as well as the exclusion of women and the maintenance of that absence through various means such as the use of women as scapegoats, was a demonstration of male power and virility, yet at the same time it also revealed the fear that women might break down men's defences, dissolve their group and thus undermine their confidence and identity, and drag them off into domesticity and femaleness. It could thus be seen as a defensive reaction to the divisiveness and threat of women—yet that danger is also seductive and attractive. The treatment of women could be likened to the way in which the Liverpudlian sense of humour was characterized earlier—as revealing an 'I'll-put-you-down-before-you-put-me-down' attitude. Similarly, the masturbatory imagery at gigs was described earlier as an assertion of men's independence from women, a declaration of the fact that they don't need women. Women, as far as the music scene was concerned, were thus strongly present in their absence.

Conclusion

In this book I have attempted to delineate and discuss rock culture in Liverpool as a way of life, with its own conventions, rituals, norms, and beliefs among struggling, grass-roots bands situated at a particular point in time within the particular socio-economic, political and cultural conditions of one British city environment. Discussion focused in detail upon actual social practices, processes, and interactions in musical creation and performance 'on the ground'. On a more abstract level, analysis covered social and cultural processes common to musical creators and performers generally, highlighting the continuing importance of live performance and collective, interpersonal creativity in a highly commercial and technological environment.

The book also portrayed a male world of fantasy peculiar to rock music and perpetuated by the mass media, which present images of rock stars' wealth and leisure, glamour and sexuality, creativity and power. It is a world that glosses over the operations of capitalist society and the social relationships conditioned by it, and it contrasts harshly with the distinctly non-glamorous realities of life for the majority of bands on Merseyside. Performances were often plagued by mishap. Band members were burdened with obligations, responsibilities, sacrifices, and hardships, and were manipulated by 'sharks' and threatened by commerce and women, both of which attracted and seduced but seemed ultimately deceitful and divisive.

The bands featured in the book were constantly negotiating the shifting ground between fantasy and reality. The threads between the two worlds were tenuous, usually held by whimsical individuals, fickle public taste, and the twists of fortune. The bands thus seemed endlessly poised between success and failure, caught between original creativity and the demands of the record industry. Consequently, some adopted what Frith termed 'the ideology of "folk" in rock'. Polarities common to that ideology were highlighted, such as rock/pop; meaningful/superficial; authentic/false; truthful/deceitful; art/entertainment (non-art); creativity/commerce. The deconstruction of such oppositions revealed underlying preoccupations and motivations, thereby bringing into question other familiar distinctions such as music/non-music; order/disorder; pure/impure; dirty/clean.

Art and creativity were revered against the divisive social pressures of commerce, femaleness, and domesticity. Commercial 'entertainment' was thus conceptualized as an injection of the profane into the sacred, the contamination of the pure with the impure, which necessitated the sealing off of the pure and sacred from the impurity and profanity that threatened it. Yet in reality there is no such thing as 'pure' music or art. All art reflects contradictions, tensions, aspects of the social environment within which it was made, and is thus a combination of creativity and commerce, pure and impure. The pure/impure dichotomy is generally made in order to express, resolve or order experience. 'It is only by exaggerating the difference between within and without, above and below, male and female, with and against, that a semblance of order is created' (Douglas, 1966: 4.) Pollution, whether in the form of sound, noise, money, or woman, presents a danger and threat to order, to that which is pure.

The production of meaning through popular culture by the band members demonstrates that although they may have been driven by, or submerged in, fantasy they were not entirely dominated or deceived by it. Their response to it was creative and manipulative and it inspired their music-making, which was dictated by circumstance yet at the same time free of it. Through it they were able to transform their own reality and perhaps create further fantasies and illusions. Their culture was for them a learning process. It helped them establish, enrich, and deepen relationships, teaching them about team-work as well as their own egos. It enabled them to develop their creative potential and use music not only as a means of communication with others but as an outlet for frustration and expression. It encouraged personal development, providing a series of goals and standards and a sense of purpose and motivation which often strengthened self-confidence and identity, and it provided a means of exploring and ordering aspects of the bands' environment.

The bands used their music as a boundary marker to identify themselves and their allegiance with others, but also to express their difference from others. Their music demarcated social relationships, men and women, honesty and deceit, pure and impure. It has been emphasized that such expressions and meanings are thoroughly relativistic and that music is therefore a contested and shifting boundary marker. Thus Gary's musical tastes conflicted with those of Trav and Dave; the Jactars and Crikey it's the Cromptons! distinguished themselves from the 'musos'; they and the small circle of bands they admired were seen to be 'indie' and 'alternative' as opposed to bands that were 'pop' or 'commercial'; and as 'indie' bands they expressed an ideology familiar throughout the history of rock and to musicians and artist of different eras and genres.

The rock music 'scene' in Liverpool was thus divided by cliques, factions, feuds, and rivalries, yet at the same time united by age, gender, a common ideology, mythology, and gossip grapevine, and a web of interlinking networks and band genealogies as its members moved between bands and music-related occupations. They generally faced a common predicament: trapped between creativity and commerce and confronted by the same industry with its familiar 'gatekeepers'. They therefore formed, in a sense, a 'community'.

Despite the wealth of music-making activity on Merseyside, the region's music industries badly needed support and improvement. Many businesses struggled to survive and there were gaps in provision in various sectors including: record labels, live performance, publishing, manufacture, printing, management, and the provision of advice and information—particularly regarding the legal, business, and marketing aspects of the music industry. However, after my research was completed, the City Council began working alongside the private sector in an effort to regenerate the city's economy through leisure and tourism. It drew up an 'Arts and Cultural Industries Strategy', and plans and feasibility studies were initiated for the development of local film, television, and music industries

This reflected the growing national interest in the role of popular music in education and social policy. It put more pressure upon Liverpool's rock community to organize itself and articulate its needs and interests, promoting itself as a valuable economic resource and political voice in order to compete with other social and cultural groups within the city for funds and facilities. Its most famous members were playing a new role in this. The Beatles, for example, continued to be a tourist attraction and a John Lennon memorial concert was staged on a large scale at the Pierhead. Meanwhile, Paul McCartney intiated plans for a local institute for the performing arts. Struggling artists of the 1960s have become policy makers of the 1990s, patrons of the rock culture they helped shape and characterize.

Through the mass media rock music appears to many as a commercial and superficial product. It is also said to break through international barriers as though the world really was one 'global village'; promoting, through its lyrics and ideology, an illusion of community. Yet throughout this book rock has been presented as culture in a very tangible sense, defining particular groups and communities in a social, economic, political, as well as cultural manner, and situating them geographically, historically, and ideologically.

Postscript

In September 1988 I returned to Liverpool to take up the post of Research Fellow at the newly established Institute of Popular Music at Liverpool University. I gave members of the Jactars and Crikey it's the Cromptons! the draft of my book to read. It is now almost five years since I first met them but both bands still exist. The Jactars are in their sixth year. Trav thinks the band's longevity reflects a point made in the book: that they are less desperate for fame than other bands. They recently started to perform again after almost a year of not performing, and in December 1989 they did a John Peel Session for Radio One, performing again in London the following month—a gig which was reviewed in *Melody Maker*. The same paper published an interview with them the following April. In 1987 they released a 12″ single entitled 'Wadlow' (financed by a bank loan and a loan from Probe, which distributed the record), and recently released a mini-album entitled 'Pull'. They haven't been going out of their way to attract attention from record companies, but they have been contacted by one or two companies.

In February 1990 they went to Germany for a week, performing four gigs on a tour financed by a recently established Liverpool agency. Dave described the tour as 'interesting'. Their van broke down but they particularly appreciated the experience of performing in East Berlin just before the Berlin Wall came down. They emphasize how much their music has changed since I conducted my research, particularly since Huw joined. Dave says it has become much closer to how they always wanted it to be, and Trav suggests that it has shifted from 'mainstream indie style' to a less commercial style.

Huw now lives in Liverpool with his girlfriend and their baby. He, Dave, and Trav are still unemployed, though Trav worked part-time with the mentally handicapped for a while and recently completed an 'access' course which will enable him to begin working for a degree in Theology at a local college. They still see Gary occasionally. He has had several jobs since leaving the Jactars and now drums with a heavy metal band. Dave still lives in Liverpool and plays with a band called Barbel as well as with the Jactars. Trav recently split up with Karen but they still see each other and live near each other in

Bikenhead on the Wirral. Tog left the band at the end of 1989 and no longer plays. He took a course in computers in Liverpool and now has a job at the computer training centre that ran the course. He still lives in Liverpool in the same flat. Pete, who played bass with Crikey its the Cromptons!, performed quite regularly with the Jactars, but they now have a new guitarist and Dave plays bass.

It cannot be easy to read about oneself and one's relationships in such an unexpected context. However, members of the Jactars responded to the text in typically diplomatic manner and to my relief and gratification their comments were generally positive, although Tog felt I had misrepresented his tastes in music and made too much of them, suggesting that they were much broader than I had indicated and more compatible with those of Trav and Dave. Trav and Dave were flattered to have been written about in such detail. The text seemed like a diary of a particular period in their lives. They thought it captured their attitude to music-making and the music business quite well and were appalled at the attitudes of other bands featured in the book. Reading my description of the Jactars' music-making process had, said Dave, inspired him and made him think more positively about the music. He even discussed ways in which they might use the book to the band's advantage.

Regarding my discussion on the relation of women to their music-making, Dave said he didn't necessarily disagree with what I had written, but pointed out that my views and observations stemmed from my personal background and outlook which needed to be emphasized. As a woman I obviously concentrated upon the absence of women. Likewise, Tog said that my conclusions were not those he would have drawn himself but were my own opinion and valid as such. Trav said he couldn't object to what I had written because I was dealing with a 'subconscious level', but pointed out that since women were excluded from many aspects of society the analysis might well be true, though it wasn't a conscious attitude on their part. As far as his lyrics were concerned, he said that whilst he had always thought of them as genderless, after reading the book he saw them in a different light and thought the observations on them were probably quite accurate.

The membership of Crikey it's the Cromptons! has changed over the past four years. According to Tony, the original band 'had a chance but blew it' because of social problems within the band, naïvety, and because his own 'head was in the wrong place'. The band recorded a 12″ single entitled 'Mouthing Off' and a mini-album entitled 'Head on the Block' (both largely financed by Dave T.) but the band's members became disinterested. Tony formed a band

called Armpit with others from Vulcan Studios and also began to
write and sing his own material as a solo performer because, he said,
singer/songwriting was now fashionable. He has written some
'excellent commercial songs' and wants to go into the studio with a
'whole load of musicians [he's] never played with before'. Meanwhile
Pete, whom Tony sees occasionally, plays with another band and
Huw, whom Tony rarely sees, concentrates solely on the Jactars.
Karen, whom Tony sees very occasionally, works in Liverpool's new
Tate Gallery and is not currently performing with any band.

Tony is in regular contact with Dave T., who still lives in London
working in insurance. Together they continue to sporadically
perform and rehearse as Crikey it's the Cromptons! with two other
musicians, though they hope to do a lot more in the future. In June
1989 they performed seven gigs during a two week tour of Germany,
also financed by the above-mentioned agency. Dave T. thought it
went very well with 'reasonable' audiences. They were also inter-
viewed that same year in *Record Mirror*. Tony thinks the band is
very good but finds it 'impossible' to get reviewed in the music press
and says the 'independent scene' finds the music too noisy. Armpit
should be more acceptable but has only had one brief review and
Tony is unsure how best to promote it. He is always eager to show
me his tapes and lyrics for Armpit with titles such as 'Food Monster',
'Trifle Underpants', 'Buttock Business', and 'Scrape out the Inside of
my Head with a Spatula.' He emphasizes how much happier he is
now that both sides of his personality are fulfilled through music-
making. Armpit is an outlet for the 'wackier' side whilst his solo
work satisfies the more serious side.

Tony is still unemployed but described in detail all the various
activities he is involved in. He spent a year taking Art A level at a
local college but his entry was 'ungraded' because 'stuffy people
marked it'. He has, however, developed an interest in video,
photography, and performance art and hopes to do some freelance
writing for music papers. He has produced three editions of his own
fanzine entitled 'Pulpa Pulpa' and has once or twice organized rather
bizarre performance art evenings held at different venues. He calls it
the Squadge Club. He suspects he will have to conform at some
point—'but not now'.

Tony's response to the text was again typical. He enjoyed reading
it, bits of it amused him, and he thought it was generally good and
representative. (I discovered that he had in fact photocopied bits of it
and distributed copies to some people working in the local music
scene, telling them that a book had been written about him.) He was
anxious, however, to point out how much he had since matured and

developed and was more interested in discussing his current activities than his views on the book and what he liked or disliked about it. Bits of it, he said, had made him cringe and feel embarrassed. That period of his life was now a thing of the past and he has moved on. He has lost touch—'out of choice'—with his old friends from the Wirral. He saw some of them recently and was shocked at how racist and sexist they were. He says he now feels a lot wiser and knows better how to deal with people in the music business. He has also become more aware of musical arrangement and how to perform to an audience. He insists that he has become more relaxed on stage and points out that many have told him that what he does on stage now is 'brilliant'.

I was particularly concerned to learn of Karen's response to the book. She had not been around much when I first got to know members of the Jactars and Crikey it's the Cromptons! because of a disagreement between her and Tony, and her presence was sporadic throughout the year, which made her difficult to get to know. In addition, when I talked to her three years later she admitted that she had slightly resented my presence and had initially been unnerved by it and had not, therefore, made much effort to be friendly. She acknowledged that this probably contributed towards her being presented throughout the text in a passive role, and pointed out that she was not always as passive as she seemed (e.g. she sometimes got Tony back in the pub afterwards when he was drunk). She suggested, however, that my representation of her had been sexist in that whilst I presented the Jactars' passive personalities, behaviour, and manner-isms in a positive light, passivity on the part of women had been viewed derogatively. However, Karen still praised some aspects of the text and thought it generally OK.

Appendix

Tongue (By Trav)

> Your tongue is loose you think it fits
> You talk with your mouth instead of your fists
> You polish your teeth with bloodstained hands
> To settle your mind I will pay you in kind
>
> Nomadic eyes never to lose sight of the fools
> Your precious tools
> Never to fail never to ask
> They know your face they carry out your tasks
>
> Keep to one nation keep to one God
> In it for comfort we've had it so hard
> It's been the same you've heard it before
> If you crack under stress
> Put it on the Bill of progress
>
> Into a fast stream move like a dead leaf
> Fall for their motives soiled hands no teeth
> Hear me out and through heat up the water to
> Open the pores skin ripped by claws
> Sat on a high-chair read nursery rhymes there
> Request a performance I have been taunted
> Tanned in the desert tortured on rocks
> Sleeping through wars sanity is taken by force

Forced to Violence (By Trav)

> Pain is one almighty burst of pleasure
> Cuts out the air you can only gasp
> The pleasure never lasts
>
> At times it was more than he could take
> His words were forced and faked
> Forced to violence against his nature

The girl didn't love him
Had to break her

Love is an immense feeling of loneliness
How many shot and missed
Hard knuckles dig in bodies twist
The pain comes during the kiss

Break the Skin (By Trav)

You are now a man
With nothing but your mouth
Inside the heart is beating
Break the skin relieve the tension

You now have a friend
But it's too good to last
On cold wintry evenings you can sit
And touch her
But beauty has danger
And death as its neighbour

Shadows and shapes
All sizes are all to be seen
Sitting and quizzing and puzzling
And then giving up the game
Except for the few the freaks
They never could tame
Don't ignore it it's you
You're to blame

Put your heart in your mouth
Put your brain in your chest
You'll find some things aren't very easy
But don't look aghast
When you see people twisting and screaming
Twist and scream
You'll know what they mean

Inside the heart is beating
Kill it off
But do it discreetly

That Sound (By Trav)

I only have their words now
The men live no more
I only have their words now

But they're more powerful
Induce more thought
Create more to see
With more beauty
Than anything around me

I only have that sound now
Coming through so clear
The sad crowd shout
But I can't hear
They threaten to hurt
But they can't get near

I only have that sound now
Ringing in my ear

No Fair Catch (By Trav)

I'm so self-conscious
You're so simple
Keep away from people
They're caught in the middle
There is no fair catch
There is no fair game
You iron my shirts
I don't know your name
This life for some
Is one big game

I was brought up by a man
And I perfected an art
A technique of drawing
With curves and arcs
I wanted to live
So I did it on their terms
Digging up the flowers
To get to the worms

Deepest Respect (By Trav)

Everyone here has the deepest respect
She just can't understand
She feels so low
She will not talk
She will not raise her eyes
I see her alone in the quietest of spots

Things not Seen (By Dave)

You may believe that you and me
Share no more than passing memories
You don't know what this world means
To a man with no mind who cannot see

Your charms are as strong as stronger still
As the strongest person with the strongest will
And without doubt you're new to the game
And I could be tempted again and again *[repeat]*

I could put my hand in the fire as fuel
But I'd never do this as a rule
But you don't know the meaning of the words
And I don't know things not seen
And things not heard

To My Toes (By Dave)

I can't trust you 'cause I can't trust myself
I'm stacking away thoughts like books
On a shelf
I caught you hook line sinker and all
But the horse has bolted
And we can't shut the door

I'd love to believe you
From my head to my toes
To climb your head like a climbing rose
But the seeds we planted are designed to grow
Like weeds in a garden they won't let go

The marks on your back
Just keep getting clearer
They shine through your eyes
Breeding knowledge and fear

But I've read the papers
That would disturb you I know
The truth is apparent how far should I go
I hold the cards
The rod and the line
I could reel you in this time

But I unhooked your lip and I let you swim
You're loving the pleasure and
You're loving the sin

CRIKEY IT'S THE CROMPTONS!' LYRICS

Week-Old Socks (By Tony, May 1985)

So I'm drunk but it's no reason for abuse
You hit. I strike back.
And life rolls on
And problems pop up like gone by friends

CHORUS: It's no way to make a living
Sane as houses but offa my box

Alias Smith or Jones it's still me-ee
Heart in brass. Head in hand
And a promise could be a lie
But who cares if life floats by

[*chorus repeated*]

I'm a Fiend for You (By Tony, Apr. 1985)

I'm a lovable hound so you found so you said
Incorrigible rogue is what you said went to my head
I seem to be alright in bed so you said so you found
Not easy to resist, hope you realize what you could'a missed

You could crush me like a flower
You know you have the power

Do you know what you have, what I can give it's all for you
You know the score for ever more you with me
We can see what we see shut out the rest who cares
We will stay as one have no lies have no secret affairs

You could crush me like a flower
You know you have the power

The Loneliness (By Tony, Jan. 1984)

I don't want to go out by myself
Bored and anxious, sometimes isolated
I feel detached from conversations
People ridicule and reject me at times
People take advantage if they can
The women I meet end up hurting me
I feel frustrated, emotionally empty
I can't correct mistakes I've always made

CHORUS: On the tight rope grabbing at hidden ropes

Bedlam (By Tony)

> Twenty-one and I haven't even started
> Bedsit bedlam where will it end
> My life is in your hands
> Please make it quick, make it quick
> God what a feeble one. I'm a chromatic aberration
>
> I feel I've aged so very quickly
> Death, love, hate, come into proportion
> My life is out of my hands
> Just take me quick
> Let me out to have feelings of disgust and shock, self pity and petty hate
> Let me out. I wanna get out
> Before you let the sun in make sure it wipes its shoes
> I'll sin until I blow up.

You Know Every Sin (By Tony, Mar. 1985)

> Your cruel black heart eats at mine
> If you follow this deceitful line
>
> No I'm not a religious man
> But hopeful I am
> If there's a heaven I want it
> Cos you'll never get there
>
> Pulling at my skin
> You know every sin
>
> You took a bite at my heart
> Tried to fuck up my mind
> Should have known you were unkind
> Knowing a hand's goin' to pull me out
>
> Pulling at my skin
> You know every sin
>
> [chorus repeated]

Surfin' Tuna Fish (By Tony, 1985)

> Like a devoted swimmer
> I'm crawling for satisfaction
> Limbs turned into fins
> I just can't get a haddock
>
> Share the kiss of fish
> I'd like to blow my stacks
> Sold your child

To get a little higher
Destructed by desire

Share the kiss of fish

Happy virgins are losers
Or so I've read
So many lacking beauty
Gotta get a little higher

Share the love of life

One Death after Another (By Tony, Mar. 1985)

People are scared of the truth
That's why they shun from reality
Crawl under the carpet in a nuclear war
Get under the table when an argument starts

CHORUS: One death after another (x 3)
Lock myself in my room
Then there's less chance of one death after another (x 3)

Give me a pill to relax me
I don't want to be part of this society
All they offer is false comfort
I can see through political lies

The Secret of a Philatelist (By Tony and Huw)

I need to lick you all over
To stop you rusting ohh
It's not small rocks and stones
For which I'm lusting
Fill the holes that leak
With my rubber scalpel
And by Thursday week
You'll be under my spell

CHORUS: It will go on and on . . .

I wouldn't molest you unless you wanted me to
And then it would be just for fun
A penny black tattoo
All down one side
Rubber solution glue
Who knows where it may hide
The tiny envelopes
On each of her toes
Continue up my legs
And finish on your nose

Discography

SOME OF THE RECORDED MATERIAL REFERRED TO IN THE TEXT

BARBEL, *One Horse Planet*, mini-album (Pink Moon, 1989; cat. no. PMM 4).

CRIKEY IT'S THE CROMPTONS!, *Mouthing Off*, 12″ single (Crompton, 1988; cat. no. CROMP 1).

—— *Head on the Block*, mini-album (Crompton, 1990; cat. no. CROMP 2).

DA VINCIS, THE, *Eating Gifted Children*, mini-album (Pink Moon, 1988; cat. no. PMM 1).

—— *Pull*, 12″ single (Pink Moon, 1988; cat. no. PMT 2).

HALF MAN HALF BISCUIT, *Back in the DHSS*, album (Probe Plus, 1985; cat. no. PROBE 4). (Also on cassette and compact disc.)

—— *Trumpton Riots*, single (Probe Plus, 1986; cat. no. TRUM XI).

JACTARS, THE, *Wadlow*, 12″ single (Brilliant Genius, 1987; cat. no. VULC 002).

—— *Pull the Plug*, mini-album (Pink Moon, 1989; cat. no. PMM 5).

Jobs for the Boys, compilation album of Liverpool bands (Natalie, 1985; cat. no. LIE1).

ONE LAST FLIGHT, *Ménage à Trois*, single (Skysaw, 1985; cat. no. SKY 4).

PIECES OF GLASS, *What you tell me*, single (Inkling, 1980).

Twist and SAMBA, compilation album of the Sefton Area Musicians and Bands Association (Quickstep, 1986; cat. no. QUICKSTEP 001).

Ways to Wear Coats, compilation album of Vulcan bands (Brilliant Genius, 1987; cat. no. VULC 001).

Bibliography

ADORNO, T. W., and HORKHEIMER, M. (1977), 'The Culture Industry: Enlightenment as Mass Deception', in *Mass Communication and Society*, ed. J. Curran, M. Gurevitch, and J. Wollacott (London, Edward Arnold).

ATTALI, J. (1985), *Noise: The Political Economy of Music* (Manchester, Manchester Univ. Press).

BARRAULT, J. (1972), 'Best and Worst of Professions', in *The Uses of Drama*, ed. J. Hodgson (London, Eyre Methuen).

BECKER, H. S. (1963), *Outsiders: Studies in the Sociology of Deviance* (New York, The Free Press).

—— (1982), *Art Worlds* (Berkeley, Univ. of California Press).

BENJAMIN, W. (1970), *Illuminations* (London, Cape).

BENNET, H. S. (1980), *On Becoming a Rock Musician* (Amherst, Univ. Massachusetts Press).

BLACKING, J. (1973), *How Musical is Man?* (London, Faber and Faber).

—— (1979), 'The Study of Man as Music Maker', in *The Performing Arts: Music and Dance* (The Hague, Mouton).

—— (1981), 'Making Artistic Popular Music: The Goal of True Folk', *Popular Music, i* (Cambridge, Cambridge Univ. Press).

BRAUN, M. (1964), *Love Me Do: The Beatles' Progress* (Harmondsworth, Penguin).

BURCHALL, I. (1965), 'The Rhymes They Are A-Changing', *International Socialism*, 23: 16–18.

BURCHILL, J., and PARSONS, T. (1978), *'The Boy Looked At Johnny'* (London, Pluto Press).

BURNS, E. (1972), *Theatricality: A Study of Convention in the Theatre and in Social Life* (London, Longman).

CHAMBERS, I. (1985), *Urban Rhythms: Pop Music and Popular Culture* (London, Macmillan).

CHANNON, H. (1970), *Portrait of Liverpool* (London, Robert Hale).

CHAPPELL, H. (1983), 'Mersey Dreams', *New Society*, 6 Oct.: 5–6.

CLOVER, C. (1985), 'Rock and the Revolution', *the Spectator*, 2 Mar.: 14–15.

COFFMAN, J. T. (1972), 'So You Want to be a Rock'n'Roll Star!: Role Conflict and the Rock Musician', in *The Sounds of Social Change*, ed. R. S. Denisoff and R. A. Peterson (Chicago, Rand McNally).

COHEN, A. (1974), *Two-Dimensional Man* (Berkeley, Univ. of California Press).

COOPER, M. (1982), *Liverpool Explodes!* (London, Sidgwick and Jackson).

DAVIES, H. (1985), *The Beatles* (London, Jonathan Cape).

DOUGLAS, M. (1966), *Purity and Danger: An Analysis of Concepts of Pollution and Taboo* (London, Routledge and Kegan Paul).

DUNNING, E. (1986), 'Sport as a Male Preserve: Notes on the Social Sources of Masculine Identity and its Transformation', *Theory, Culture and Society*, 3: 1.

DURANT, A. (1984), *The Conditions of Music* (London, Macmillan).

EDGE, B. (1984), *Joy Division and New Order: Pleasures and Wayward Distractions* (London, Omnibus Press).

ESSLIN, M. (1976), *An Anatomy of Drama* (London, Temple Smith).

FINKELSTEIN, S. (1976), *How Music Expresses Ideas* (New York, International Publishers).

FINNEGAN, R. (1986), 'The Organisation and Functioning of Small Local Bands in a Modern English Town' (unpublished paper for Kent Popular Music Conference).

—— (1989), *The Hidden Musicians: Music-Making in an English Town* (Cambridge, Cambridge Univ. Press).

FISCHER, E. (1963), *The Necessity of Art* (Harmondsworth, Penguin).

FLETCHER, C. (1966), 'Beats and Gangs on Merseyside', in *Youth in New Society*, ed. T. Raison (London, Hart-Davis).

FRITH, S. (1980), 'Music for Pleasure', *Screen Education*, 34: 51–61.

—— (1981), 'The Magic That Can Set You Free: The Ideology of Folk and the Myth of the Rock Community', *Popular Music*, I (Cambridge, Cambridge Univ. Press).

—— (1983), *Sound Effects: Youth, Leisure, and the Politics of Rock'n'Roll* (London, Constable).

—— (1986), 'Art versus Technology: The Strange Case of Popular Culture', *Media, Culture and Society*, 8: 3.

—— and MCROBBIE, A. (1978), 'Rock and Sexuality', *Screen Education*, 29: 3–19.

GIFFORD, LORD, BROWN, W., and BUNDY, R. (1989), *Loosen the Shackles: First Report of the Liverpool 8 Inquiry into Race Relations in Liverpool* (London, Karia Press).

GROF, S. (1977), 'The Implications of Psychedelic Research for Anthropology: Observations from LSD Psychotherapy', in *Symbols and Sentiment*, ed. I. Lewis (London, Academic Press).

HADFIELD, J. A. (1972), 'Drama in Dreams', in *The Uses of Drama*, ed. J. Hodgson (London, Eyre Methuen).

HARDY, P. (1984), 'The British Record Industry', *IASPM UK Working Paper*, 3.

HARGREAVES, J. (1986), 'Where's the Virtue? Where's the Grace?, *Theory, Culture and Society*, 3: 1.

HARKER, D. (1980), *One For the Money: Politics and Popular Song* (London, Hutchinson).

HEBDIGE, D. (1979), *Subculture: The Meaning of Style* (London, Methuen).

HERMAN, G. (1971), *The Who* (London, Studio Vista).

HUGHES, D. J. (1973), 'Pop Music', in *Discrimination and Popular Culture*, ed. D. Thompson (London, Pelican).

JACKSON, A. (1969), 'Sound and Ritual', *Man*, 3: 293–9.

KEIL, C. (1966), *Urban Blues* (Chicago, Univ. of Chicago Press).

KENT, G. (1983), A View From the Bandstand (London, Sheba).

KERRIDGE, R. (1984), 'Innocent Abroad', *New Society*, 2 Aug.: 60–1.

KETTLE, M. (1981), 'The Toxteth Troubles', *New Society*, 9 July: 60–1.

LAING, D. (1969), *The Sound of Our Time* (London, Sheed and Ward).

—— (1985), *One Chord Wonders* (Milton Keynes, Open Univ. Press).

LANE, T. (1986), 'We are the Champions: Liverpool vs the 1980s', *Marxism Today*, Jan.: 8–11.

—— (1987), *Liverpool Gateway of Empire* (London, Lawrence and Wishart).

LANGER, S. (1951), *Philosophy in a New Key: A Study in the Symbolism of Reason, Rite and Art* (London, Oxford Univ. Press).

LAW, I. (1981), *A History of Race and Racism in Liverpool, 1660–1950*, ed. J. Henfrey (Liverpool, Merseyside Community Relations Council).

LEIGH, S. (1984), *Let's Go Down the Cavern* (London, Vermilion).

LÉVI-STRAUSS, C. (1970), *The Raw and the Cooked* (London, Cape).

LIENHARDT, G. (1985), 'Self: Public and Private. Some African Representations', in *The Category of The Person*, ed. M. Carrithers, S. Collins, S. Lukes (Cambridge, Cambridge Univ. Press).

MCGREGOR, C. (1983), *Pop Goes the Culture* (London, Pluto Press).

MCROBBIE, A. (1978), 'Working Class Girls and the Culture of Femininity', in *Women Take Issue* (London, Hutchinson).

—— (1984), 'Dance and Social Fantasy', in *Gender and Generation*, ed. A. McRobbie and M. Nava (London, Macmillan).

MARCUSE, H. (1979), *The Aesthetic Dimension* (London, Papermac).

MARSH, P. (1977), 'Dole Queue Rock', *New Society*, 20 Jan.: 114.

MARTIN, B. (1981), *A Sociology of Contemporary Cultural Change* (Oxford, Basil Blackwell).

MASSER, F. I. (1970), 'The Analysis and Prediction of Physical Change in the Central Area of Liverpool', in *Merseyside Social and Economic Studies*, ed. R. Lawton and C. M. Cunningham (London, Longman).

MEADE, M. (1972), 'The Degradation of Women', in *The Sounds of Social Change*, ed. R. S. Denisoff and R. A. Peterson (Chicago, Rand McNally).

MERRIAM, A. (1964), *The Anthropology of Music* (Evanston, North western Univ. Press).

MITCHELLS, K. (1967), 'The Work of Art in its Social Setting and in its Aesthetic Isolation', *Journal of Aesthetics and Art Criticism*, 25/4 372–4.

MOORE, S. F., and MYERHOFF, B. G., eds. (1977), *Introduction to Secular Ritual* (The Netherlands, Van Gorcum).

PARKINSON, M. (1985), *Liverpool on the Brink* (Hermitage, Berks. Policy Journals).

PLACKSIN, S. (1985), *Jazz Women* (London, Pluto Press).

RIESMAN, D. (1957), 'Listening to Popular Music', in *Mass Culture*, ed. B. Rosenberg and D. M. White (New York, The Free Press).

RUSSELL, D. (1987), *Popular Music in England, 1840–1914: A Social History* (Manchester, Manchester Univ. Press).

SARTRE, J. P. (1976), *Critique of Dialectical Reason* (London, NLB).

SAVAGE, J. (1984), 'Sweet Nothings', *New Society*, 6 Sept.: 241.

SHARRAT, B. (1980), 'The Politics of the Popular? From Melodrama to Television', in *Performance and Politics in Popular Drama*, ed. D. Bradbury, L. James, and B. Sharrat (Cambridge, Cambridge Univ. Press).

SHAW, F. (1978), *My Liverpool* (Wirral, Gallery Press).

SHEPHERD, J. (1987), 'Music and Male Hegemony', in *Music and Society: The Politics of Composition, Performance and Reception*, ed. R. Leppert, and S. McLary (Cambridge, Cambridge Univ. Press).

Social Survey of Merseyside (1934), ed. D. C. Jones (London, Liverpool Univ. Press).

STEWARD, S., and GARRATT, S. (1984), *Signed, Sealed and Delivered: True Life Stories of Women in Pop* (London, Pluto Press).

TAGG, P. (1979), 'Kojak—50 Seconds of Television Music: Toward the Analysis of Affect in Popular Music', *Studies from Gothenburg University, Department of Musicology*, ii, (Gothenburg, Gothenburg Univ. Press).

TAYLOR, J., and LAING, D. (1979), 'Disco-Pleasure Discourse: On Rock and Sexuality', *Screen Education*, 31: 43–8.

TAYLOR, R. (1985), 'It's Magic', *New Society*, 14 Ma.: 404–6.

THEWELEIT, K. (1987), *Male Fantasies* (Cambridge, Polity Press).

TURNER, V. (1957), *Schism and Continuity in an African Society* (Manchester, Manchester Univ. Press).

—— (1969), *The Ritual Process* (Chicago, Aldine).

—— (1977), 'Variations on a Theme of Liminality', in *Secular Ritual*, ed. S. F. Moore and B. G. Myerhoff (The Netherlands, Van Gorcum).

—— (1983), 'Dionysian Drama in an Industrializing Society', in *Celebration of Society: Perspectives on Contemporary Cultural Performance*, ed. F. E. Manning (Canada, Bowling Green Univ. Press).

WHITE, A. (1983), 'Convention and Constraint in the Operation of Musical Groups: Two Case Studies' (Ph.D. thesis. Univ. of Keele, unpublished).

WILLIAMS, R. (1976), 'Communications as Cultural Science', in *Approaches to Popular Culture*, ed. C. W. E. Bigsby (London, Edward Arnold).

WILLIS, P. (1978), *Profane Culture* (London, Routledge and Kegan Paul).

WILMER, V. (1987), *As Serious As Your Life: The Story of the New Jazz* (London, Pluto Press).

WRIGHT, C. (1983), 'The Record Industry', in *Making Music*, ed. G. Martin (London, Pan Books).

Index